Teach®
Yourself

Understand
Scottish History

David Allan

Hodder Education

338 Euston Road, London NW1 3BH.

Hodder Education is an Hachette UK company

First published in UK 2011 by Hodder Education

First published in US 2011 by The McGraw-Hill Companies, Inc.

This edition published 2011.

British Library Cataloguing in Publication Data: a catalogue record for this title is available from the British Library.

Library of Congress Catalog Card Number: on file.

10 9 8 7 6 5 4 3 2 1

The publisher has used its best endeavours to ensure that any website addresses referred to in this book are correct and active at the time of going to press. However, the publisher and the author have no responsibility for the websites and can make no guarantee that a site will remain live or that the content will remain relevant, decent or appropriate.

The publisher has made every effort to mark as such all words which it believes to be trademarks. The publisher should also like to make it clear that the presence of a word in the book, whether marked or unmarked, in no way affects its legal status as a trademark.

Every reasonable effort has been made by the publisher to trace the copyright holders of material in this book. Any errors or omissions should be notified in writing to the publisher, who will endeavour to rectify the situation for any reprints and future editions.

Hachette UK's policy is to use papers that are natural, renewable and recyclable products and made from wood grown in sustainable forests. The logging and manufacturing processes are expected to conform to the environmental regulations of the country of origin.

www.hoddereducation.co.uk

Typeset by MPS Limited, a Macmillan Company.

Printed in Great Britain by CPI Cox & Wyman, Reading.

Contents

Meet the author

Welcome to *Understand Scottish History*!

History is about all aspects of the past as it has been experienced by human beings. But it is also about seeking to understand previous events. Analysis and explanation rather than simply description is therefore essential: historians ask *why* things happened as they did and want to know what the implications turned out to be.

In *Understand Scottish History*, we'll be looking in this way at one country's past. Scotland, however, is not just any old country. Certainly it is old – very old, in fact. And it has not always been a single country. The gradual emergence of Scotland as a nation, and its continued survival in the face of severe internal and external threats, is an important thread throughout much of the Scottish story.

But the human occupants of the country we now know as Scotland have had a truly remarkable past. Some parts of it are fantastically well-documented, as befits a people who have had a major impact on the rest of Britain, Europe and the world. Other parts, especially in the earliest times, are now bafflingly obscure, wrapped in legend and penetrable, if at all, only with great difficulty.

As a professional historian with a particular focus on Scotland, I want to introduce you to this complex and fascinating story. In just 15 chapters, we'll travel from the country's first geological beginnings to its peculiar social and political problems in the early 21st century.

I hope you'll enjoy the journey.

In one minute

Scotland's small size belies a history of unrivalled colour and richness. Few small countries have also had such an impact on the wider world.

Much of Scotland's history has been dominated by a remarkably varied landscape and even more varied human settlement. The Highlands and Lowlands in particular have long produced contrasting cultures and politics.

A succession of occupants, invaders and immigrants, often in conflict with one another, have had profound effects too: Celts, Britons, Romans, Picts, Angles, Scots, Vikings, Normans, Irish, English, Chinese, Pakistanis and Poles – all have left, and some are still leaving, their distinctive marks.

A dominant feature of Scottish existence, shaping politics, internal organization and even the self-image and identity of the population, has been the experience of living beyond the reach of those who have dominated the British mainland's southern and more prosperous regions.

The Romans, in never properly subduing Scotland, ensured that the ancient Caledonians and Picts would develop in their own way. Later and for far longer, the English, as near neighbours, one-time invaders and present political partners, have similarly exerted a powerful influence, usually unintentionally. Over many centuries, to be Scottish has primarily meant not being English. And Scotland's distinctiveness, in not being like England, matters more to its people than almost anything else.

Heroic achievements have also marked out Scottish history. Those who fought successfully against English encroachment – Sir William Wallace and Robert the Bruce – are remembered still as patriots. But even Scotland's great losers – Macbeth, Bonnie Prince Charlie and Mary, Queen of Scots – have striking dramatic allure.

The Scots, however, have been as prominent in the arts of peace: writers like Sir Walter Scott and Robert Burns, scientists and engineers like Lord Kelvin and James Watt, and philosophers and economists like David Hume and Adam Smith, achieved and still retain world renown. Vast numbers of Scottish emigrants and empire-builders, meanwhile, helped shape countries like Canada, Australia, India and the United States.

Scottish history is in this sense a part of everyone's history.

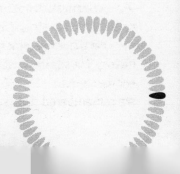

1

Scotland before the Scots

In this chapter you will learn:
- **about the earliest inhabitants of the land that became Scotland**
- **about the coming of Christianity and the invasions of the Vikings**
- **how Scotland came into existence during the ninth century.**

First footprints

The earliest people in Scotland were certainly *not* the Scots.

The very first evidence of a human presence is actually given by the frustratingly faint signs left by what must only have been temporary encampments. One was set up near modern Biggar, a town in the Borders that, probably significantly, lies by the Tweed and the Clyde, two major rivers rising in the Southern Uplands: excavations in 2009 revealed a cache of flint tools for killing and butchering wild animals from around 8500 BC. A more extensive contemporary habitation, indicated by the stake-holes of a raised structure as well as by some stone implements and discarded and carbonized hazelnut shells, was found in 2008 at Cramond, again a riverside site, where the Almond meets the Forth above Edinburgh. A mixture of animal bones, redundant sea shells and tools found at Sand in Wester Ross and apparently from around 7500 BC also hints tantalizingly at a group of Mesolithic people fleetingly setting up camp. Such hunter-gatherers, with their migratory lifestyle and still-limited impact on the land, are always likely to remain a fascinatingly elusive quarry for archaeologists.

Old stones, new stones

The advent of the Neolithic, however, is much more impressively documented, because of the substantial structures that people were now starting to construct.

Neolithic culture in Scotland generated some of the earliest permanent habitations for which evidence survives. It is most brilliantly illuminated by the remarkable concentration of stone dwellings and other substantial structures in Orkney. Two spectacular constructions stand out and now form the core of a UNESCO World Heritage Site.

At Skara Brae on Mainland, the largest Orkney island, is the best-preserved group of Neolithic stone houses anywhere in northern Europe: built around 3100 BC, it comprises ten large buildings made of local flagstones. Nearby at Maeshowe is a massive chambered stone cairn and a passage grave beneath a 24-foot high grass mound. Archaeological evidence confirms that the people responsible for these complexes lived in a farming community, used grooved-ware pottery, regularly herded domesticated sheep and cattle and grew wheat and barley with great success.

The arrival of metal

The Bronze Age, which in Scotland started around 2000 BC, was in some ways not a revolutionary departure from the Neolithic, notwithstanding the introduction of mining, smelting and metalworking techniques that lends it its familiar archaeological label. In particular, the large-scale physical evidence looks not dissimilar to what had already been seen in Scotland for thousands of years. It is the much smaller artefacts, however, that are more obviously different. These speak eloquently of the period's greater wealth and more sophisticated material culture. Nothing previously seen compares with the rich, varied and skilful artefacts in the Migdale Hoard, found near Bonar Bridge in Sutherland.

By about 700 BC, Scotland's inhabitants had already entered the Iron Age. As the name suggests, this extended the range and quality of metalware available in everyday life as well as for ceremonial use. But this did not simply mean iron: indeed, the unearthing in 2009 of four gold torcs (neck-rings) in a field in Stirlingshire, items with an obviously Mediterranean provenance, was another reminder of the widening cultural networks, and the material sophistication, that this period brought to Scotland.

More typically, however, the Iron Age was associated with increasingly elaborate social and economic arrangements in everyday life.

We certainly find more evidence of fortified settlements and other defensive structures (such as the drystone 'brochs' that sprang up at hundreds of locations). This perhaps implies the emergence of better-defined tribal identities like the Votadini, whose ramparted fortress at Traprain Law to the east of Edinburgh is the period's outstanding monument, and, less attractively, more scope for inter-communal tensions.

They came, they saw, they conquered

The first Roman penetration of Scotland, conventionally bringing down the curtain on the Iron Age, was by any standards a decisive moment, not least because the Romans finally provide us with the earliest descriptions of Scotland and its inhabitants. In this sense Scottish history only gets properly underway once Roman authors begin writing about a country to which, when referring to its northern parts, they also gave its first recorded name: Caledonia.

The first identifiable individual from Scotland – the first Caledonian, so to speak – is an unnamed king of Orkney who joined other British leaders in submitting to the Emperor's overlordship at Colchester, following the Romans' arrival in England in AD 43. It is probably best to think of him as representing the increasingly well-developed power structures through which Iron Age society had already organized itself along tribal and geographical lines. It certainly suggests that even in the far north, political leaders already knew about – and could participate in – transformational developments at the opposite end of their island.

Not until the protracted series of campaigns beginning in AD 71, however, did the Romans probably venture into Scotland itself. But in that year Quintus Pettilius Cerialis, provincial governor of Britannia, sent his legions northwards.

Quickly establishing relations with the Votadini (who became reliable allies) and subduing the neighbouring Selgovae, the tribe occupying the coastal region along the Solway, the Romans soon confronted the Caledonii, who inhabited Britain north of the Tay. It was 30,000 warriors of this stubborn people that the legions, under the new governor Agricola, routed in the famous Battle of Mons Graupius in the summer of AD 84.

Insight: The lost victory

Much fun has been had in the fruitless attempt to locate Mons Graupius. In the absence of archaeological finds indicating a misplaced ancient battlefield, the arguments are based on likely routes for invading armies, the pattern of known Roman encampments and the presence of appropriately mountainous topography. Contenders include Bennachie and Megray Hill, both in Aberdeenshire, the Gask Ridge in Perthshire, and as far away as Sutherland and/or Caithness. Troublingly, it has even been proposed that this great triumph was invented by Tacitus to burnish the reputation of his politically ambitious father-in-law Agricola.

Despite this comprehensive military victory, the Romans' grip on Scotland was neither firm nor comprehensive. Moreover, given the complex tribal politics, the costly infrastructure and manpower permanent occupation would have required and the obvious harshness and limited agricultural value of the country, it may well be that the Romans were wise indeed in their periodic retreats to the comfort and safety of the south.

Yet under successive dynasties, notably the Antonines in the early second century and again under Septimus Severus early in the third, Scotland was nevertheless subjected to renewed Roman incursions, re-garrisoning and at least partial occupation, which in each case must have lasted for many years at a time. This is why, although modern Scots pride themselves on their country never having been conquered, the familiar signs of Roman military power remain visible in the landscape of central and southern Scotland.

Most strikingly, there are the walls – not just Hadrian's famous edifice, mainly in stone, built after AD 122, that runs from the Solway to near Newcastle in north-east England and delineates what was then the northern frontier of Britannia, but also the less well-known Antonine Wall, engineered from around AD 139, comprising a ditch and embankment that marks, defends and controls a more ambitious boundary of Roman control at Scotland's narrowest point, between the firths of Clyde and Forth. There are also the characteristic roads, especially Dere Street, running from York to near modern Falkirk, but also several others in the Border hills and Central Lowlands.

Imperial authority was also expressed across the southern half of the country through the building of more than 150 army encampments, many of them recently revealed by archaeologists to have been more than once re-engineered – a fact which in itself suggests continuing strategic usefulness over time.

The Romans, however, clearly brought more than raw military might. Large numbers of their coins have also been found. So have a vast array of other artefacts, ranging from elaborate brooches to scrap metal hoards. This strongly suggests that Romans and natives co-existed peacefully, trading and interacting regularly, for much of the time.

Archaeological evidence from places like southern Perthshire even confirms that wheat was being cultivated immediately after the first Roman invasion. Agricultural output as a whole also increased. This in turn implies not just a growing population but also an expanding economy and relatively settled conditions at precisely the times and places the Romans were present.

....

Insight: Nailing the Ninth

Some claim that, in a doomed attempt to pacify the Caledonians around AD 117, the Romans lost the famous IXth Legion (Hispana). Most recently as the subject of the Hollywood film *The Eagle* (2011), this claim is based on a mixture of error and wishful thinking. Archaeological evidence places the IXth on the Rhine in 121. And though it disappears from records before 200, if it did indeed meet a violent end (which is mere speculation) better hypothetical cases exist for known campaigns in Palestine from 132 or the Danube in 162. There is no evidence at all, despite what some Scots now want to believe, that the cream of Rome's army was annihilated by their country's ferocious, freedom-loving ancient inhabitants.

....

Roman influence probably even helped forge Scotland's native tribal groupings into larger and more structured political entities. This was especially important after the last major occupation early in the third century AD. Retreating once more behind Hadrian's Wall, Severus's army left a country whose southernmost regions remained in the hands of the familiar old tribal societies but the rest of which was controlled by a substantial confederation of natives brought together in part by the long-term presence of the Romans. The latter also began describing these people in a new and intriguing way – as the Picts.

Painted people?

The Picts are one of the great mysteries in Scottish history. Even their name, from the Latin *pingere* 'to paint', which first crops up in the Roman writer Eumenius in AD 297, may simply have been a nickname awarded by the legionaries to slightly eccentric northern neighbours who often decorated themselves with tattoos or dyes. What the Picts actually called themselves is a puzzle. Nor can we even be sure when or how they began to recognize themselves as a single, coherent people.

About a number of things we can nevertheless be reasonably confident. First, 'Pict' was a name given to people, many of them previously known as Caledonii, who had long inhabited Scotland to the north of those regions periodically occupied by the Romans. Second, the Picts were a Celtic people. As a result, their Brythonic language was probably rather like that of more southerly tribes, such as the Votadini – subsequently known in their own tongue as the Goddodin – with whom the Romans had peacefully interacted.

Third, the Picts enjoyed a highly sophisticated artistic culture, albeit one that operated within relatively narrow confines. For they have left us some marvellous standing stones decorated with complex symbols and evocative pictures of people and animals, such as the Dupplin cross from Perthshire and the Aberlemno cross-slab from Angus.

The easiest way of confirming the former presence of the Picts in different parts of the modern Scottish landscape is simply to look for place names beginning 'Pit-' such as Pitlochry, Pitsligo and Pitlessie, particularly densely congregated, as we would expect, in eastern

Scotland north of the Forth. In search of the Picts we can also rely on the contemporary observations of Irish, Welsh and English writers, above all Bede in the early eighth-century *Ecclesiastical History of the English People*, and on later Scottish materials – although it should be borne in mind that the latter were written by those whose power, language and culture had eventually obliterated Pictish civilization. These sources all make it clear that for several centuries after the final withdrawal of the Roman armies the dominant political structure in most of Scotland was a Pictish kingdom known as Fortriu. This was almost certainly focused on the Moray and Easter Ross areas in the north-east (though it was long believed to centre on Strathearn in Perthshire) and extended its power as far south as the Forth.

While there has also been a convention of regarding Fortriu as synonymous with what we now call Pictland (or Pictavia) as a whole, there were clearly also some other smaller Pictish kingdoms at various times. Among these were Fib in modern Fife, the Circinn in Angus, which probably existed in some sort of dependent relationship with Fortriu.

The Angles' angle

As should by now be clear, the word 'Scotland', in the periods we have so far been discussing, is simply a convenient shorthand label applied to that northern part of the Britain that later fell under the control of a people called the Scots, after whom it was eventually named.

Although the Picts were the leading political presence across most of the Dark Ages, other peoples also exercised a significant influence in Scotland that would last far into the future.

One such group were the English, or, to give them their early name, the Angles. By the mid-seventh century, their territories would include all those parts of modern south-east Scotland up to the Firth of Forth as well as modern England as far south as the River Humber. Edinburgh itself, then a small fortified settlement called Dunedin or Din Eidyn, was thus for a time effectively part of an emerging English domain: Din Eidyn itself is simply a Celtic name meaning 'the hill fort of the sloping ridge'.

The English advance to the Forth was profoundly important for Scotland's future. In particular it ensured the early and permanent use of a version of the English language in the districts close by the later Scottish capital.

Insight: Language matters

Whether Scots is really a language in its own right or just another version of English is an unresolved – and unresolvable – question. Since, in the old joke, a language is a dialect with a flag and an army, the claim appeals most to those favouring Scottish independence. But a confusing history hardly helps. The names Welsh, English, French, German and Italian all denote both a people and their language. By contrast, the widely-spoken tongue today known as Scots (revealingly called Inglis before 1500) descends from Anglo-Saxons who settled post-Roman Berwickshire and the Lothians. The Scots people, however, who eventually gave their name to the whole country, originated in the west Highlands and spoke an ancestor of modern Gaelic – now intelligible to barely one per cent of Scotland's population.

However, this English encroachment did not go unchecked. In fact, history records more than one significant battle between the Angles and the different Celtic groups their expansionism increasingly brought them up against. One such encounter forms the dramatic subject of a major poem called 'The Goddodin', which, since it commemorates the heroic deeds of their Brythonic-speaking brethren, survives today, despite its obvious origins in what is now Scotland, as the earliest recognized work of medieval Welsh literature.

A larger-scale Anglo-Celtic confrontation, of even more far-reaching significance for future British history, is actually described in some detail by Bede and confirmed once more by Irish and Welsh sources. This time dateable with extraordinary precision to Saturday 20 May 685, it took place at somewhere afterwards known in English as Nechtansmere ('Nechtan's lake'). Here, the Picts, led by King Bruide, inflicted a crushing defeat on the previously all-conquering Northumbrian army of King Ecgfrith.

This decisive Dark Age Armageddon effectively freed the Picts from subservience to the kings of Northumbria. It allowed them to reinforce their own influence at least as far south as the Tay. At the same time it dealt a severe blow to English hopes of finally absorbing the lands north of the Forth. If Scotland, as we now know it, had not one but several moments of birth – or at least identifiable points when the eventual emergence of a distinct kingdom and sense of national identity in northern Britain became likely – then Nechtansmere, for all that its details are shrouded in uncertainty, needs to be numbered among them.

Celtic connections

Another important post-Roman Celtic people clearly operating independently of the Pictish hegemony were those other Brythonic-speaking Britons who developed the kingdom of Alt Clut, later known as Strathclyde. The people of Alt Clut, like the Goddodin, had been much affected by a long and probably overwhelmingly fruitful relationship with the Romans. This kingdom's core territory stretched from Galloway in the far south-west up towards the Firth of Clyde in the north. Here a fortress built on another of the Central Lowlands' imposing volcanic plugs, at Dumbarton, emerged as the kingdom's main stronghold.

Crucially it was in the lands of Alt Clut that something else of immense long-term significance for the history of Britain seems to have happened. This was the emergence of the first identifiable church in Scotland.

The coming of the cross

The best-known story of how Christianity became established in their country remains present – and still important to many – in the Scottish public's imagination. It gives pride of place to St Columba, an Irish missionary of royal stock who after 563, working from the southern Hebridean island of Iona, today the principal pilgrimage destination for Scotland's Christians, ministered to the inhabitants of Pictland.

In a nation which has for centuries defined itself by not being a part of England, and which in more recent times has become increasingly proud of its affinities with other Celtic peoples, particularly the Irish, the centrality accorded to this determined and visionary figure from Donegal is perfectly understandable. Yet the history of Scottish Christianity almost certainly did not begin with Columba.

To start with, the far west had longstanding cultural ties with Ireland, which had itself known Christianity since before the missions of Palladius and St Patrick in the early 430s. Roman cultural influence must also have been an important factor in bringing Christianity to Scotland. There were definitely believers in southern Britain even in the mid-second century. London and York actually had bishops by 314. And tradition has long maintained that it was at Whithorn in southern Strathclyde that the first church in the future Scotland was constructed, shortly before the end of the Roman period.

This church was reputedly founded by St Ninian, a British-born bishop about whom no fact is certain but who, like Patrick, is said to have been greatly moved by his experience of Christianity in France and to have studied at Rome. Whithorn later became a key pilgrimage site, revered by medieval Scots as a place of considerable sacred significance for Scottish Christianity. And even nearly a millennium and a half afterwards, when Pope Benedict XVI came to Scotland in 2010 for only the second ever visit by an incumbent pontiff, it was, significantly, on 16 September, the Feast Day of St Ninian, that he chose to arrive in the country.

The survival of Pictland as well as of Alt Clut, despite the power and ambitions of the Angles to the south and east, had confirmed at least one thing: the future of these peoples did not lie simply as an integral part of an English-dominated confederation extending throughout mainland Britain. But which of the competing groups occupying the diverse terrain between the Southern Uplands and the Pentland Firth would eventually manage to place their own stamp on this landscape as a whole?

As things turned out, the answer lay in the far west, in and around Iona itself, among the islands and along the jagged coastline where there existed yet another culturally-distinct population, mainly set apart by being Gaelic speakers with strong links to Ireland. These people, obscure and peripheral though they would have appeared at the time to Pictish or English observers, would eventually give their name to the entire country: they were the Scots.

The Scots before Scotland

If the traditional story of their migration as a people from Ireland is literally true, the Scots may at first perhaps have been more interested in raiding and exploring than in settling and exploiting the country they would eventually dominate. But, finding it agreeable and profitable, they would soon have realized the benefit of coming in numbers and putting down roots. Yet there are aspects of the migration story that do not ring true. For example, we know that there had been constant cultural and economic traffic between the northernmost parts of Ireland and the westernmost parts of Scotland from very early times.

What is beyond doubt is that, at some point during the fifth century, a people known as the Scoti, as the Romans had latterly described them (perhaps borrowing from the Old Irish word *scuit*, meaning 'wanderer'), began to acquire an enhanced prominence. Soon they became a recognizable force in what would later become Argyllshire, the island of Bute and the western districts of Inverness-shire. The name that this emerging group gave to their newly established kingdom, however, was, interestingly, not Scotland: in Gaelic it came to be known instead as Dálriata (or Dálriada).

Insight: A Pharaoh's daughter

The story that later Scots told themselves about their origins, and which helped reinforce their identity as a people, was highly elaborate. The Scots came to believe that their own ancestors had come not from Ireland at all. Rather their roots lay, just like the Romans, in the eastern Mediterranean of antiquity.

Here it was that a Pharaoh's daughter called Scota had been married to an exiled Greek warrior-prince called Goidel Glas or Gathelus (whose name helpfully singled him out as the father of the later Gaels). The happy couple had then sailed to Spain, founding the no-less-conveniently-labelled Galicia. Finally, their ambitious and adventurous descendants had moved on first to Ireland (in some versions of the story led by a second Pharaoh's daughter, yet another Scota) and then at last to Scotland itself, under a first king called Fergus Mac Ferchard.

With their keenness to locate their own distant origins in the arrival of ancient heroes in new lands, the Scots were a typical European people.

A kingdom of the west

Dálriata's sixth-century capital lay at Dunadd (meaning 'fort on the river Add') near modern Kilmartin in Argyllshire. There were other significant centres of power and influence in Dálriata, however, reflecting what was clearly a common Gaelic practice of recognizing subordinate kings and multiple tribal kindreds. Dunaverty in Kintyre, for example, seems to have been home to a dependent dynasty of rulers. Dunseverick in Antrim, meanwhile, was probably Dálriata's principal seat of government, at least before the kingdom's centre of gravity shifted decisively to Scotland.

Using a mixture of archaeological evidence, the more plausible tales that later Scots told about their origins and the writings of other early chroniclers elsewhere in the British Isles, we can reconstruct at least the outlines of this kingdom's early history as it emerged as an influential force in northern Britain.

We know a little about the checks that early Dálriata received, ensuring that its energies would be channelled with more lasting effect in some directions than in others. At Degsastan in around 603, for example, probably somewhere on the English side of the modern border, the raiding Scots under Aedan Mac Gabrain were defeated by the Northumbrians under Aethelfrith. This setback may well have helped establish clear limits to Dálriata's influence to the south.

Similarly we are told that under Domnall Brecc the Scots, who still controlled Antrim, fought a number of unsuccessful battles in Ulster, including at Mag Rath (near Moira in modern County Down) in 637. These reversals perhaps added to the growing sense that it was in Scotland not Ireland that the main focus of Dálriata's interests now lay.

It was in a further defeat, this time at the hands of Owen, King of Alt Clut, that Domnall was finally killed in 642 at Strathcarron (probably in the valley of the modern River Carron in central Scotland rather than the Highland glen of the same name). Again the Scots' early attempts to advance outside the western Highlands appear to have come to naught.

Whatever else the future held for Dálriata, this setback, one among many for a kingdom that lost at least as many battles as it won, certainly would not have suggested to a contemporary observer that the Scots, in forming a kingdom in their own name, would eventually come to dominate northern Britain as a whole.

Conflict and co-operation

At the risk of reading history backwards, by far the most interesting question to ask about Dálriata's evolution, because it sheds valuable light on what came afterwards, is: what can we say about the Scots' dealings with the Picts? After all, this was a relationship out of which in time a unified kingdom, the crucible of Scotland itself, would finally be made.

From an early stage there was tension and conflict between these two Celtic peoples, a situation which helps explain the conventional historical narrative in which Scotland was supposedly created by the defeat of the native Picts and their subjection to the rule of the once-immigrant Scots. Chroniclers record a major battle as early as 558 when a certain Brude of the Picts emphatically defeated the Scots under Gabran. Two centuries later Dálriata again tasted bitter humiliation when Ungus, Nechtan's successor as King of Fortriu, actually occupied Dunadd in the 730s. Nor should we be surprised by this pattern of regular reversals for the Scots at the hands of their Celtic neighbours. For neither imperial Rome nor the powerful rulers of Northumbria had successfully subdued the Picts.

There are also tantalizing hints, however, that, for all the underlying tensions and their regular confrontations with each other, the Scots and Picts were on occasion able to identify common interests as Celts exposed to the threat posed by English expansionism. At Nechtansmere, for instance, when Northumbrian hopes of extending their influence throughout northern Britain were decisively crushed, it is believed that Scots from Dálriata as well as Britons from Alt Clut may have fought alongside the triumphant Picts.

Even more significant is the evidence for what anthropologists call acculturation – which is to say, the steady seepage of one group's culture into another's, gradually eroding existing differences and encouraging greater homogeneity. As a result, we need to be extremely careful before accepting the conventional wisdom that the creation of something called Scotland – or as it was initially known, the unified kingdom of Alba (pronounced 'Al-a-pa') – was the result simply of the Gaels having defeated and extinguished the Pictish kingdom in the aftermath of some sudden but decisive encounter on the field of battle.

Father of the nation?

Steadily increasing cultural and social intimacy between Scots and Picts, then, was almost certainly a key factor in Scotland's eventual emergence. But short-term political and strategic circumstances must also have played an important part.

No figure is more important in this process than the man we know as Kenneth Mac Alpin (or *Cinéad Mac Ailpín*, in his Gaelic manifestation), who was finally crowned King of the Picts at Scone in Perthshire, long an important Pictish site, in 843.

Traditionally viewed as the last King of Dálriata who had either secured the Pictish throne by right of conquest (the orthodox interpretation between the 13th and the 19th centuries) or else, benefiting from close family ties, had succeeded by rightful inheritance in the female line (an explanation favoured for much of the 20th century), scholars now choose to emphasize instead Kenneth's essentially Pictish identity. In particular it bears endless repetition that even when Kenneth died on 13 February 858, according to contemporaries he did so as 'King of the Picts' and not as king of an entity called Alba, much less as a declared King of Scots.

The two peoples and two kingdoms, then, were coming perceptibly closer together. But despite being accelerated by important figures like Kenneth, who embodied the increasing cultural and familial connections between Picts and Gaels, especially at the elite level, this was a slow, fitful and as yet incomplete process.

Our own attention must now turn to what may well have been the most important catalyst in the final disappearance of both Pictavia and Dálriata and their absorption into something called the kingdom of Alba. This was the arrival in Scotland of the Vikings.

Men from the north

Few historical groups are as recognizable as the Vikings – the name conjuring up unmistakable images of flowing blond locks, shaggy beards, horned helmets, fearsome weaponry and high-prowed longships.

Climate change, the Vikings' technically innovative longships and population growth in Scandinavia are all cited as possible reasons why these invaders harried, harassed, occupied and ruled many of the islands and coastal regions of north-western Europe between the late eighth and mid-11th centuries.

Whatever the underlying causes, the first arrival of the Vikings can be dated with some accuracy, thanks to the writings of terrified British chroniclers, to the year 794. Just months after they had violated the monastic calm of Lindisfarne off the north-east coast of England – in an attack of shocking brutality that writers claimed had been foreshadowed by fiery dragons in the sky – the same culprits also sacked Iona, Scotland's holiest island.

Here, in a pattern of devastation that recurred twice more in the next 12 years, the Vikings, with a ready eye for rich pickings and easy targets, attacked the monastery and plundered its treasures. In 825 the Vikings returned again. This time they murdered the abbot and all his companions when they tried to defend their precious relics. Another abbot again fell victim as late as 986 during an attack on Iona by Scandinavians who had established a major forward base at Dublin.

Colonization and settlement were from an early stage an integral part of the Scandinavians' interest in the British Isles. And Shetland and Orkney, nearest to Norway and accessible by sea, were probably the first parts of Scotland to be occupied.

What happened to the existing Pictish populations of Shetland and Orkney when the Vikings began to occupy them is an interesting question. Some historians follow the chronicles produced by the Vikings and their descendants, who tell of the killing or enslavement of the native people, or else talk chillingly of the islands as effectively uninhabited when the Norse arrived: the overwhelmingly Scandinavian place names in modern Shetland and Orkney add to the grim suggestion of near-genocide at the hands of bloodthirsty invaders. Other scholars favour less melodramatic explanations. For peaceful co-existence, intermarriage and steady integration may well have been the mundane norm, albeit with a dominant Scandinavian overlay eventually eradicating the Celtic culture of the Picts. The simple truth, however, is that we do not know.

Putting down roots

Lacking substantial contemporary records, archaeological evidence is our main source for the gradual expansion of Scandinavian settlers across Scotland in the ninth and tenth centuries.

It is certain that, for very obvious reasons, those districts most readily accessible by sea tended to be especially exposed to Viking colonization. Their cemeteries, for example, characterized by pagan grave-goods, occur from an early stage not only in Shetland and Orkney but also across the Western Isles and in the mainland's western and northernmost extremities. Ship burials beneath earthen or sandy mounds, the most atmospheric of memorials to a significant Viking life, are also found from the ninth century, notably one on Colonsay – where a warrior was buried with his horse and a formidable collection of weaponry – and three on nearby Sanday, all in the southern Hebrides.

Hoards of precious items, presumably buried as a precaution in a time of heightened instability but never recovered, fill out more details of Viking settlement. Most of those with clear Scandinavian origins occur across the same arc of coastal regions running right around from the far north to the far west. Particularly fine examples were found at Skaill on Orkney (including fabulous silver brooches, necklets and armlets) and on the Hebridean islands of Tiree and Islay – the latter two, each containing silver ingots as well as coins, dateable with reasonable accuracy to around 975.

Insight: The Lewis chessmen

A collection of 78 walrus ivory chess pieces and 14 round 'table men' found in a sandbank at Uig on the Isle of Lewis in 1831 provide the single most stunning and familiar images of Scotland's Scandinavian past. Dating from the 12th century and originating probably in western Norway around Trondheim, the chess pieces are of exceptional quality, wondrously carved figures with expressive faces and gestures. Most were immediately purchased for the British Museum in London, with a few later ending up in Edinburgh – a division that now irks many Scots and has been the subject of recent attempts by the Scottish National Party to have the set reunited in Scotland.

Scandinavian buildings have also been found, sometimes in significant groupings. At Brough of Birsay, a small island off the Orkney mainland with an earlier Pictish settlement, a number of Viking structures were erected from the ninth century onwards, comprising a mixture of residential, agricultural and communal facilities, and eventually, once the inhabitants had been converted to Christianity, even a Norse church. At Jarlshof in Shetland, too, where there had been Bronze Age occupation, Viking settlers constructed what is today the best-preserved such site in Britain, an elaborate farm complex, including a smithy, a bath-house and a large hall.

The fact that the smaller materials found at Jarlshof include just a single spearhead but a range of domestic artefacts such as dress-pins, combs and loom-weights nicely emphasizes that those who lived there were now long-term occupants organized into a settled and reasonably prosperous community. Certainly there is no hint that they still saw themselves as their Vikings forefathers had – as wandering seaborne warriors bent on a life of fleet-footed raiding.

Contested cultures

Clearly the Vikings gradually put down substantial roots in some districts. Probably they intermarried with the natives while also establishing distinctive resident populations who spoke Norse and observed the peculiar customs of their Scandinavian ancestors. As a result, there remained ample scope for antagonism between these newcomers, with their Nordic culture and social organization, and the country's pre-existing Celtic power structures – notably the Picts of Pictavia and the Scots of Dálriata.

In the first place the Scandinavians' political identity, backed by a substantial military capability, became and remained a critical factor. Most obviously, a powerful and distinct earldom of Orkney and Shetland (initially the domain of a Norse *jarl* or lord) also dominated Caithness and Sutherland in the far north. Indeed, this continued to operate, eventually under the auspices of the kingdom of Norway, until its final re-absorption into Scotland, by an agreement between the two countries, as late as the 15th century.

Similar autonomy was established by the tenth century in the Western Isles and adjacent parts of the mainland – whose rulers at times extended their grip as far as Ulster and the Isle of Man. Originally these were strong-willed Norse leaders like Ketil Flatnose, the first to call himself King of the Isles. But as elite intermarriage slowly Gaelicized them, this line of independent regional rulers soon became known as the Lords of the Isles, resulting eventually in Celto-Scandinavian figures such as the famous Somerled in the 12th century (whose own sons were in later times claimed as the common Scottish ancestors of Clan MacDougall and the MacDonalds).

> ### Insight: Blood ties?
>
> Clans, from the Gaelic *clann* ('children'), are usually imagined as extended Scottish families sharing a common surname and ancestor, historically living under a chieftain on defined territories. The truth, however, is less romantic. As surnames spread downwards from the medieval elite, many Scots borrowed from landlords or powerful neighbours: few modern Campbells, MacDonalds or MacLeods are biologically related. Some, like Armstrong and Home, today treated as authentic clan names, originated in the non-Gaelic south. Others, like Smith and Brown, were occupational or descriptive and occur as widely in England. It is the marketing of tartan goods, as well as interest in exploiting Scotland's diaspora and exaggerating the country's Celtic identity (while downplaying ethnic ties with the English), that explains most modern myth-making about the significance of Scottish surnames.

Scotland's internal development was also affected by the simultaneous Scandinavian penetration of Anglo-Saxon England and of Ireland. Dumbarton, for example, Alt Clut's capital, was captured by Vikings in 870 after a long siege by Ivarr the Boneless and Olaf the White, the magnificently named joint kings of Dublin. This old British fortress now became a Scandinavian strongpoint on the Clyde. It was later claimed, implausibly but dramatically, that 200 ships carried off the captives into Irish slavery. What remained of Alt Clut became known as Strathclyde and was centred on Govan on the south side of the river.

Subsequently, in the 11th century, the kings of Scots would again have to deal with the uncomfortable realities brought by Scandinavian power elsewhere in the British Isles. In particular, the English reign of King Cnut (or Canute), along with the brute force available to his Scandinavian earls of Northumbria, set limits to the ability of Scotland, even after it had finally swallowed Bernicia and the formerly Anglian districts that now comprise Edinburgh and the Lothians, to extend its influence much further south into England.

The interaction between the Vikings, the Scots and the Picts, was, however, the most important process for Scotland's future. Especially in the early period, Scandinavian power evidently transformed Scottish politics. As we have seen, the Vikings probably eliminated Kenneth Mac Alpin's rivals to the Pictish throne in a great battle fought somewhere north of the Tay in 839. Other kings, like Constantín I, also paid a grisly price for confronting the fearsome Scandinavians on the field of battle. Yet the Vikings were not only a destructive force. Ultimately it was almost certainly the stresses imposed by their presence, and the threat that they posed to the older Celtic societies, that finally galvanized the emergent kingdom of Alba.

In effect, the Vikings presented the Scots and the Picts, hitherto locked in an often troubled embrace, with what amounted to a make or break situation. That Scotland first came into existence during the ninth century, and that it still exists today, might therefore be in significant measure an unintentional by-product of the arrival of those terrifying blond-haired raiders whose mighty longships first crunched into the sandy beaches of Iona in the summer of 794.

THINGS TO REMEMBER

▶ Human occupation in Scotland has obscure but distant origins, mainly revealed only by modern archaeology.

▶ By the late Iron Age a rich material culture and well-developed tribal societies had emerged.

▶ The Romans never occupied Scotland permanently but they created a significant infrastructure in the Lowlands and influenced the country's economic and social structures.

▶ The Picts, a name given to the Brythonic-speaking northern and eastern Celts never subjected to direct Roman control, founded the kingdom known as Fortriu.

▶ A similar Celtic people dominated Strathclyde in the south and created the kingdom of Alt Clut.

▶ English-speaking Northumbrians settled the post-Roman south-east by the sixth century but failed to advance into the rest of the country.

▶ Christianity arrived in Scotland by different routes, some Roman-influenced from the south, others Irish-based and Celtic.

▶ The Scots of Dálriata were later seen as post-Roman invaders from Ireland (with mythological Mediterranean origins) but in practice they and their distinctive Gaelic tongue may have been long present on Scotland's western fringes.

▶ The Vikings brought fear and destruction but also new settlers who influenced the formation of the kingdom of Alba.

▶ Kenneth Mac Alpin and his successors as kings of Alba probably represent a successful fusion of the Scottish and Pictish elites.

2

Building a kingdom

In this chapter you will learn:

- *about the slow consolidation of the kingdom of Alba*
- *about the historical Malcolm, Duncan and Mac Bethad (Macbeth).*

A union of peoples?

The formation of Alba was clearly a slow and uneven process. It was by no means inevitable. Nor, though, was it remotely inexplicable.

Essentially it was the outcome of changing social and political relations between the Scots and the Picts. This in turn was substantially made possible by the intense pressure exerted by the Scandinavians who between 800 and 1050 represented the primary existential threat to the two leading rival Celtic kingdoms that had emerged in post-Roman northern Britain.

In reconstructing even the basic outlines of this process of unification, we are once again at the mercy of inadequate, sparse and often also potentially misleading sources. Most, indeed, were produced externally, in Ireland, England, Wales or Scandinavia, and frequently at a significantly later date, by people with only indirect knowledge of earlier Scottish events.

Yet about some of the most important features of Alba's emergence – including several of its rulers, now among the best-known names in all of Scottish history – we can be slightly more confident.

Kingship and kin

All the evidence confirms that kingship in Alba was a perilously hard-edged business. Success or failure was not only of political significance but was also literally a matter of life and death for those who wore the crown.

Donald II, the son of Constantín I, reigned from 889 to 900. This clearly marked a decisive moment in the monarchy's development, since he was the first who, when he died, was described by the Irish chroniclers as King of Alba. Donald's immediate predecessor Giric, later (and inaccurately) known as Gregory the Great and afterwards credited (equally inaccurately) with conquering Ireland and England, may also have been an important factor in this process of unification. Some historians have argued that it was in fact Giric who helped bring about the successful fusion of Scots and Pictish rulership. Either way, by the end of the ninth century Alba was at last acquiring recognizable coherence.

Donald II, reputedly killed by Viking invaders at Dunnottar on the north-east coast, was succeeded by Constantín, another Mac Alpin and probably Donald's cousin. The most striking fact about Constantín II, as he came to be known, is that, in an age of constant warfare and ever-present danger for kings who were surrounded not only by powerful external enemies but also by ambitious rival kinsmen, he appears to have enjoyed the longest and most secure reign of any early Scottish monarch. Certainly from 900 until his voluntary abdication in 943, Constantín II was a crucial figure. He further strengthened the identity and internal organization of what was now called Alba – it was first so described in the Irish-based *Chronicles of the Kings of Alba* in 903, just three years into his reign. He also made his kingdom recognizably the dominant political structure throughout northern Britain.

Constantín II and the consolidation of power

Partly because of his longevity but also because Alba's growing prominence attracted increasing interest outside Scotland, more can be said about Constantín II than about any of his often shadowy predecessors.

Above all, the viability of any kingdom at this time rested on winning the acceptance of a single king's, and ideally a single dynasty's, rule over a defined area. And bringing this about across those former territories of the Scots and the Picts that were not under Scandinavian control seems to have been the understandable focus of Constantín's efforts.

In unifying Alba in part by making it more consistently Gaelic in culture and ethos as well as in its leadership, Constantín's reign was of considerable long-term significance. Certainly the aggressive cultivation of Irish-style Columban Christianity was a powerful force for cultural integration across the kingdom. This deliberate process was spearheaded by a group of monks known in Gaelic as the *Céli Dé* or 'servants of God' (later widely anglicized as Culdees), whose influence, starting first at Iona but then fanning out across the rest of Alba, was very strong over the next three centuries.

The use of the Culdees actually made much sense in Scotland in particular. Kenneth Mac Alpin had appointed a bishop at Dunkeld and Constantín probably granted oversight of the entire kingdom to a bishop at the pilgrimage shrine at St Andrews in 908. But in practice Alba lacked any proper diocesan organization of its own. It was in this unusually fluid situation that the Culdees were able to use centres like St Andrews and Loch Leven in Fife, Dunkeld and Abernethy in Perthshire and Monymusk in Aberdeenshire to spread their distinctive form of Celtic Christianity far and wide throughout the formerly Pictish lands.

Constantín II also played a noteworthy part in wider British history as he sought greater authority and influence for Alba. Much of the time, as for his predecessors, this seems to have meant dealing with Scandinavian incursions into the kingdom. In 904, for example, a Viking force sacked Dunkeld before being defeated somewhere in Strathearn. At Corbridge near Hadrian's Wall in 918 Constantín fought alongside Ealdred, the exiled English ruler of Northumbria, in the defeat of Ragnall, its dangerous new Viking lord and close ally of the Dublin monarchy.

But the greatest external threat came from the English, and especially the West Saxon (or Wessex) dynasty – the descendants of Alfred the Great who were then unifying England under their own power.

Around 921, the *Anglo-Saxon Chronicle*, England's best-known surviving source, records that, along with Constantín, the kings of Viking Dublin and Strathclyde met with Edward, Alfred's son, and accepted him as their superior. Interestingly and significantly, this is also the first occasion on which the word *Scottas* is used in the *Chronicle* to describe Constantín's subjects: again this hints that a single political and cultural identity was now visible to those observing northern Britain from the outside.

On 12 July 927 at Eamont Bridge in northern England, Constantín, along with King Owen of Strathclyde, once more met with an English monarch, this time Athelstan, Edward's son, and repeated his acknowledgement of West Saxon overlordship. Clearly caught, like other British rulers, in some sort of subordinate relationship to England's monarchy, he even appeared periodically at Athelstan's court, including at Buckingham in 934 where a document described him explicitly simply as *subregulus* (i.e. an under-king). By this time Athelstan had successfully expanded his authority throughout Northumbria, and perhaps as far as the Firth of Forth, sweeping all before him: Alba, for all its growing coherence and relative internal stability, therefore seemed to face domination from without.

It was in 937 that, along with the Viking ruler Olaf Guthfrithson of Dublin and in association once more with Owen of Strathclyde, Constantín finally rebelled and invaded Athelstan's territory. The aim was surely simple enough: to limit once and for all the expansionary power of the kings of England. Unfortunately for this uniquely broadly based Celto-Scandinavian coalition, it was an utterly disastrous decision. At the bloody and decisive Battle of Brunanburh, whose precise location, like so many military engagements in this early period, is now lost to history, but which probably took place either near Bromborough in modern Cheshire or near the River Humber in Yorkshire, Constantín and his allies were crushed by Athelstan's army.

Unlike so many kings in this era, Constantín II's power in Alba nonetheless endured. And even more unusually, he ended his days peacefully. Retiring to the Culdee monastery at St Andrews in 943, when he died there nine years later his body was conveyed to Iona for burial alongside his ancestors.

Successful successors

Constantín II's reign was followed by several others that, while certainly shorter and individually less eventful, helped further consolidate the kingdom of Alba.

Gaelicization remained a consistent theme of the period. Norse was retreating to the northern and western fringes while the once-dominant Pictish was starting its long march towards complete extinction. By the tenth century it is therefore probable that most of Alba's population were making everyday use of the same Gaelic language.

Cultural change was also at work in other ways that helped reinforce Scottish identities. Not just the kings, who continued to be buried on Iona, but also the kingdom's elites increasingly cultivated a strongly Gaelic profile. Often this meant adopting a complicated, substantially mythological Dalriatan pedigree. Distinctively Scots socio-political organization spread too: the first references to a *mormaer*, a Gaelic regional ruler answerable to the king, occur in the early tenth century, in relation to an unnamed officeholder who fought at Corbridge and then to one Dubacan, apparently responsible for Angus, killed at Brunanburh.

The church likewise increasingly built with confidence on its specifically Scots heritage. This in turn gradually eroded the older traditions of Ninian among the Picts and of Northumbrian Christianity in the south and east. Instead there emerged a new and more organized Irish-influenced structure that exploited St Columba's charismatic legacy within a framework of greater ecclesiastical jurisdiction. Continuing to expand the status and power of the Culdees, the great culture carriers of Gaelic Christianity, was probably also a key priority for the later Mac Alpins.

Yet there remained obstacles to Alba's successful consolidation. Internal threats continued to come from rival members of the Mac Alpin family, to whom Celtic traditions of alternating successors from different branches of the wider bloodline offered obvious encouragement. Other challenges were posed by regional powerbases that provided concentrations of support for those wishing to reject the authority of the monarch: the fact that Alba was itself in the process of emerging from out of several constituent parts ensured that there were always several viable examples. Of course, where both threats also came together, the consequences for the monarchy were necessarily even more worrying.

One who was successful in dealing with them was Malcolm I, seemingly Donald II's son and Constantín II's immediate successor. Malcolm was forced to lead his army into Moray where he killed Cellach, a rebellious local leader, who may well have been taking advantage of the strong regional identity in the north-east dating from the times when this had been the original heartland of Pictish Fortriu.

Malcolm II, the last of the Mac Alpins, whose lengthy reign lasted from 1000 to 1034, faced similar challenges. His rule was marked by intermittent conflict with Northumbria, now under Scandinavian control, including a major victory alongside his Strathclyde allies at Carham in 1018, the most important consequence of which was the lands of Lothian down to the Tweed – essentially the eastern part of the modern Anglo-Scottish border – being ceded to Scotland. By marrying his daughter to the Norwegian Earl of Orkney, he also managed briefly to acquire control over the Northern Isles through his grandson Thorfinn Sigurdsson.

It was probably under Malcolm that Strathclyde was finally absorbed by Alba. Little is known about this process but by the mid-11th century it was clearly complete: even the distinctive Cumbric language of the region, a version of Brythonic, rapidly vanished. Moray, however, was very different, remaining a troublesome rival powerbase within Alba, as the mormaer Findláech and his family demonstrated.

Today we rarely think of Findláech and his ambitions for the Scottish throne. But those of his son will never be forgotten: this was Mac Bethad – better known to us as Macbeth.

Thanes, murders, witches?

On Malcolm II's death in 1034, the throne passed from the direct Mac Alpin male line to those whose claims rested initially on female descent. In the first instance this meant Duncan I, the son of Malcolm's daughter, whose claim was underpinned by his having been designated as Malcolm's *tànaiste* (tanist or chosen heir) from among the eligible candidates.

Duncan's reign was brief and unhappy. It was scarred by a reckless invasion of England in 1039 in retaliation for a Northumbrian attack on Strathclyde, which culminated in an unsuccessful siege of Durham and a humiliating retreat. The sources offer few details but Mac Bethad, described as *dux* or leader, had already come to the fore following Duncan's accession and may have been the principal power behind the young king's throne. The disastrous English expedition may even have been masterminded by the older and more experienced Mac Bethad.

What we do know is that Duncan next invaded Moray in an apparent attempt to curtail Mac Bethad's over-mighty influence. This too proved to be a mistake – fatally so for Duncan. At Pitgaveny near Elgin on 14 August 1040 he was killed in battle. Mac Bethad, whose own claim rested on his mother or grandmother having been a daughter of Malcolm II, now became king.

At this point we need to forget Shakespeare's version of events, based as it is on late-medieval distortions and fabrications. The real Mac Bethad's reign was regarded by near-contemporaries as a tolerably good one. Not the least of his achievements that the famous play ignores was surviving for fully 17 years the perennial threats offered by both internal and external enemies.

Mac Bethad faced the customary challenges, including an uprising by Duncan's father Crinan whom he killed in battle at Dunkeld in 1045. He was even sufficiently secure on the throne that he allegedly risked leaving the country, making a pilgrimage to Rome in 1050. But the persistent problem of resistance to central authority, particularly on the kingdom's fringes, remained. Mac Bethad certainly appears to have struggled in his dealings with Orkney in particular: Thorfinn Sigurdsson seemingly defeated Mac Bethad both at sea and on land in asserting his independence from a King of Alba whose sovereignty he refused to recognize.

Even greater dangers came from elsewhere. In 1052 the court of Alba provided sanctuary for exiles from England's political crisis. Two years later the Northumbrians, perhaps in retaliation, invaded Scotland, inflicting major losses on Mac Bethad's army. Unconnected with this, there was then a rising by Duncan's son Malcolm, clearly a plausible claimant to the throne, who had been brought up safely either in England or in Orkney. This was what finally brought about

Mac Bethad's death in battle on 15 August 1057 at Lumphanan in Aberdeenshire. The next year Mac Bethad's son Lulach was also killed in Strathbogie, the crown passing into the hands of the victor.

Shakespeare's brooding anti-hero is, of course, an utterly compelling figment of a brilliantly original poetic imagination. The real Mac Bethad, however, was no tyrant, or at least no more so than other near-contemporary British kings. Nor, clearly, was he vanquished, as the play suggests, at Dunsinane in Perthshire, by Macduff, a man 'from woman's womb untimely ripp'd'. But in one respect the familiar dramatic finale captures a deeper truth. For the death of Duncan's successor did mark the discernible end of a chapter in the history of Scotland and in particular of Scottish kingship. A new one would now be written by different hands, and would lead the country as a whole in a strikingly different direction.

THINGS TO REMEMBER

▶ Alba – the early kingdom of Scots – was more than anything else a political entity defined by acknowledgement of the legitimate rule of its kings.

▶ We know little about many of the individual kings but they were largely successful in building loyalty and a growing sense of cohesion in Alba.

▶ The kings actively tried to promote unity by spreading Gaelic identity and organization and by sponsoring a strongly Gaelic form of Christianity.

▶ Other Celtic influences, especially from Brythonic speakers like the once-dominant Picts and the inhabitants of Strathclyde, were slowly eliminated through aggressive Gaelicization.

▶ Alba still experienced internal tensions, with rival candidates for the crown within extended royal families as well as regional powerbases often built on older ethnic and cultural differences.

▶ Mac Bethad – Shakespeare's model for Macbeth – was a challenger from Moray who provided successful kingship for 17 years.

Norman Scotland

In this chapter you will learn:

- *how the Normans came to Scotland and increasing Normanization altered the kingdom's elite, importing new families who would dominate Scotland's future history*
- *about the reforms of St Margaret and her son David*
- *about Scotland's struggles to remain separate from the politics of her southern neighbour while subduing treachery at home.*

Canmore and kingship

The beneficiary of Mac Bethad's elimination, better known as Malcolm Canmore or simply as Malcolm III, is not always well understood. Yet it is beyond dispute that Canmore was of considerable importance to Scotland's development.

Above all, Canmore engineered a marked shift in Alba's cultural and political orientation. The earlier phase of Gaelicization under the Mac Alpins had united its inhabitants not least by encouraging them to look west to their Celtic heritage rather than south to English and French influences. But this process largely came to an end by the mid-11th century. And Canmore was the most important single ruler responsible for this development.

Insight: Counting kings

Long tradition accords Malcolm III the name 'Canmore' (from the Gaelic *ceann mór* for 'big head'). Modern scholars, however, have made the case for misidentification, arguing that the first ruler to bear this name was in fact his great-grandson Malcolm IV (died 1165), who was so-called in a

Norman knights had first sought refuge in Scotland, as we noted, under Mac Bethad. But under Canmore this trickle became a flood, helped by the Norman conquest of England and also encouraged by Canmore's own connections in the south.

These early Norman arrivals included heavyweight landed dynasties like the Sinclairs (from St-Clair-sur-Epte in Normandy) and the Flemings (as the name implies, originally from Flanders). But this was about much more than merely transplanting a few elite families. This group would actually take the lead in the kingdom's feudalization under Canmore and his successors. These Continental practices, already imposed on England by the Conqueror, ultimately transformed landholding, social relations, elite culture and political power across much of Scotland too.

The same decisive reorientation was seen also in Canmore's second marriage in 1070 to Margaret, who began life as the Hungarian-born sister of an uncrowned English prince in exile. This was a crucial moment. For it meant that Scotland's royal dynasty were tied thereafter not only to the old English royal house whom the Conqueror had overthrown but also, once Henry I had married Edith (known in England as Maud or Matilda), Canmore's daughter with Margaret, in 1100, to the Norman and Plantagenet kings of medieval England – through whose veins therefore coursed the blood of the Mac Alpins as well as that of the West Saxons.

Canmore's own relations with the English monarchy were understandably cagey, not least because the wider implications of William's victory in England took time to become clear across the rest of Britain.

Canmore actually met him at Abernethy in 1072, prudently repeating the submissive gestures made by Constantín II – acknowledging William's overlordship and even handing over a son of his first marriage, Duncan, another future ruler, as a hostage. Canmore formally agreed peace with William once again in 1080. But punctuating these periods of edgy mutual toleration between ambitious monarchs with widely differing resources were periodic eruptions of violence. Scottish forces, for example, harried Northumbria on several occasions while the English more than once raided deep into Strathclyde.

St Margaret and the soul of Scotland

Margaret's influence on her adoptive country was also profound. Certainly it is no coincidence that she was soon canonized – becoming Scotland's only royal saint and for centuries second only to St Andrew, an apostle whose historical connection with Scotland is much more tenuous, in popular esteem.

Margaret's reputation for piety and devotion, which began with a youthful interest in becoming a nun and continued with extensive charitable donations and personal care for the poor, was richly deserved. But she was also determined to clarify and purify Scottish Christianity, hitherto the unwieldy and confusing product of disparate Irish, Pictish, Northumbrian and Roman influences.

A key reform under Margaret's direction was the widespread celebration of Easter communion. She also emphasized observing the Sabbath by abstaining from work and attending mass. Both measures served to tie ordinary Scottish believers into the routine liturgical life of the national Church.

Her piety also had more tangible consequences. One was the construction of St Margaret's Chapel, the first Scottish building in the Norman style, still today at the heart of Edinburgh Castle. Another was her encouragement of the cult of Scotland's patron saint at St Andrews, instituting free passage for pilgrims crossing the Firth of Forth at what duly became North and South Queensferry.

Simultaneously Margaret tried to resolve the linguistic ambiguities that were the accidental legacy of the Scottish Church's complicated history. Latin now replaced local Celtic dialects as the universal medium for mass. As a result, while the everyday use of Gaelic continued to spread, especially north of the Forth and Clyde, and while French and English were becoming common among the elites, ecclesiastical reform meant that a visitor from anywhere in western Europe would have been able to understand the key Christian ritual when it was performed in Latin in a Scottish church.

Margaret was also greatly attached to Continental forms of monasticism. This too began to reorient Scotland's religious life away from its traditional ties to Iona and Ireland and towards France and England. In particular, it represented – although there is evidence that Margaret herself was sympathetic to them – a long-term challenge to the formative role of the Culdees. Fittingly, since it was already a major royal centre and where she herself would be buried in 1093, the first Benedictine community was established at Dunfermline in Fife in the 1070s, with monks secured by Margaret with the help of the Archbishop of Canterbury.

Even more important, perhaps, Margaret's passion for the fashionable new forms of monasticism would also be transmitted to her sons, Canmore's successors. This in turn would decisively alter the character and organization of the Scottish Church.

Duncan, Donald and Edgar

Canmore's own sons provided four of the next five kings, their names signifying the cultural and political shifts that his reign had begun. Duncan II, who reigned for several months in 1094 and whose mother was Thorfinn's widow, Canmore's first wife, had a Celtic name recalling earlier kings of Alba. Later came the reigns of Margaret's offspring, all, significantly, with names indicating their affinity with English and European traditions of rulership – Edgar (1097–1107), Alexander I (1107–1124) and David I (1124–1153).

When Canmore was killed, along with his chosen successor, Edward, Duncan's half-brother, during yet another invasion of Northumbria in 1093 (a personal tragedy that hastened Margaret's own death just four days later), the crown was seized initially by Canmore's brother Donald Bane, who became Donald III after having expelled Margaret's children and her English allies from Edinburgh.

Donald, however, rapidly faced a reaction in the form of an invasion from Duncan. Having spent many years in England as a hostage, having been knighted by the Conqueror's successor William Rufus and having also acquired an English wife, Duncan II was strongly backed in his successful challenge by Norman knights from England.

Yet Duncan's reign proved the most fleeting of intermissions. Perhaps because of his obvious unfamiliarity with Scotland, his excessive reliance upon Norman support and a corresponding lack of Scottish allies, especially among the old Celtic elites north of the Forth, he too faced almost immediate rebellion. Donald, who had survived Duncan's *coup*, provided a focus for the malcontents and for what it is tempting to interpret as a Gaelic backlash against the kingdom's steady anglicization. Duncan himself was quickly murdered by the mormaer of Mearns and Donald III was reinstated before the end of 1094.

Donald himself, however, soon met the same fate as Duncan, when another of his Canmore nephews, Edgar, Margaret's eldest son, similarly exploited his family's strong connections with England, and particularly with its Norman feudal elite, to devastating effect. Aided by his English uncle and assisted by Rufus's knights, Edgar invaded Scotland in 1097. Although the exact circumstances received conflicting treatment from the various chroniclers, it is clear that Donald, whether he was blinded and imprisoned or simply assassinated, was swiftly eliminated as a political threat to Margaret's descendants.

Amidst the familiar treachery and bloodshed, however, there were also symbolic changes taking place in Scotland that would be of great significance for the country's future. First, Donald III was the last monarch to be laid to rest among his Gaelic ancestors on Iona: all later kings would be interred on the mainland, usually in churches or monasteries founded on the Norman model by Margaret and her descendants. Second, Duncan II, despite the extreme brevity of his reign, became the first King of Alba to bear the Latin title *Rex Scottorum* – making him, in the English translation that soon became widespread, the first to be identified as 'King of Scots'.

Edgar's tenure, notable chiefly for his being forced to confirm to Magnus Barelegs the Norse king's rightful possession of Kintyre and the Western Isles, appears to have made a largely peaceful contribution to the country's growing anglicization. Certainly he was the first of a series of Scottish rulers who knew the English court and the English kings very well.

In 1098 Edgar founded the Benedictine priory at Coldingham in Berwickshire under the auspices of Durham Cathedral. Initially staffed by English monks, this community commemorated St Ebba, one of Northumbrian Christianity's great early figures. Edgar also seems to have chosen to make Edinburgh Castle his political and administrative centre, retaining Dunfermline, where he, like his mother and most of his family, would be interred, as the Scottish monarchy's principal religious site.

The first Alexander

Unmarried and childless, Edgar was succeeded in 1107 by his brother Alexander I. But he also ensured that their younger brother David would be granted substantial authority across the south of Scotland – essentially in Lothian and the former Strathclyde, the latter itself now fully absorbed into the territories of the King of Scots.

Alexander's rule in many ways marked a continuation of the previous reign. In keeping with the reputation of Margaret and her sons for ostentatious acts of piety (it should be noted in passing that he had in fact been named not after the ancient Greek ruler but after a recent pope), there were additional monastic foundations from Alexander, this time at Scone in Perthshire and on Inchcolm in the Firth of Forth, an island on which in 1123 he had been shipwrecked and cared for by a hermit. Run by the Augustinians, the most fashionable and influential of the recently-established European monastic traditions, the first occupants were brought from their existing communities in England.

The Tironensians, a mainly French order, were also encouraged. The first arrived at Selkirk in 1113 under strong encouragement from David, in his capacity as prince of the Cumbrians, before moving on to Kelso once he was on the throne. Alexander also revived the ancient see at Dunkeld, with its Columban associations. And he helped defend the independence of the Bishop of St Andrews – recognized since at least Constantín II's time as the Scottish Church's *de facto* leader – from the aggressive claims of the Archbishop of York.

Alexander, however, for all his pious gestures, justified his conventional nickname 'the Fierce' by displaying considerable military and political authority. One potential threat, fortunately neutralized peacefully, came early in the reign from David, with whom an unseemly dispute over the latter's claim, backed by their brother-in-law Henry I of England, to additional lands in Upper

Tweeddale, was settled by negotiation. But elsewhere, Alexander's soldierly prowess was tested to the full.

He was particularly relentless in subduing the wayward rulers of outlying parts of the kingdom, especially the mormaers of Mearns and Moray – the latter, of course, the family of Mac Bethad and Lulach and therefore representatives of Alba's old ruling house. Attacked when holding court at Invergowrie near Dundee, Alexander pursued them into the far north, beyond the Grampians, finally defeating them near Beauly.

Like his recent predecessors, Alexander enjoyed a close and generally cordial relationship with England's Norman kings. Indeed, following Edith's union with Henry I and also his own happy marriage to Henry's illegitimate and intensely religious daughter Sybilla (who sadly died young and childless), Alexander was also a member of their immediate family. In cementing these personal and cultural ties with England, however, he had in fact set Scotland on a course that would in succeeding centuries have the most explosive consequences.

David I

Alexander having died without legitimate sons, it was David, Margaret's youngest son, whose name recalled both a recent Hungarian ruler and the greatest of biblical kings, who eventually succeeded in 1124.

David's time as prince of the Cumbrians had given him an impressive powerbase across Lothian and Strathclyde as well as further strengthening his connections with England. This influenced how he ruled as king.

In particular, David bolstered Scotland's emerging feudal elite with yet more Norman imports. These included the Bruces, from Brus in Normandy, whom he established in Annandale; the Comyns, who left northern France for Durham and then for Roxburghshire; the Douglases, transplanted from Flanders to Lanarkshire; the Lindsays, who moved from that part of Lincolnshire from which they took their name to Lanarkshire; the Ramsays, who left Huntingdonshire to establish a new stronghold in Midlothian; and the Oliphants, who came from Normandy via Northamptonshire before becoming major landholders in Roxburghshire and Perthshire. Most importantly, though no one could have known it at the time, it brought the Fitzalans, who came from Brittany via England, to whom David granted a lordship in Strathclyde: this family later became royal stewards – and thus, it turned out, the progenitors of Scotland's royal House of Stewart.

David's strong ties to England also brought his own marriage, encouraged by Henry I, to the hugely eligible Matilda, the Earl of Northumbria's daughter. This was how he inherited the Huntingdon earldom and estates – which in turn simply reinforced his personal contacts within a cross-border network of Norman knights and landowners.

In his immediate claim to Scotland's throne, however, David faced some difficulties. There was an uncle, Malcolm, customarily regarded as Alexander's illegitimate son. Only with Henry I's help and with his own Norman knights to the fore was David able to march into central Scotland, defeat Malcolm and have himself formally crowned at Scone in 1124.

David was also confronted by the familiar threat of hostile subordinates in the kingdom's well-defined outer regions. The mormaers of Moray in particular were recalcitrant opponents, and it was with them that the defeated Malcolm took sanctuary.

For his part David initially had to accept serious limits to his authority. North of the Forth was effectively loyal to Malcolm, around whom resistance to the new monarch, associated with the French-speaking court of Henry I rather than with the Gaelic-speaking heartlands of his own kingdom, was able to gather. Indeed, David's early reign was marked by regular visits to his English estates and a continuing closeness to Henry that probably did nothing to persuade Scottish doubters.

In 1130, however, David's army, again backed by Henry and by Norman mailed knights, crushed Malcolm's forces at Stracathro near Brechin, killing Óengus, Lulach's grandson and mormaer of Moray, in the process. Malcolm himself was captured in the far west by Henry's fleet. Four years later this dangerous rival was safely detained in Roxburgh Castle. From here Malcolm disappears from the historical record, the silence inviting us to reach a sinister conclusion about his fate.

The removal of Malcolm and the subduing of Moray confirmed David's hold on the crown. But it had also underlined his dependence on an Anglo-French elite of warrior landowners who needed to be systematically imported, promoted and rewarded. This in turn increased Scotland's entanglement in English politics, especially in the conflicts which erupted following Henry I's death in 1135. David found himself involved partly because of personal loyalty to Henry's daughter and intended heir, his own niece Matilda, in her fight with her usurping cousin Stephen. But David was also interested in the opportunities it brought to extend the Scottish crown's territories into northern England, particularly in Northumberland.

Within days of Stephen's coronation in December 1135, a Scottish army had entered England. This occupied Carlisle and Newcastle before the first Treaty of Durham was signed: Carlisle was ceded to David, as was confirmation of his son's rights to the earldom of Huntingdon which Stephen had previously annulled. Poor relations continued, however, leading to re-invasion and David's demand that Stephen hand over the earldom of Northumbria. After a victory at Clitheroe in Lancashire the Scots were defeated in the Battle of the Standard, fought near Northallerton in Yorkshire in 1138. In the resulting treaty David's original demands were largely met. His rights to the two English earldoms were acknowledged and Scotland continued in possession of Cumberland and Northumberland.

This may well be why on David's death at his new seat of power at Carlisle in 1153, he was described in Irish chronicles as 'King of Scotland and England' – an exaggeration, surely, but also an indication of his success in pushing his influence southwards. Another terminological innovation may also capture something significant about David's view of kingship: for the first time the Scottish king's official Latin title starts to alternate between the older *Rex Scottorum* (King of Scots) and the new *Rex Scotiae* (King of Scotland) – emphasizing rule over a defined territory rather than leadership of a community of people and perhaps hinting at a Norman-style king sitting atop a feudal pyramid of property owners.

At home, David's mature kingship saw a broader programme of consolidation designed to transform and so to integrate the most troublesome parts of the kingdom. This was especially obvious in the truculent north. Burghs – chartered towns with a legal right to internal self-government and to hold markets – were founded at Elgin and Forres. These were simultaneously new centres of royal administrative power and an attempt to divert local energies into productive commercial activity. David's is also the first reign during which we first hear of something like a Parliament: the earliest known organized meeting of Scotland's lay and ecclesiastical leaders with their king probably took place at Edinburgh Castle around 1140.

Monasticism too played a part in David's campaign to increase the cohesion of the kingdom. A new Benedictine priory was founded at Urquhart in Moray, initially using monks from Dunfermline. Kinloss, a Cistercian house first established towards the end of the reign, also formed part of the same programme. In the far north, where the Scandinavian legacy made integration more testing, David formed a bishopric of Caithness in the 1140s and appointed a Scottish incumbent. He also married a lord's son from Atholl with the daughter of the Earl of Orkney in an attempt to extend royal power over the Northern Isles.

David's programme for the Scottish Church, like his importation of a feudal elite, can be thought of as essentially a process of continuing Normanization. Episcopal power, long weak in Scotland, was a key component. As prince of the Cumbrians he had appointed a new Bishop of Glasgow, turning the diocese into the kingdom's second most important ecclesiastical jurisdiction. As King David also gave regular diocesan powers to old Gaelic bishoprics like Dunblane, Dunkeld and Brechin. He even pushed this progressive territorialization of church authority to its logical conclusion by extending the parish system in the localities.

Monasteries, with their substantial wealth, wide local influence and imposing architecture based on foreign designs and often built with the help of immigrant craftsmen, physically embodied David's approach. His strategic foundations in outlying regions like Moray and Ross were accompanied by an even greater number in the kingdom's core areas, especially in the Borders and Central Lowlands. Among those founded either by David himself or by his feudal allies and associates were Kelso (a transfer from Selkirk), Jedburgh, Holyrood, Lesmahagow, Newbattle, Dryburgh and, above all, Melrose, established by English Cistercians in 1137.

Yet despite the ways in which Normanization also entailed anglicization, David was also determined to maintain the traditional independence of the Scottish Church. This was crucial, since despite St Andrews' long-standing *de facto* primacy within Scotland, ultimate legal supremacy was claimed by the Archbishop of York from 1125 – not only over the southernmost dioceses of Glasgow and Galloway, which had in earlier times come under direct English influence, but even over the whole Scottish Church which notably lacked its own archbishopric. The disagreement, which the papacy failed to settle, rumbled on for years. It was also further complicated by David's occupation of much of northern England and his own ambitions to control both the York archdiocese and the powerful Durham bishopric.

Such ambiguities in Anglo-Scottish affairs were, of course, greatly exacerbated by the cultural and political reorientation of Scotland that had taken place in the period of almost a century between Canmore's accession and David's death. As things turned out, they also pointed the way to the considerable difficulties between the two kingdoms that would scar succeeding centuries.

THINGS TO REMEMBER

▶ Malcolm Canmore's reign began a shift away from his kingdom's Celtic roots and Irish influences towards new connections with England and France.

▶ Normanization altered the kingdom's elite, importing new families such as the Bruces, Comyns and Stewarts, who would dominate Scotland's future history.

▶ Another key Norman legacy was feudal landholding and social organization.

▶ Anglo-French influence transformed the Church, especially under Margaret and her sons, making it less Celtic and more Continental in character.

▶ The Canmores successfully increased the kingdom's internal unity and cohesion by using institutional developments – burghs, bishops, monasteries – to extend royal control across the country.

▶ Relations with England were complicated by personal ties between the rulers and by the Normanization of Scotland's elite.

▶ David I became a particularly powerful figure on the British stage, ruling a defined territorial kingdom in Scotland but also holding English lands and titles.

4

The golden age

In this chapter you will learn:

- *about the period of stability that followed the rule of David I*
- *how Alexander III loosened the Scandinavian grip on the north and west, and presided over a largely peaceful land, before his sudden death brought chaos.*

Looking forwards and backwards

David's four immediate successors ruled throughout a period of nearly a century and a half during which a crucial watershed in Scotland's development had clearly been passed. Above all, the existence of a unified realm under these mainly long-lived and well-regarded kings had been substantially settled. Ultimately neither Malcolm IV (1153–1165), nor William I (1165–1214), nor Alexander II (1214–1249), nor Alexander III (1249–1286) had cause to doubt that they ruled over a widely recognized and functioning political entity called the kingdom of the Scots.

It is not hard to see why this era, and in particular the final part of it in Alexander III's long reign, would later be regarded as a time when Scotland had been peculiarly blessed. Certainly what came afterwards strongly encouraged sentimental nostalgia for the relative calm and stability before 1286.

Clearly, though, while such a favourable interpretation is psychologically understandable given subsequent events, it is important that we should also ask whether it is really historically accurate.

The last of the Malcolms

Malcolm IV, David's grandson, was in some ways lucky to have become king at all. His father Henry, Earl of Huntingdon, had been the expected successor, but the latter's death in 1152 had left Malcolm as the heir. Crowned Malcolm IV at Scone on 27 May 1153, he was in questionable health and just 12 years old.

Malcolm justified his Canmore inheritance. Known for his piety, he founded the Cistercian monastery at Coupar Angus. Government was also further consolidated. Sheriffs – judicial and administrative officers who had exercised royal power throughout England since Anglo-Saxon times – now appeared in Scotland in places like Linlithgow, Forfar and Dunfermline, initiating the county system of local government.

Malcolm also faced the same threats as his predecessors. His youthful inexperience (he acquired the unwelcome nickname 'the Maiden') hardly helped. Nor did his continuing encouragement of influential immigrants whose prominence affronted traditional interest groups: the Hay family, yet another Norman dynasty with a great Scottish future ahead of it, first appeared at Malcolm's court and quickly married into the Celtic aristocracy. Together with the usual plentiful supply of rival claimants to the throne with plausible blood connections and useful regional power bases, these factors served to invite serious challenges to Malcolm's kingship.

These came from different directions. In the first year of the reign the famous Somerled, independent ruler of the Celto-Scandinavian lands of Argyll and the Hebrides, attempted to extend his own authority eastwards, in league with some of Malcolm's distant Gaelic relations. Somerled's diversion by other disputes initially helped Malcolm, before the royal army, marshalled by Walter Fitzalan ('the Steward') and the Bishop of Glasgow, defeated and killed Somerled and many of his invading force at Renfrew in 1164. There were also risings in two of the kingdom's most distinctive outlying regions, Galloway and Moray, as well as a rebellion by the mormaer of Strathearn in 1160. In each case Malcolm exploited the royal military power and political authority accumulated by his immediate predecessors to see off the challenge.

But Malcolm's most intractable problem, and one which eventually damaged his posthumous reputation, came predictably from elsewhere. For Henry II unsurprisingly resented Scottish occupation of the territories taken by David and was in a position to manipulate Malcolm's dual status as a neighbouring monarch and as the holder of lands and aristocratic titles in England itself.

Malcolm was duly forced to do homage to Henry at Chester in 1157. Allowed to retain the earldom of Huntingdon, he was, however, made to surrender Cumbria and Northumberland, including the city of Carlisle and the prestigious earldom of Northumbria, which thereafter remained in English hands. Malcolm even went on to serve in Henry's French campaigns, being knighted for his loyalty in 1159. Such an honour, of course, appeared less flattering to many Scottish observers, suggesting that their own ruler, already stripped of hard-won lands and titles, had accepted his subordination to the King of England.

A Lion or a lamb?

Malcolm IV, when he died unmarried at Jedburgh of natural causes in 1165, aged just 24, was a rather diminished figure, having ceded territory and status to a powerful rival king. His brother and successor William, however, one of Scotland's longest-reigning sovereigns, would be remembered quite differently.

Insight: Symbol or substance?

Long after his death, and probably not before 1300, William I became known, as he still is today, as 'the Lion'. Yet this was probably more to do with his having placed a lion on the Scottish royal standard than because of a particularly ferocious temperament or unusual military prowess. Indeed, William's success, such as it was, lay very much in his longevity as King of Scots rather than in any great or lasting victories.

Some features of William's reign followed the recently established pattern. There were attempts to extend the reach of government – as, for example, by conferring royal burgh status on Dumfries (chartered in 1186), Ayr (1205) and Perth (1210). Highly visible acts of piety were also undertaken – including the foundation of the great Tironensian abbey at Arbroath in 1178 that would play such an important part in Scotland's later struggles against

English domination and where William himself would eventually be laid to rest. Again, too, there were continuing problems with rebellions in Galloway and Ross, which William regularly needed to tackle.

William's principal aim from the moment of his coronation, however, was to recover what Malcolm IV had lost – particularly the earldom of Northumbria, previously in his personal possession. But in this ambition he was thwarted. Captured on 12 July 1174 at Alnwick in Northumberland in an ill-advised skirmish that formed part of a doomed wider revolt against Henry II in which William and the Scots had participated opportunistically, he was first imprisoned in Newcastle and then at Northampton before eventually ending up in one of Henry's imposing castles in Normandy.

Humiliated even more than Malcolm had been, some of the key southern strong points in William's kingdom, including the castles at Edinburgh, Stirling and Berwick, came into the uncontested possession of Henry's forces. He was even obliged to raise funds to pay both for the cost of the English occupation and a ransom for his own release.

It is hard to think of a Scottish monarch so comprehensively humbled as William was by being made to sign the Treaty of Falaise in 1174, explicitly acknowledging English overlordship in Scotland and also placing the Scottish Church firmly under the Archbishop of York. By the next year William had himself sworn his fealty to the kings of England and as late as 1186 he married an aristocratic English wife, a granddaughter of Henry I, specifically chosen for him by Henry II: reinforcing the Scottish king's submission, Henry ensured that the bride's dowry, given as a gift rather than as an entitlement received as of right, was none other than Edinburgh Castle.

The long-term implications of William's embarrassment were fortunately more limited. Henry's successor Richard the Lionheart, desperate to fund the Third Crusade, permitted the Scots to annul the Treaty of Falaise through the Quitclaim of Canterbury in 1189. A one-off payment of 10,000 silver marks ended the English occupation and released Scotland formally from subordination. The Pope, lobbied by William's bishops, also agreed that the Scottish Church should remain independent.

In truth, William the Lion's reign ought to have taught some sobering lessons about the increasing power and ambitions of the kings of England and the growing difficulties that their Scottish counterparts would face in resisting them.

Another Alexander

Without being unduly cynical, Alexander II's reign looks in many respects like those of most of his predecessors back to Canmore – a mixture of trials and tribulations inside and outside the kingdom, some noteworthy royal strengths offset by significant weaknesses, and, in the long-term view, a number of promising developments.

On the one hand Alexander faced continuing difficulties with certain parts of Scotland which since the early 11th century had most resented the Normanization of kingship and culture. Ross and Moray, under their Gaelic mormaers, as well as Galloway, with its powerful Gaelic lordship and links with England, all became the focus of resistance at different points. The most dramatic incident in these struggles was the savage murder of a baby girl, the last representative of the MacWilliams, descendants of Canmore who claimed both Moray and the Scottish crown: on Alexander's orders her brains were smashed out against the market cross at Forfar in 1230.

Even more problematic was Alexander's relationship with the King of England, hardly helped by the still-simmering disputes over both Cumberland and Northumberland. Initially Alexander followed his father's example in taking advantage of King John's weakness. He sided with the rebel English barons and with the French, even sending a Scottish army into England that reached Dover unopposed before John was forced to sign Magna Carta in 1215.

After Henry III's accession, however, and the return of more settled conditions south of the border, Alexander's approach largely mirrored that of his pragmatic uncle Malcolm IV. His response to Henry, whose ten-year-old sister Joan he married in 1221 (she died childless in 1238), was simply to avoid unduly antagonizing the English monarch. Instead he offered reasonable concessions with good grace. The greatest fruit of the new mutual understanding was the Treaty of York in 1237. This drew a boundary between the two kingdoms, never again substantially altered, which followed the natural barriers of the Solway in the west and the Tweed in the east.

Other aspects of Alexander's long reign also continued some of the more constructive trends of the previous century. New royal burghs were chartered at the old Strathclydian capital of Dumbarton (1222) and at Dingwall in Ross (1226). The first Parliament of Scotland for which any documentary record of the proceedings survives also occurred when Alexander brought together his leading barons and bishops at Kirkliston near Edinburgh in 1235.

Alexander also encouraged the further settlement of the English elite north of the border. It was now that the Umfraville family, originally from Normandy and lately settled in Northumberland, took possession of the earldom of Angus. It was also at this time that the Balliols, with deep roots in Picardy but more recently in County Durham, first married into the Celto-Scottish aristocracy of Galloway, acquiring great power and influence in the south and west.

Least surprisingly, we once again find a descendant of St Margaret enthusiastically establishing monastic houses. In Alexander's case we can attribute the foundation not only of the Cistercian abbey at Balmerino in Fife (1227) but also of the Dominican friaries in Edinburgh and at Berwick (both 1230) and of the priory at Pluscarden in Moray (again 1230) to his personal intervention.

When Alexander died in 1249 he was buried, appropriately, in Melrose Abbey, and was succeeded by his son Alexander, the late-born child of his second marriage to the French noblewoman Marie de Coucy.

The happiest of times?

The reign of Alexander III, more than that of any other Scottish monarch, has often seemed to later ages to reveal Scotland as its best – stable, secure and, above all, independent.

The evidence, perhaps surprisingly given what had gone before, largely supports this interpretation.

Ascending the throne at just eight and married at ten to Henry III's daughter Margaret, Alexander's kingship began auspiciously.

He declined Henry's attempt to have him do homage for his Scottish kingdom and, as he grew into adulthood, the settlement arrived at by his father appeared likely to endure.

Alexander made significant strides during his reign towards finally loosening the Scandinavian grip on the north and west. On coming of age in 1262, he was bold enough to demand that King Haakon of Norway formally transfer sovereignty of the Western Isles to Scotland. And when Haakon responded, not surprisingly, with a seaborne attack, Alexander's army fought him in the indecisive Battle of Largs in Ayrshire in 1263, a reversal for the previously confident Norwegians which effectively demonstrated the impossibility of their continuing to defend their claim to the islands off Scotland's west coast. Accordingly in 1266 they agreed by the Treaty of Perth that Alexander, in return for a cash payment, could assume control over the Hebrides. Two decades later he bestowed the Lordship of the Isles upon the MacDonald chieftain, in whose family it would thereafter descend.

Alexander, then, was a determined and successful political operator who, through good judgment and the astute deployment of royal power, made a conspicuously effective King of Scots. He was less fortunate, however, in his personal life.

Margaret died in 1274, having provided him with two sons who predeceased him and a daughter Margaret, who married Erik, Haakon's successor as King of Norway. She too predeceased Alexander, leaving just her own half-Norwegian daughter, again Margaret, whom in 1284 he had been forced to take the precaution of having recognized by Parliament as the heir-presumptive. Alexander's second wife, Yolande of Dreux, actually fell pregnant immediately following their marriage in 1285. But tragically this child was still-born. As a result Alexander's granddaughter Margaret, in Norway and as yet some way short of her third birthday, was in early 1286 his most likely hypothetical successor.

It was therefore very fortunate that the King of Scots was just 44 years of age and apparently in rude health.

Scotland's ruin

The night of 19 March 1286 was dark and stormy, with snow and rain carried on a strong northerly wind. Alexander III had spent the day in Edinburgh but he was now riding on horseback, against the advice of several people, as he finally neared Kinghorn on Fife's southern coast. What happened next had repercussions that had been predicted a day earlier by Thomas of Ercildoune, also known as Thomas the Rhymer. This prophetic vision of Alexander's fatal fall down steep ground onto the beach below is worth quoting in all its melodramatic glory:

> *Alas for the morrow, day of misery and calamity! Before the hour of noon there will assuredly be felt such a mighty storm in Scotland that its like has not been known for long ages past. The blast of it will cause nations to tremble, will make those who hear it dumb, and will humble the high, and lay the strong level with the ground.*

Over the edge, in a national as well as a personal calamity, went not only Scotland's able and secure king but also its best chance of peace and stability. The next 200 years would instead be marked by chronic upheaval and warfare as rival claimants to the throne struggled for dominance and opportunistic English interventions regularly threatened the kingdom's very existence.

THINGS TO REMEMBER

▶ The period between David I and the death of Alexander III has always seemed relatively stable and prosperous for Scotland.

▶ Kings nonetheless faced difficulties as traditional interests – as always, mainly rival kinsmen and claimants with regional power bases – resisted the intrusion of Norman culture and practices.

▶ Scotland's kings sought greater cohesion and control by founding monasteries and burghs and by importing and advancing English and Norman allies.

▶ Numerous attempts were made by England's monarchs to assert feudal superiority over the king and kingdom of the Scots, which the latter sometimes conceded but at other times managed to reject.

▶ The tragic loss of Alexander III without an acknowledged adult male heir greatly increased the kingdom's vulnerability to internal rivalries and English ambitions.

5

A nation compromised

In this chapter you will learn:
- *how the 200 years that followed Alexander's death were marked by severe internal instability and powerful external threats*
- *about Sir William Wallace's battles against Edward I, his victories and his eventual defeat and death.*

The fair Maid

If the decades before 1286 came to be seen as Scotland's lost golden age, the centuries that followed were more like an age of steel.

Not that violence and political instability were new. Kings of Scots in particular were no strangers to vindicating their authority on the battlefield, sword in hand. Most rulers, as we have seen, had faced a combination of challenges not only from inside the country, especially from ambitious kinsmen and from over-mighty subjects on the kingdom's periphery, but also from outside – above all from English monarchs eager to assert their own sovereignty over all of mainland Britain.

What was different from 1286 onwards was that English power on an unprecedented scale, deployed in such a way as to worsen political uncertainty and exploit growing divisions within Scotland itself, now placed the kingdom's independence in grave jeopardy.

Alexander III's accidental death in March 1286, an unmitigated disaster which left his infant granddaughter Margaret, the so-called 'Maid of Norway', in formal possession of the crown, illustrates this vulnerability vividly.

Given Margaret's extreme youth and location overseas, royal power following Alexander's unexpected demise was delegated by Parliament to four barons and the bishops of St Andrews and Glasgow – collectively designated the Guardians. Had Margaret's claim been unchallenged, this cumbersome arrangement would still have been difficult to sustain in the long run. But there were actually several other potential successors waiting expectantly in the wings. And not all of them could resist the obvious opportunity that Margaret's age, her gender and her absence now presented.

Late 1286, for example, saw a rising in the south-west, led by two Robert Bruces, father and son, respectively 5th Lord of Annandale and Earl of Carrick. The father was David I's great-great-grandson and actually Alexander III's closest living male relative. A regent during Alexander's own minority, he had even been named the king's preferred successor before Margaret's birth. The Lord of Annandale, then, was a thoroughly credible claimant.

Yet the Bruces' revolt was soon quelled. Other contenders, some with equally powerful claims, were also kept at bay by the Guardians. Somewhat uneasily but quite successfully, the kingdom was governed in this way for nearly three more years, effectively deferring some of the most serious issues about how, when and with what consequences Margaret might eventually rule Scotland.

One thorny question, however, affecting all young elite females at this time, did need to be grappled with. This was the politically sensitive matter of pre-determining her future marriage. Margaret's father, the King of Norway, wanted her engaged to Edward, infant son and heir of Edward I, King of England.

Eventually in 1290 the Scots Parliament and the English ruler signed the Treaty of Birgham. It decreed that Margaret, whose claim to the Scottish crown the English formally acknowledged, would reign as queen of Scots in her own right. It also agreed that, while any offspring with Prince Edward would inherit both thrones, Scotland would remain a separate kingdom, governed independently and not subject to England's jurisdiction.

What no one could have anticipated, however, was what happened next. Margaret, finally travelling by ship to Scotland, died at Orkney, aged just seven, apparently of natural causes, in the autumn of 1290.

With the leading candidate suddenly removed from the game, the field of play had been dramatically levelled. This completely unexpected development had one utterly predictable outcome. For it encouraged a host of other competitors for Scotland's crown to enter the fray.

Candidates for kingship

In some ways the extent of the political uncertainty created by the tragic deaths of both a reigning monarch and his designated heir in quick succession can be gauged from the fact that no fewer than 14 contenders now stepped forward. Each staked a claim in what has become known as the Great Cause – 'cause' being the Scots law term for a 'case', with competing parties exchanging legal arguments before a court.

Some possessed only flimsy justifications and must privately have doubted their own chances. Robert de Pinkeney, for example, great-great-great-grandson of David I, was undermined by being reliant upon an allegedly illegitimate great-grandmother. Not a man to allow implausibility to stand in the way of ambition, even King Erik of Norway advanced a claim based on being Margaret's father and the previous king's son-in-law.

Stronger arguments were also heard. As well as the Bruces, there was John Comyn (known as the 'Black Comyn'). His case, as the great-great-great-great-grandson of Donald III, again involved relatively remote royal ancestry. Yet it was reinforced by the fact that he was also a Guardian and, as Lord of Badenoch, the head of Scotland's pre-eminent baronial family with extensive landholdings in the north and east. Comyn, as a consequence, was a man of substance, whatever the strict legal merits of his argument.

In the event, however, Comyn threw his considerable weight behind another claimant. This was his brother-in-law John Balliol. Comyn's decision to back him was characteristically shrewd. For Balliol's claim was actually stronger than Bruce's because the latter, although tracing his ancestry back to David I through one fewer generations, was dependent upon his mother Isabel who had been the younger sister of Balliol's grandmother Margaret.

According to the law of primogeniture whereby elder children and their descendants enjoy superior claims to property and titles – a system of inheritance common among the Scottish elite since Normanization began in the 11th century – the undeniable fact that Margaret had been born before Isabel rendered Balliol's case more persuasive than that of Bruce.

One other aspect of the Great Cause requires comment. This was the role played by Edward I. For the threat of civil war between the supporters of the two leading Scottish contenders seems to have convinced the Guardians that having the final judgment endorsed by such a powerful and authoritative external judge would help contain the threat of internal instability.

Before agreeing to help, Edward insisted that the Guardians acknowledge his overlordship. In the end they conceded this point. Edward was also allowed temporarily to occupy the principal royal fortresses, another clear sign both of his aspirations for Scotland and of the weakness of those charged with defending the kingless kingdom. A court of 104 'auditors' or judges was then appointed, 24 by Edward and 40 each by Balliol and Bruce. Edward himself sat as president of this unique court as the arguments unfolded in the Great Hall of Berwick Castle.

On 17 November 1292 it was announced that Balliol, clearly in possession of the stronger legal claim, had won. Importantly, this judgment enjoyed the support not only of Edward but of the majority of Scottish nobles, including even some of the Bruce auditors. To all intents and purposes with the consent and good wishes of those who most mattered, Balliol therefore became King John and was crowned at Scone on St Andrew's Day.

The trouble with John

It is hard to approach John's reign with an open mind, given the distaste in which he came to be held. Even before his death he was being mocked as 'Toom Tabard' ('empty jacket') – an embarrassing nickname perhaps referring to the Scottish royal insignia that Edward later had stripped from John's knightly apparel but probably also indicating that many Scots eventually saw him as a nonentity, a stuffed shirt, a mere hole in the air.

John's misfortune was to have been from the outset the King of England's man. Yet this was to a great extent unavoidable in the circumstances. Most of Scotland's leaders, the Bruces as well as the Guardians, had formally submitted to Edward I as a condition of his role in the Great Cause. It therefore seems unlikely that anyone who acquired the Scottish crown through such a compromised process would have been able to ignore this reality and exercise substantial independence.

Edward, no shrinking violet in exercising his sovereign rights, hardly helped. His treatment of John, emphasizing the Scottish king's inferior status, made it more likely that, sooner rather than later, the traditional elites, long accustomed to being the biggest fish in a relatively small pond, would react against the King of England's attempts to transform them into comparatively minor and peripheral players on a much larger stage.

Insults to John and to Scottish pride came thick and fast. Less than a month after his coronation, he was required to do homage to Edward at Newcastle as King of Scots. John was also informed that in any internal Scottish disputes, Edward, as feudal superior, would decide. Military burdens were added in 1294, including providing men and money for the on-going English campaign in France. Even the Treaty of Birgham was now repudiated, as John was forced to accept both the theory and the practice of English suzerainty.

These accumulating slights were what led to a decisive event at Stirling in July 1295. A group of Scots nobles and clergy, comprising four earls, four bishops and four barons, constituted a council of advisors, presumably to guide John and to protect the kingdom's autonomy from Edward's depredations. Crucially, they sought and received a treaty of mutual aid with King Philip IV of France, to be sealed by marrying John's son and heir to Philip's niece – the formal beginning of the famous 'Auld Alliance' and a flagrant breach of what Edward understood as his Scots subjects' solemn obligation to fight alongside him against France.

John's council also took direct action against those most closely associated with English domination. Ironically, given the role that the Bruce family would soon take in Scotland's battle for independence, it was the Earl of Carrick, son of the competitor in the Great Cause, who was immediately caught out. For Carrick was at this stage a vital ally of Edward, who in 1295 even entrusted him with command of strategically sensitive Carlisle Castle. Accordingly the Bruce lands in Annandale were confiscated by John and handed to his Comyn backers after Carrick refused to participate in a general Scottish call to arms.

That the loyalties of Scotland's elite were divided in this way ought not to shock us. Partly this happened because feudal noblemen always naturally prioritized their own families' interests, which frequently differed from those of the monarch and his immediate henchmen. Partly too the varied responses reflected the effects of Normanization since the 11th century as well as the extensive intermarriage in recent times between the English and Scottish elites. The fact that Patrick, Earl of March and previously another contender for the crown, aligned himself with Edward, while his wife, Marjorie, a Comyn, garrisoned March's own castle at Dunbar for John, only illustrates in extreme form the acute conflicts of allegiance that could result.

Edward's response to the actions taken by John's council was considered, direct and brutal – in other words, entirely in character. An English army crossed the border, sacked Berwick and then on 27 April 1296, led by the Earl of Surrey and with the Earl of Carrick prominent on Edward's side, defeated John's army near March's castle. This incursion appeared even more significant in retrospect since it began a period of more than 150 years during which the two kingdoms' forces fought regularly over Scotland's continued autonomy: not for nothing is 1296 customarily taken as the beginning of what are still known to the Scots as the Wars of Independence.

The death toll may actually have been quite limited on the field of battle at Dunbar, in what appears to have been largely a cavalry engagement. But several Scottish earls, including some of the Comyns, were captured and carried off to England as prisoners. Facing overwhelming military odds, James the Steward then surrendered Roxburgh Castle, the last great Scottish fortress in the Borders. The English king, at the head of his army, occupied Edinburgh, taking the castle after a brief siege. Stirling, whose key castle the Scots made no attempt to defend, was the next to fall, followed by Perth.

At Montrose on 8 July the inevitable conclusion was reached. King John of Scotland, having already contacted Edward to offer his surrender, abdicated in person before the King of England. This is where the Scottish royal arms were ripped from John's jacket by the Bishop of Durham in a humiliating gesture symbolizing his effective loss of monarchical status.

Flushed with victory, Edward now had the Stone of Destiny removed from Scone and convened a Parliament at Berwick in August 1296 where he received homage from much of the Scottish nobility, including not only the Earl of Carrick but also his son, another Robert Bruce. The Earl of Surrey as governor and Sir Hugh de Cressingham as treasurer were put in charge of running this previously errant and insubordinate part of Edward's realm.

Effectively Scotland seemed to have been bent successfully to the King of England's ferocious will. Having earned for himself the name *Malleus Scottorum* (Hammer of the Scots), Edward's triumph over those whom he saw not as foreign enemies but as rebellious subjects appeared complete.

Wallace's glory

This was not, however, the end of the matter. For this first part of the Wars of Independence would finish not with meek acceptance of Edward's control over Scotland but rather with a bold campaign of resistance, ultimately unsuccessful but utterly memorable and inspirational for later generations, that etched itself forever into the Scottish consciousness.

One leader of this uprising was Andrew Moray, who hailed from a respected knightly family with Flemish origins which had arrived in the north-east in David I's time. His ancestors' successful assimilation into the peculiar culture and society of the part of Scotland from which they soon took their name meant that Moray seems to have sympathized with its ancient traditions of independent-mindedness and hostility towards centralizing Scottish regimes – whether run by a proud descendant of Mac Alpin or by an ambitious King of England.

Moray's principal colleague was from a quite different social background. He was a minor landowner, sufficiently obscure that we can only guess that his family originated either in England or in Wales and that his birth, usually said to have taken place at Elderslie, was probably in Ayrshire or Renfrewshire (there are villages with similar names in both counties): this was the indomitable William Wallace.

It is widely believed that Wallace's dramatic arrival on the national stage was preceded in May 1297 by his slaying of William Heselrig, sheriff of Selkirk – allegedly because, according to Blind Harry, who wrote a sympathetic poetic biography in the 1470s, the Englishman had murdered his wife, Marion. There are also several other tales, none well-documented, of Wallace's early taste for extreme violence, such as his purported killing of the son of an English aristocrat in a quarrel in Dundee, as well as his yearning for vengeance for the death of his father and brother at the hands of English soldiers. Yet another story, partly supported by one slightly ambiguous contemporary legal record and perhaps helping to explain the repeated English accusation that Scotland's national hero was in fact little more than a common thief, even has Wallace involved in a robbery at Perth as late as June 1296. Whatever the truth, when Wallace, who was certainly not a man to turn the other cheek, finally emerges into the light of recorded history in the summer of 1297, he does so as the leader of resistance to Edward across central and southern Scotland.

Insight: Black Earnside

Wallace's victory at Black Earnside, commemorated by a recently installed plaque near Newburgh in Fife, epitomizes the problems with his story. Contemporary English records date this episode to September 1304, towards the end of Wallace's career. The plaque, however, follows Blind Harry's long-posthumous narrative, which suggests June 1298, before the Battle of Falkirk. The site is also slightly ambiguous: the English reference confirms losses to Wallace at 'Yrenside' which could potentially be Ironside in Angus; and while Blind Harry's account of 'Black-Ern Side' certainly places the action in Fife, it also raises suspicions about its own accuracy by offering far too much precise detail for a description composed 200 years later.

How far their rising was planned in detail and in advance we do not know. Some historians have seen the series of rebel actions across Scotland as clear evidence of a co-ordinated national rising. Others have emphasized that an unpopular regime, once its authority was being successfully flouted by charismatic opponents, would be likely to experience successive waves of spontaneous resistance by unconnected groups eager to mount their own challenges.

What we do know is that Wallace's military capabilities first shone brightly when defeating English forces in small-scale engagements, such as one at Scone, where he fought alongside Sir William Douglas, in the process taking much treasure with which to fund subsequent adventures. Edward's army managed a bloodless victory in July 1297 at Irvine in Ayrshire, where a large Scottish force, riven by dissension between competing noblemen, ultimately saw its leaders, including James the Steward and the young Robert Bruce of Carrick, re-affirm their loyalty to the English ruler – the 'capitulation of Irvine' as it was called. But the momentum overall remained very much with the rebels.

Andrew Moray had simultaneously waged war against Edward in the north. Castle Urquhart on Loch Ness was brazenly attacked by Moray in May 1297: it fell later in the summer. Other English strongholds in the north-east were soon in Moray's hands and supporters of Edward forced to flee. In one particularly bold move, which Blind Harry typically credited to Wallace but for which Moray, who controlled rebel operations in the area, seems almost certain to have been responsible, English ships at anchor in Aberdeen harbour were burned.

The response of Edward, who was campaigning against the French in Flanders, was to charge the Comyns and the Bishop of Aberdeen with defeating Moray. The evidence suggests that they were not especially enthusiastic about this. Indeed a brief and inconclusive encounter between the respective forces at Enzie in late August 1297 hints strongly at a reluctance by both Scottish parties to engage in serious hostilities against each other.

Edward was left with little choice but to seek to re-impose control in Scotland with a substantial English force. Commanded by Surrey and Cressingham, it was this army that took the fateful decision to march towards Stirling, site of the strategic bridge across the Forth giving access to central and north-eastern Scotland. Here Moray and Wallace, previously besieging Edward's castle at Dundee, waited patiently on the north bank.

The battle, fought on 11 September 1297, brought them a stunning victory. First allowing just enough of the English cavalry and foot soldiers to cross the river, the Scots infantry, an experienced and confident force by now, attacked ferociously. The normal medieval military assumption that well-trained armoured horsemen would defeat soldiers on foot was undermined by the skilful ways in which

Wallace and Moray deployed the forces available to them at the Battle of Stirling Bridge.

Surrounded by a determined enemy and with a narrow crossing behind them, the English army on the north bank was trapped and cut to pieces. Cressingham himself fell in the melee, the chroniclers recording that Wallace subsequently had his skin flayed and a strip turned into a baldrick for his sword. The remainder of the English army to the south of the river observed the carnage. Surrey, who would later be much criticized for it, decided on a full-scale retreat to Berwick, rather than attempting to defend his own riverbank against the onrushing Scots.

Stirling Bridge has always been regarded as a glorious high point in Scotland's medieval history. It certainly encouraged successive generations to believe in the real possibility of national independence despite England's far greater military resources. And yet its aftermath was in reality somewhat mixed.

To start with, Moray seems to have been incapacitated in the battle and disappears hereafter from national affairs: it is usually assumed that he must have died later in the year from wounds incurred at Stirling. Wallace, for his part, was able to complete the business of throwing off Edward's grip on Scotland by such actions as the capture of the Dundee garrison and slaughtering the occupants of the castle at nearby Cupar in Fife. He was rewarded for his astonishing achievements by being knighted by a group of admiring Scottish noblemen, possibly including young Bruce. He was also appointed Guardian, the first to hold this office on his own – nominally acting still to defend Balliol's sovereign rights, of course, but arguably increasingly representing much of the wider kingdom and its population.

Less productively, Wallace followed his victory at Stirling Bridge with a foray into Northumberland and Cumberland which, lacking siege equipment and having no clear strategic focus, achieved little on the ground. It may well have been designed to show that the reach of the Scots' military power was more extensive than the English monarch had ever imagined. It certainly encouraged other Scottish leaders into decisive action: Bruce in particular seems to have abandoned his previous oaths to Edward at this point and to have burned the castle at Ayr in order to deny it to the English. The raid into England also, however, confirmed for Edward the need to take personal charge of the next attempt to bring the Scots to heel.

On 1 April 1298 Edward himself crossed the border at the head of a powerful army of 15,000 men. Harrying the south of the country around Edinburgh, the aim was to bring Wallace to battle. The initial response of the resistance was sensibly to avoid a set-piece encounter on unfavourable terms against an experienced and well-equipped adversary. Indeed, Wallace's aim was rather to make life difficult for the English army by destroying potential food supplies and encouraging it to move deeper and deeper into Scotland without forcing a major engagement. But, of course, some kind of confrontation would in the end still be required if Wallace wanted Edward's invasion to be defeated.

This eventually took place at Falkirk, on the road from Edinburgh just a few miles short of Stirling, on 22 July 1298. It was a disastrous defeat for Wallace in which the military reputation of the victor of Stirling Bridge was badly tarnished.

Part of the problem this time around was that, while Wallace no longer had Moray by his side, Edward was an infinitely superior battlefield commander and tactician to either the timid Surrey or the arrogant Cressingham. Wallace also faced an opponent whose allies within Scotland included many figures of national significance. The late-14th-century Scottish chronicler John of Fordun even places Bruce himself back on Edward's side, although this is generally seen as an inaccuracy. The earls of Angus and Dunbar, however, were definitely Edward's allies, helping him with vital intelligence on Wallace's intentions.

The English monarch also had the benefit of a contingent of Welsh archers and Italian crossbowmen. The medieval equivalent of mobile heavy artillery, these elements gave him the destructive firepower with which to pulverize the Scots' densely packed formations from a safe distance before the remnants were put to the sword at close quarters by his armoured knights, themselves battle-hardened veterans of Edward's French wars. In the slaughter at Falkirk, several of Wallace's closest allies fell, including second-in-command Sir John de Graham and Macduff, the Earl of Fife's son.

In the short term Edward's crushing victory was even less successfully exploited than had been Wallace's at Stirling Bridge. Lacking supplies and with elements in his feudal host deserting him, Edward had no option but to retreat to Carlisle. Wallace, meanwhile, resigned as Guardian and was replaced by Robert Bruce and John Comyn, a pairing capable at least in theory of uniting the kingdom's major factions in the struggle against English overlordship.

Wallace's story after Falkirk is less happy. In 1299 he was in France seeking military support from Philip the Fair. He also tried to secure political assistance from the Pope: some believe that Wallace actually visited Rome in person. But, returning home in 1303 to conduct guerrilla operations in the Borders against forces loyal to Edward, who by now once again enjoyed the support of significant numbers of the Scottish elite, Wallace was eventually betrayed on 5 August 1305 by John de Menteith at Robroyston near Glasgow and handed over to his enemies. Conveyed to London he was immediately put on trial for treason in Westminster Hall.

There, in what became famous words of defiance, Wallace contemptuously rejected the principal charge by insisting (plausibly, for unlike many Scots, and the Bruces in particular, he had never actually taken oaths to Edward) that the English monarch had no legitimate claim on his loyalties: 'I could not be a traitor to Edward, for I was never his subject'. The outcome, though, was a foregone conclusion.

On 23 August Sir William Wallace was dragged naked through the streets of London tied to a hurdle and then at Smithfield, the traditional place of execution, was subjected to a traitor's death: he was first partially hanged by the neck; then, cut down while still alive, his entrails were drawn from his body and burned; and finally he was beheaded and his body quartered so that the parts could be sent for public display in different parts of Edward's kingdom.

THINGS TO REMEMBER

▶ The sudden deaths of Alexander III and Margaret produced a bitter contest for the succession.

▶ Edward I's role as an arbitrator exacerbated the problem, further splitting the divided Scottish elite and encouraging him to extend his control over Scotland.

▶ John Balliol, although fairly chosen by Edward, proved unable to resist the English king's ambitions and was gradually undermined and marginalized.

▶ A national resistance campaign emerged, involving parts of the traditional elite but also new groups represented by Sir William Wallace.

▶ Wallace's stunning victory at Stirling Bridge ultimately proved inspirational but it was not immediately decisive and, following his subsequent defeat at Falkirk, his career finally ended in his grisly death.

6

<hr>

The wars of independence

In this chapter you will learn:

- *how after Bannockburn Robert Bruce was able to attract broad support from the Scottish elite*
- *about the Declaration of Arbroath.*

<hr>

Edward's interventions

The years after Falkirk were hard for the defenders of the Scottish kingdom's independence.

After Wallace's resignation, the country's fortunes were initially in the hands of men whose difficult personal relationship symbolized Scotland's internal problems. The two principals, the younger John Comyn (the 'Red Comyn', son of the 'Black Comyn') and Robert Bruce, were deadly rivals from implacably opposed families. Their selection as Guardians therefore represented not a plausible recipe for consensus so much as an attempt to minimize instability by treating the kingdom's two major factions as equals. This point was underlined with the addition of a supposedly neutral third figure, William de Lamberton, appointed Bishop of St Andrews under Wallace's influence because of his strong support for national independence.

This awkward compromise was sorely tested by Edward's continued aggression. The King of England's army campaigned regularly in Scotland and had a number of notable successes. Caerlaverock Castle, for example, the Maxwell family's fortress in Dumfriesshire, was attacked in July 1300. Edward's army, which successfully captured this vital Border stronghold, included 87 of his leading barons and was equipped with a large trebuchet (or catapult) called the Warwolf that was reputedly capable of hurling 200-lb missiles against the castle walls.

In August that year Pope Boniface VIII wrote asking for an end to his violent assaults on Scotland but Edward only entered into a truce with the Scots at the end of the campaigning season. One result of the tensions created by Edward's interventions, and by the unsatisfactory nature of a shared Guardianship, was the resignation first of Bruce late in 1300, to be replaced by Sir Ingram de Umfraville, and then of both Comyn and Lamberton as well as Umfraville in May 1301. They were replaced by Sir John de Soules, who like Wallace before him became sole Guardian. His selection as a neutral figure was merely a different answer to the same question of how to deal with the fact of a bitterly divided Scottish elite.

The summer of 1301 brought no respite, the English capturing Bothwell in Lanarkshire despite the close attentions of Soules' forces. Edward then advanced on Linlithgow to the west of Edinburgh, which he had previously used as a forward base in the Falkirk campaign. Having built a substantial fortification, he even felt comfortable spending Christmas in residence there with his son, the future Edward II.

In January 1302 he again signed a truce and many Scottish nobles now took the opportunity to make their peace with him. The details of some of these personal dealings are sketchy but Bruce in particular appears once more to have renewed his oaths to Edward. The best explanation is that with Soules and many other leading figures still seeking Balliol's reinstatement and with the latter now released from his English prison by Papal intercession and actively seeking French military support for a victorious return, Bruce's own claim to the Scottish throne, a dynastic ambition always at the heart of his strategy, looked in growing jeopardy. It may also have mattered that Bruce's father was dying and feared for the family's prospects if his son persisted in defying a powerful monarch who, it still seemed on balance, was likely to dominate Scottish politics for the foreseeable future.

It was at this time, with many members of Scotland's elite prudently inclining back towards Edward (who in 1302 was confident enough to hold a Round Table tournament at Falkirk, deliberately echoing King Arthur's claim to rule all of Britain), that the French king also seriously undermined the cause of independence. With a revolt at home and in urgent need of better relationship with England, it is perhaps no surprise that Philip IV decided to cut the Scots loose and, through the loss of his influence, the Papacy also ceased to provide diplomatic support. So critical was this that Soules appears to have travelled to Paris to plead with Philip. In his absence and with Bruce evidently not to be relied upon, Comyn was re-appointed to assist him as Guardian. But in May 1303 Philip and Edward signed a formal peace treaty nonetheless. Scotland, in short, stood alone once more.

It was in this situation that Edward continued to pressurize the Scots into collective submission. In the summer of 1303 his army marched via Edinburgh, Perth and Dundee to Aberdeen, which he reached in August, and then moved on into Moray and Badenoch before returning to over-winter at Dunfermline. Edward's easy movement through the country's heartlands, unmolested by Scottish forces, was a clear indication of his forbidding military strength. Yet in the final analysis, of course, this impressive feat was still not quite the same as permanently occupying and successfully pacifying Scotland.

By February 1304 all significant figures except Soules (still in France) and Wallace (in his final act as a guerrilla leader) had formally made their peace with Edward and outwardly accepted his overlordship. The outlines of a permanent settlement were also visible after Comyn in particular submitted to Edward's authority in return for an agreement that certain laws and privileges traditionally enjoyed by the Scottish elite would be protected. Wallace's hounding, capture and execution the next year has to be seen in this context: the special hatred reserved for him by Edward was because he was the last person of consequence to reject an arrangement that would finally allow the King of England to impose his will on Scotland.

With Wallace dead by August 1305, it appeared that Scotland as a whole was at last beginning to adjust to life under English rule. A Scots Parliament had confirmed Edward's sovereignty in May and appointed representatives to negotiate the complete assimilation of Scotland into his kingdom's political system. With the Guardianship in abeyance, Edward's nephew the Earl of Richmond was placed in charge and given oversight of key Scottish military sites. He was to be assisted by a council of leading noblemen and bishops including Lamberton, Comyn and Bruce, all sworn to be Edward's men.

Edward, to all intents and purposes, looked to have won.

Destiny calls

One reason why the situation was not quite as desperate for the cause of independence as at first sight it appeared was that Bruce in particular, encouraged by the increasing certainty that Balliol would not return, had clearly not abandoned his own family's claims to the throne. As a result, Edward continued to treat Bruce, long recognized as the most devious and unpredictable of the rival claimants, with some suspicion: in 1305 he explicitly required him not to maintain his castles in an offensive posture and took back some of the lands that he had earlier been given. Nor was Edward incorrect to doubt Bruce's sincerity. For ever since June 1304 he and Lamberton had been in a secret pact to support each other's political objectives. Crucially, this linked the Bruce claim to the crown of an independent Scotland with the desire of the leading bishops to maintain an independent Scottish Church.

Yet the trigger for Bruce's decision to lead the fight against Edward's occupation was seemingly trivial and may not even have been premeditated. At a meeting inside the Greyfriars Church at Dumfries on 10 February 1306, Bruce, in a fit of temper following a verbal altercation, stabbed John Comyn in front of the high altar. Comyn was then finished off by a Bruce retainer, Roger de Kirkpatrick.

This single episode transformed everything. It was the most spectacular act of sacrilege imaginable and in religious terms required the immediate help of Lamberton and other leading bishops with whom Bruce was already allied. The murder obviously also ended any prospect of the rival Scottish dynasties living together peacefully under Edward's overlordship. Bruce now either had to surrender himself to Edward and face the consequences or take whatever steps were required to make himself king in his own kingdom.

More immediately, however, the murder ensured that Bruce would initially be an outlaw. Three nights sleeping rough while Comyn's men hunted him through the hills of southern Scotland were merely a foretaste of what was to come. Absolution came from Robert Wishart, Bishop of Glasgow, before whom Bruce knelt to confess his mortal sin. Rather than seeking his excommunication, Wishart, in consort with Lamberton, instead encouraged other Scots to regard Bruce as their rightful king. Wishart also hurriedly led him to Perth so that he could be crowned at Scone on 25 March 1306, in the presence of several bishops and leading earls.

In another fascinating illustration of the split loyalties that so often divided the Scottish elite, the coronation was re-enacted two days later because the arrival of an important participant had been delayed. This was Isabella MacDuff, who, because her brother was in English captivity, was allowed to exercise her family's traditional right as earls of Fife to place the crown on the new ruler's head. It was therefore a woman who literally transformed mere Robert Bruce into Robert I, King of Scots.

Brave as well as independent-minded, Isabella was the wife of Comyn's cousin the Earl of Buchan, from whom she clearly differed violently on the question of the crown's rightful ownership. Her husband John pursued his family's revenge for the murder at Dumfries and became a natural leader among Edward's Scottish allies. Isabella, however, inspired the Scots' resistance to English rule by crowning the rival claimant and defiantly overturning the original judgment in the Great Cause.

Robert's early experiences as king, for all that he must have longed for the moment, must have fallen short of his original expectations. Mainly this was because the vengeance of Edward and the Comyns was so swift. There followed a prolonged period during which Robert and his entourage were in fear of their lives and were even forced to flee the kingdom whose monarch he had so recently become. This was what happened after their defeat by Aymer de Valence, future Earl of Pembroke and brother-in-law of the Red Comyn, when surprised at Methven in Strathearn on 19 June 1306.

First Robert escaped to Strathfillan in the southern Highlands. But here he and his small army were again defeated at a place afterwards known as Dalrigh ('the Field of the King'), this time at the hands of the powerful MacDougall clan, associates of the Comyns and relations of Balliol. Next he hid in the Atholl mountains, taking the precaution of sending his wife, Elizabeth, and some of his other supporters to Kildrummy Castle in Aberdeenshire. Finally Robert himself fled to the greater safety of Ireland's northern coast along with a few hand-picked men, to plot a guerrilla campaign against overwhelming military odds.

The year 1307 was another unhappy one for Scotland's newly crowned king. Edward marched north, having his clergy also declare Robert excommunicated for his sins. The fugitive's estates were given to families loyal to the English monarch. Worse, Edward's forces successfully besieged Kildrummy: some of the male defenders, including Robert's brother Nigel, were hanged, drawn and quartered; the women, who initially escaped to Tain and were captured there by Comyn's supporters, were transported to prisons and publicly displayed in wooden cages, open to the elements, for the next four years – Mary Bruce, the Scottish king's sister, at Roxburgh, Isabella MacDuff at Berwick. For her part, Elizabeth Bruce, probably more because she was the daughter of Edward's ally the Earl of Ulster than owing to her disputed royal status, was treated more gently, being taken to England and placed under house arrest. Even so, she did not meet her husband again for eight years.

Military events were more encouraging for the new monarch. From Rathlin Island the Bruces returned to Scotland in two separate parties. Robert and his brother Edward conducted hit-and-run operations from the Carrick hills that they knew so well, before defeating Aymer de Valence in a carefully chosen pitched battle at Loudoun Hill in Ayrshire on 10 May. He followed up this success by moving north to attack the Comyn-held castles at Inverlochy, Urquhart, Nairn and Inverness, leaving Edward in charge in Galloway while his ally James Douglas harried Bruce's enemies in the Borders. Later in the year Robert also attacked the Comyns' strongholds in Ross-shire and Aberdeenshire. But Robert's other two brothers, Alexander and Thomas, were less fortunate on their return to Scotland. Landing at Loch Ryan in the far south-west with their supporters, they were swiftly captured by a MacDougall ally of Balliol and were executed at Carlisle by the English.

The long-term outlook for Scotland was changed significantly by an event which took place just south of the border on 7 July 1307: the death of Edward I from dysentery and his replacement by his far less imposing and less able son Edward II. Yet in the short-term nothing much changed, as the King of Scots continued his aggressive and highly mobile campaign against both Comyn and the English forces. In May 1308 Robert defeated the Earl of Buchan's army decisively in a major engagement at Inverurie, attacked Buchan's estates, captured the key English garrison at Aberdeen and then routed a MacDougall force in the Pass of Brander in Argyllshire, reversing the result at Dalrigh two years earlier and at the same time eradicating the last important Comyn stronghold, the traditional MacDougall fortress at Dunstaffnage. As this run of victories showed, Robert's mastery of guerrilla tactics and the flexible nature of the military resources available to him – particularly when set-piece battles were avoided and fast-moving, roving strikes against enemy strongpoints were made instead – allowed him gradually to extend his influence over most of Scotland, especially north of the Tay.

By March 1309 the credibility of Robert's claim to sovereignty throughout his kingdom was underlined when his first Parliament met at St Andrews. His authority in Scotland was further strengthened when the clergy, meeting in council, formally recognized him as King of Scots. Over the next few years, he made steady progress towards effective domination of the country, largely untroubled by Edward II's weak rule or by the badly damaged Comyns (the Earl of Buchan himself had died in 1308).

English-held fortresses fell to him in succession, gradually eliminating the military basis of Edward's flimsy hold on Scotland: Linlithgow (1310), Perth (1312), Roxburgh (taken by James Douglas in March 1314) and Edinburgh (captured in the same month by Robert's nephew Thomas Randolph, later Earl of Moray). Only Stirling, with its strategic fortification at the very heart of Scotland, held out. Defended by Sir Phillip Mowbray, it was besieged by Edward Bruce who had reached an agreement with the occupants at Easter 1314, perhaps unwisely, that they would surrender to him unless relieved by an English army before 24 June.

It was in this situation that Edward II, although embroiled in conflict with his English barons, ordered preparations in the late spring of 1314 for a major counter-offensive.

Bruce's moment

Edward II had clearly concluded that relieving the garrison at Stirling, which held the key to central and northern Scotland, was worthy of a full-scale expedition. Similar recognition of the castle's decisive importance explains Robert's willingness, after years of avoiding pitched battles against the much larger and better-equipped English forces, to risk a conventional engagement.

On 17 June 1314 Edward's force of approaching 20,000 men, including perhaps as many as 3,000 cavalry, set out from Berwick and began its march into Scotland. The leaders of this great feudal host once more reflected the divided loyalties of the Scottish elite in particular. For among those riding at Edward's side were Robert's old enemy the Earl of Pembroke, Sir John Comyn of Badenoch (son of the Red Comyn), Henry de Beaumont (who had recently inherited the earldom of Buchan through his new Comyn wife), several MacDougalls, the Earl of Angus (an Umfraville whose mother was a Comyn) and even Sir Ingram de Umfraville (former Guardian of the kingdom and a staunch Balliol supporter).

Inside two days they were at Edinburgh. Three further days saw them at Falkirk, readying themselves to approach Stirling itself.

For its part Robert's army, just 7,000 strong, had already been drawn up in three main formations, mainly hidden from sight in the woods near the small stream known as Bannock Burn which flows across the boggy plain of the Forth to the south of Stirling. One, to the rear, was commanded by the King of Scots. His brother Edward led the centre while Randolph was in the front. Each of the Scottish formations was largely comprised, as usual, of spear-wielding infantrymen, along with some archers, backed up by a small separate force of horsemen under Sir Robert Keith.

On 23 June the English army moved onto the plain between them and Stirling. The English cavalry in particular were already uncomfortably bunched up, obliged by the obstacles in their way, including traps dug by the Scots, to approach the Bannock Burn by a single narrow road that limited their ability to deploy their full weight of numbers in a single manoeuvre. Mowbray, confident enough to leave the castle to meet Edward, actually advised against a battle, especially on such difficult terrain, but Edward and his other commanders ignored the warnings and pressed on. The English knights, leading from the front, therefore approached what they took to be Robert's army.

Henry de Bohun, a young Englishman, seeing Robert, wearing a crown and on horseback, at the front of his formation, attempted to charge the king with his lance. But Bohun, too hot-headed by half, was felled with one well-aimed blow to the head from the royal battleaxe. Randolph's schiltron also performed great work, untroubled by any enemy archers and so able effectively to repel the English cavalry.

As evening fell, a Scottish knight who had deserted Edward's cause also brought word of demoralization in the English camp at the day's events, news which further encouraged Robert to press home the advantage and fight once more in the morning.

On 24 June 1314 the main part of the greatest battle in Scottish history was fought to a brutal conclusion. The schiltrons, concentrating on those parts of the much larger enemy force that tried repeatedly to cross the Bannock Burn, found that their smaller numbers were no disadvantage on such a constricted site. Edward's poorly organized army, immobile and unable to mount mass cavalry charges, found it difficult to make much headway in breaking up the determined and well-drilled Scottish formations. In return, however, they were subjected to continual attack from Robert's spearmen and archers. Several prominent supporters of Edward were eventually killed in the increasing confusion, including the Earl of Gloucester and Sir John Comyn of Badenoch, before the English army as a whole turned and began to retreat.

Edward himself attempted to gain refuge in Stirling Castle but was denied entry by Mowbray, unwilling to break the terms of his agreement with Edward Bruce. Finally, the King of England reached Dunbar from where he took ship for London. Many in the English army died in the withdrawal, which was harassed by Robert's forces as well as by the wider Scottish population. Barely 5,000 of the 16,000 foot soldiers who had set out probably made it back home.

Tightening the grip

Bannockburn ushered in a period during which Robert's campaign to assert his right to the Scottish throne could be carried outside

Scotland to wherever and whenever English power, the one constant threat to the Bruce cause, could be challenged.

This explains why Robert continued the age-old Scottish strategy of attacking northern England. Yorkshire and Lancashire felt the full force of his wrath: both were invaded and forced to pay tribute to him. In 1315 Robert capitalized upon his own Irish affiliations – both through his de Burgh marriage and through his mother's Gaelic ancestry – to extend his campaign across the North Channel, ostensibly to liberate the Irish from the English yoke but also to weaken Edward II's authority and secure Scotland's south-west flank from invasion.

Ultimately this strategy was unsuccessful. Outside Ulster, with its traditional links to nearby Scotland, the invaders received only very limited encouragement from Ireland's elites, whether Celtic or Norman. Even some of the de Burghs' allies fought against Edward Bruce's army. A number of towns and monasteries, including Kells, were sacked, and there was little sign of the kind of pan-Gaelic rising against the English foreseen in Robert's optimistic early pronouncements. In fact, the violence, disruption and famine brought by the Scots only made Robert's intervention predictably unpopular with most of the natives. The whole sorry venture reached its disappointing culmination on 14 October 1318 with the Battle of Faughart near Dundalk, where Edward was killed by Anglo-Irish forces: in a grisly touch, this Bruce's head was cut off, packed in salt and sent as a trophy to the King of England.

If Bruce military power outside Scotland in reality had severe limitations, Robert's diplomatic campaign produced more durable achievements. For Robert and his advisers energetically courted international public opinion, and especially that presided over by the Church, with a letter in Latin to Pope John XXII, dated 6 April 1320, which sought the lifting of the King of Scots' excommunication. Drafted at Arbroath Abbey and signed by 51 prominent Bruce supporters, this later came to be known as the Declaration of Arbroath. The most famous statement of independent Scottish nationhood ever composed, an English translation of its inspirational central section deserves quotation in full:

Thus our nation under [previous popes'] protection did indeed live in freedom and peace up to the time when that mighty prince the

King of the English, Edward, the father of the one who reigns today, when our kingdom had no head and our people harboured no malice or treachery and were then unused to wars or invasions, came in the guise of a friend and ally to harass them as an enemy. The deeds of cruelty, massacre, violence, pillage, arson, imprisoning prelates, burning down monasteries, robbing and killing monks and nuns, and yet other outrages without number which he committed against our people, sparing neither age nor sex, religion nor rank, no one could describe nor fully imagine unless he had seen them with his own eyes.

But from these countless evils we have been set free, by the help of Him Who though He afflicts yet heals and restores, by our most tireless Prince, King and Lord, the Lord Robert. He, that his people and his heritage might be delivered out of the hands of our enemies, met toil and fatigue, hunger and peril, like another Maccabaeus or Joshua and bore them cheerfully. Him, too, divine providence, his right of succession according to our laws and customs which we shall maintain to the death, and the due consent and assent of us all have made our Prince and King. To him, as to the man by whom salvation has been wrought unto our people, we are bound both by law and by his merits that our freedom may be still maintained, and by him, come what may, we mean to stand.

Yet if he should give up what he has begun, and agree to make us or our kingdom subject to the King of England or the English, we should exert ourselves at once to drive him out as our enemy and a subverter of his own rights and ours, and make some other man who was well able to defend us our King; for, as long as but a hundred of us remain alive, never will we on any conditions be brought under English rule. It is in truth not for glory, nor riches, nor honours that we are fighting, but for freedom – for that alone, which no honest man gives up but with life itself.

This was an immensely powerful statement, simultaneously asserting the Scots' fierce loyalty to Robert and yet also their willingness to oppose him if he should cease to preserve their freedom from foreign domination. Its strong hint at some form of popular sovereignty in Scotland has also impressed many modern observers, even though it remains unclear how meaningful such a notion really was in the minds of the early 14th-century feudal elite whose grip on power it tried to advance.

The Declaration of Arbroath's impact on contemporaries is harder to assess. We know Robert's excommunication was soon rescinded. Peace negotiations were also begun with papal endorsement. But these dragged on, mainly because Robert insisted that his right to the throne be formally acknowledged, and in 1327 he renewed the French alliance and invaded northern England once more. Edward II's deposition and the regency of the young Edward III helped bring the English back to the table. In 1328 the Treaty of Edinburgh-Northampton was signed. This recognized both Robert's kingship and permanent Scottish independence while also fixing the border as it had been in Alexander III's time. Underpinning the deal, Edward III's six-year-old sister Joanna was married to Robert's son and heir David.

When on 7 June the next year King Robert I died at Cardross, he left the kingdom more secure than it had been for over four decades. But also, much more problematically, he left it with a four-year-old successor.

Insight: Bruce in bits

As was common for many deceased kings through history, Bruce's mortal remains went their separate ways. The body was interred at Dunfermline but the heart was removed at Bruce's request (apparently in penance for his sacrilegious murder of Comyn) and taken on crusade against the Moors in Spain by Sir James Douglas. Although Douglas was killed the heart was retrieved and later buried at Melrose Abbey, where recent archaeological testing has confirmed it still lies.

The boy David

While his father spent many long years plotting to seize the Scottish crown, David II was fortunate to wear it from infancy and to do so for more than 40 years.

Yet his reign was not unruffled. Indeed, this was a desperately difficult period for Scotland. For through the first half of his reign David was initially a child unable to govern in his own right; then in exile, unable to return to his own kingdom; and then finally a prisoner under Edward III's personal control.

Central to David's problems was the rapid unravelling of the Treaty of Edinburgh-Northampton, not least owing to the fact that Edward, a minor when it had been signed, considered it a shameful surrender which had unreasonably compromised his own sovereign privileges. Other factors, however, also undermined the recent settlement. Above all there were many noble families with Scottish estates whom Robert I had disinherited after Bannockburn, giving their traditional lands to his own supporters because their owners had demonstrated that their primary allegiance was to the King of England. This policy had made a certain sense to Robert, since it clarified once and for all the ambiguous loyalties dividing the kingdom's elite. As a result these decisions had been confirmed by the Treaty. Yet this plainly left a body of wealthy and influential men in England with a powerful vested interest in overturning that settlement and seeking to recover their lost Scottish inheritances.

A further difficulty for David was the familiar one during a minority or interregnum of there being a Guardian exercising authority on the king's behalf. In the first instance this meant Thomas Randolph, Earl of Moray, but after his death in 1332 the role was taken by the Earl of Mar. The latter, however, fell victim to the first invasion of Scotland led by the supporters of Edward Balliol, the most prominent of the disinherited and son of the deposed King John (who had died in French exile in the year of Bannockburn).

Edward Balliol, whose demands for a return of his family's Scottish properties were fully backed by Edward III, landed on the Fife coast at the end of July 1332. In a two-day engagement on 10 and 11 August, led by Balliol himself and by the titular Earl of Buchan, they fought and utterly defeated Mar's army on Dupplin Moor near Perth. The Guardian was killed, only ten days after his appointment, as was Sir Robert Keith, veteran of Bannockburn. This was a stark illustration of the continuing vulnerability of Scotland to English-backed interventions, for all the manifest military achievements of Robert I's reign.

The weakness of David II's position was further highlighted by Edward Balliol's coronation at Scone on 24 September as well as by the need to appoint a new Guardian, this time Sir Andrew Moray of Bothwell, the son of Wallace's celebrated colleague at Stirling Bridge who also just happened to be Robert I's brother-in-law and David's uncle. Yet even this only worked as a short-term expedient. Moray was captured at Roxburgh in April 1333, attempting to attack Balliol's supporters in Galloway. Held captive in northern England, Moray was replaced as the leader of Scotland's resistance by Sir Archibald Douglas, half-brother of the Bruce's ally Sir James. Douglas, however, lasted no longer as Guardian than his immediate predecessors, falling in battle at Halidon Hill near Berwick on 19 July 1333, beside other leading nobles like the Earl of Ross, when Balliol's forces, assisted by English archers, heavily defeated the Scots once more.

Understandably alarmed, and with Balliol in command of much of southern Scotland, David's supporters were forced to send the boy-king into a protective French exile early in 1334. He would be out of the country for seven years, living at Château-Gaillard in Normandy, while Edward Balliol – King Edward in the eyes of his Scottish allies and of the English – attempted to impose his will more widely on the kingdom that he had taken by force.

The staying power of the Bruces

Balliol's hold on Scotland, for all his ability to inflict decisive-seeming defeats in battle, was never either extensive or secure. He had genuine support in places like Fife, Galloway and the Borders. But much of the kingdom remained loyal to the Bruce cause and instinctively hostile to a man whose claim to be king was hotly disputed and who was in any case transparently dependent on English backing. Worse, Balliol's actions as King of Scots, even though they were surely unavoidable given the commitments and alliances on which his power rested, made it less likely that he would be able to win over the doubters – or indeed successfully retain all of his original Scottish supporters.

A key problem unsurprisingly turned out to be Balliol's reliance on Edward III – just as the assumption back in 1292 that Edward's grandfather was pulling his strings had proven so disastrous for the credibility of Balliol's father. This relationship was confirmed by Balliol's explicit acceptance of the King of England as his overlord. Furthermore, Balliol conceded vital Scottish interests: great Border fortresses such as Roxburgh, as well as strategic towns such as Dumfries and Berwick, and the whole area of Lothian around Edinburgh, were given to Edward III in 1334.

The precariousness of Balliol's authority was even clear in the wake of his apparently conclusive battlefield victories. For following

Dupplin Moor and his coronation in 1332, he had been forced to flee half-clothed and take refuge in England, having been surprised and attacked by nobles loyal to David II at Annan in Dumfriesshire. The campaign in 1333 that culminated in his triumph at Halidon Hill was again followed by widespread flouting of his demands across Scotland. Yet another invasion by Edward III in 1335 led to the ravaging of the countryside around Glasgow and Perth but, with the Scottish resistance again avoiding pitched battles, no effective means of imposing control presented itself. In short, a strange kind of stalemate had emerged.

With Sir Andrew Moray released from English detention and re-appointed Guardian, the Scots, encouraged by the French, attempted to negotiate a peace treaty with England. Although some were prepared to recognize Balliol if he accepted David as his heir, David himself rejected the scheme, a chain of events that led Edward III to re-invade, this time sending no fewer than three separate armies to attack towns as far distant as Elgin, Aberdeen and Glasgow. This was an important turning point, however, for it led Philip VI of France to commit openly to supporting the Scots. Edward prudently returned to England to defend his kingdom, leaving Moray and other Bruce supporters to regain almost complete control of Scotland by 1338.

In June 1341 it was finally possible for David II, now 18 years of age, to come back to Scotland and to begin governing in his own right.

A king incarcerated

David's return, however, was by no means the end of his troubles. His kingdom was war-torn and divided. Many nobles had previously sided with Edward Balliol and some of the southern districts even had rival Scottish and English administrations in place. The royal revenues had also been decimated by war and by years of non-collection, while David himself was a young and inexperienced ruler needing to establish his own authority from scratch. And nor was this all. For a combination of continuing tensions with England and the consequences of the alliance with France would soon lead to David's darkest hour.

This occurred in 1346 when, in support of his French partners, who feared that the English were about to attack them, David, probably not without some reluctance, mounted an ill-judged invasion of England designed to distract Edward III. The brief campaign, which began with the usual harrying of the north and the sacking of Hexham Priory, culminated in the Scots' defeat at Neville's Cross near Durham on 17 October, where an English army commanded by Lord Ralph Neville and Lord Henry Percy destroyed David's force, even killing the Earl of Moray into the bargain, and captured the Scottish king.

Insight: A plague on both their houses

The worst human disaster ever to afflict Scotland occurred in David's reign: the Black Death, initially called 'the foul death of England', crossed the border in 1349. Lack of contemporary records makes precise quantification impossible but a death toll of between one-third and one-half of a population of only around one million is plausible in the first two years, many succumbing horribly within days of showing symptoms. Not many fewer died in another bout in 1362–3. Shockingly, Scotland may have got off lightly. Bubonic plague, the pandemic's main component, was probably less virulent in the cool and damp Scottish climate.

Carried off to England, David would spend the next 11 years in captivity, in London and at Windsor and then latterly at Odiham Castle in Hampshire. Not until October 1357, and the payment of a ransom of 100,000 marks by the Scottish nobility under the terms of a new treaty signed at Berwick, was David in a position to return to Scotland and reclaim his throne.

Yet the payment of such a large cash sum proved problematic. It was obviously humiliating. It was also financially beyond the means of the Scots, a fact that seems to have forced David, the son and heir of the victor of Bannockburn, into a remarkable expedient. For over the next few years David continued negotiations with Edward, which had clearly begun during his captivity, with the aim of having the ransom annulled in return for making either Edward or one of Edward's sons (other than the next King of England, so that the separateness of the two kingdoms would be preserved) his own successor as King of Scots.

It is probable that David, who was childless, knew that this scheme would be unacceptable to most of the Scottish elite – and in particular that it would be opposed by the supporters of his current heir, his powerful and well-connected nephew Robert the Steward, the son of the Bruce's daughter Marjory. David's doubts were fully justified. The Scots Parliament rejected the proposal in 1364. But David continued his negotiations in secret, seeking at least to reschedule the ransom. Fortunately the war with France remained Edward's priority and in 1369 he conceded a reduced payment from David, a mere 56,000 marks.

David's second period in residence as King of Scots was characterized by his attempts, never quite successful, to restore royal authority over a kingdom in which absentee monarchy and the related emergence of potent rival sources of power had become established political facts. Robert the Steward, both as his lieutenant during David's long periods out of the country and as his close kinsman and likely successor, enjoyed immense prestige and influence. So too did the Douglas family, staunch allies of Bruce kingship but also an ambitious and assertive landed dynasty in their own right.

David recognized the realities of having to work with rather than against such weighty individuals when he granted Robert the earldom of Strathearn (the previous holder of the title had fallen at Neville's Cross) and created a new earldom in the name of the Douglases. David tried to balance these unavoidably powerful influences, however, by advancing other families as his own personal allies, notably the Erskines and the Drummonds. He even took Margaret Drummond as his second wife in 1364 (divorcing her in 1370, still without having produced a direct heir).

Yet the last decade of David's reign was nonetheless marked by tensions between the king and his over-mighty magnates. Indeed, both the Steward and the Douglases were implicated in a rebellion in 1363, obscure in origin but probably arising out of their determination to protect their own families' positions from new royal favourites. But David was in no position to punish the perpetrators. That he simply accepted their submission and re-confirmed Robert's right of succession merely underlines the weakness of the King of Scots in relation to some of his most important subjects.

When David died suddenly at Edinburgh Castle on 22 February 1371 the crown fell straightforwardly into the lap of Robert, David's 55-year-old nephew, who duly became Robert II. The kingship of the Bruces, for all Robert I's plotting and scheming, had lasted less than 70 years. Scotland would now be ruled by a new dynasty whose name was a reminder of the hereditary stewardship of the kingdom that their ancestors had held: the House of Stewart.

THINGS TO REMEMBER

▶ Edward I's control over Scotland was extensive and drew on genuine Scottish support but it was always incomplete and provoked periodic resistance.

▶ Robert Bruce was a tough-minded and able opponent with a good claim to the Scottish throne, who successfully made himself the focus of anti-English forces.

▶ From Bannockburn onwards Robert was able as King of Scots to attract broadly-based though not universal support from the Scottish elite.

▶ In the Declaration of Arbroath, the Bruces' supporters managed to identify his family's dynastic ambitions with the defence of Scottish nationhood itself.

▶ Edward III's military successes and the Balliols' revived power could never extinguish the self-belief and wider support built up by the Bruces.

▶ David II, the second and last Bruce king, faced imprisonment by Edward III and the rising power of the Stewarts and the Douglases, yet still the Scottish kingdom survived independent and intact.

7

·····

The late mediaeval kingdom

In this chapter you will learn:
- *about the rise of the House of Stewart, though the reigns of many were unstable, marred by factionalism and cut short by early death*
- *how late-mediaeval kings were notable for their learning and patronage of the arts, helping establish the Renaissance in Scotland.*

The House of Stewart

It is worth pausing at the outset of Robert II's reign to consider the significance of the Stewarts' dynastic triumph. Not only is this useful because Robert's family would eventually rule England and Great Britain too. It is also important because the family's rise and rise – from immigrant Breton landholders and respected government servants to royal status in their own right by 1371 – tells us a great deal about how politics and society in Scotland had changed in recent centuries, as well as about the ways in which it had not.

Above all Robert II's coronation completed a process that had begun in the 11th century. His crowning at Scone, like those of the two Bruces before him, reflected the effective transformation of the kingdom's elite. Once overwhelmingly Gaelic in heritage and culture, aristocratic society was increasingly dominated by those with origins in France and England, who naturally enjoyed closer cultural links with the wider European world and had far less affinity with the kingdom's Celtic roots. Inevitably this had knock-on effects at all levels of society, the most important of which was the beginning of the retreat of the Gaelic language in everyday usage and its gradual displacement outside the Highlands by something known at this time as 'Inglis' but which would eventually come to be called Scots.

The successful ascent of this re-configured national elite, however, did not, in the event, bring greater peace and tranquillity to Scottish politics. It is, after all, unlikely that high-achieving dynasties, whose members have been propelled onwards and upwards by exceptional levels of ambition and ruthlessness over several generations, will suddenly find it within themselves to live in harmony just because one kinsman in particular happens to have reached the summit. Scotland under the Stewarts, at least as much as any other mediaeval society in Europe, would demonstrate the essential truth of this observation.

Family strife

Robert II's reign began with a clear warning of the challenges to come, with William, Earl of Douglas, even leading some short-lived armed resistance to his coronation.

Afterwards, Robert recognized the need to balance the desire to entrench the Stewarts' new-found domination with sensitive treatment of important rival sources of authority. His daughter, for example, was married off to Douglas's son. The rebel earl was also given control of much of southern Scotland. Robert's own sons, meanwhile, acquired major earldoms and were allowed to command the main castles. Some of these privileges were taken from others but, in further evidence of Robert's astute management of different interests, substantial compensation was generally awarded.

Awareness of another long-term problem, and an intelligent attempt to prevent a recurrence of the disastrous uncertainty following Alexander III's demise, saw Robert have the Scots Parliament pre-determine the succession. Accordingly it was agreed in 1373 that precedence should be given strictly to male claimants descended through other males. Robert also sought to integrate the distant fringes of the kingdom. Another of his daughters married the Lord of the Isles, creating new bonds between the Stewart monarchy and the Gaelic Highlands, while his young son David was given the earldom of Caithness in the far north.

Robert's greatest problem, however, could not be so neatly solved. For castles like Berwick and Roxburgh, as well as many Scottish landowners, remained loyal to the King of England. Robert's clever response was to encourage reliable Border noblemen to harry and press the forces of occupation while denying official responsibility and avoiding large-scale confrontations. Incremental gains were the reward, like the recovery of Annandale in 1376 and Teviotdale in 1384.

Yet Robert also suffered greatly from his own strategy for extending the Stewarts' power. His fourth son, Alexander, Earl of Buchan, used violence and intimidation in the north-east in a campaign of outrageous insolence that peaked shortly after Robert's death in 1390 in the infamous sacking of Elgin, together with its cathedral and other churches. Later remembered as 'the Wolf of Badenoch', this infamous prince was a serious liability, undermining Robert's policy of trusting his own family to exert Stewart authority and at the same time demonstrating his inability to exercise effective central control. Robert's unwillingness to engage in open war against England also gradually undercut support.

These signs of weakness were what probably lay behind the decision of the king's council in November 1384 to appoint Robert's son and heir John, Earl of Carrick, as lieutenant of the kingdom. Carrick's seizure of power, though, was brief. Although his closer involvement in the Anglo-French conflict delivered the famous Scottish victory at Otterburn in August 1388, the death of his ally the Earl of Douglas in the battle provoked a struggle for the Douglas estates which was won by Sir Archibald Douglas ('the Black Douglas'), with whom Carrick's relationship was strained. This Douglas, backed by Robert II's younger son, Robert, Earl of Fife, helped sideline Carrick, triggering Fife's own elevation to the lieutenancy and bringing about Buchan's marginalization as Fife also took control in the north-east.

Robert II, however, did not long outlast the dynastic strife. He died in April 1390 and was buried at Scone where Carrick was duly crowned king.

In name only

Carrick's reign was again unsettled. The new king even changed his name on ascending the throne: born John, which unhelpfully recalled 'Toom Tabard', he thought it better instead to become simply Robert III. Yet he experienced the same challenges as his predecessors.

Like Robert II, he was marginalized by powerful magnates and undermined by disobedient family members. As a result for much of the time he was unable to exercise full regal authority.

The most important aspect of Robert III's kingship, as of so many previous Scottish monarchs, was his continual struggle to assert himself. In some ways he was reasonably successful. He achieved a degree of control over foreign policy. He also tried to check the excessive influence of his brother Fife and 'the Black Douglas' by the old device of favouring a rival, in this case the Earl of Angus ('the Red Douglas'). But Robert's rule was ultimately marred by fraught relations within his immediate family. For his son David, to whom he had passed the earldom of Carrick and then added the dukedom of Rothesay, was as ambitious as Fife, who had now become Duke of Albany. Accordingly it could have been no surprise when in January 1399 the king's council was persuaded to hand power to Rothesay, who it was agreed would become lieutenant for three years.

Rivalry between Rothesay and Albany provided the mainspring of political action for what remained of Robert III's unhappy reign. As lieutenant Rothesay inevitably challenged his uncle's powerbase in central Scotland. Once his term of office ended, however, he was incarcerated by Albany at Falkland Castle in Fife, where he allegedly died of starvation – foul play by Albany and 'the Black Douglas' is virtually certain – in March 1402.

Appointed lieutenant in Rothesay's place, Albany now dominated the government. It was in this desperate situation that Robert's 11-year-old heir James was first sent as a figurehead to challenge Albany's authority in the Douglas-dominated Borders and then, when he was forced to retreat, obliged to flee to the Bass Rock in the Firth of Forth. It was from there that James attempted to reach France by ship, a voyage interrupted off the Yorkshire coast by English vessels who consigned him to the custody of Henry IV of England.

When the ailing Robert III died on 4 April 1406, he already knew that his successor was in the hands of the kingdom's enemies.

Another prisoner

When we think of the first part of the reign of James I of Scotland it is even more than – with the similar experiences of David II – a matter of tracing the implications of absentee monarchy through two parallel stories: one is the tale of a King of Scots during his many years in English hands; the other relates Scottish developments, a narrative mainly shaped by the ambitions of those running the kingdom in his enforced absence.

James's English captivity was in fact relatively undemanding, so far as we know. It may even have had its compensations. For from his capture in 1406 until he returned and was finally crowned at Scone in May 1424, he greatly improved his education and had the chance to develop many accomplishments that, at a time when the Renaissance was spreading steadily across Europe from its Italian roots, the most sophisticated rulers were increasingly starting to display.

Ultimately James came to embody this new ideal of cultured and cultivated kingship. He became an able writer, poet and musician, this peculiar royal literary career in exile being crowned by a work known as *The Kingis Quair*, a semi-autobiographical poem, which reflects philosophically upon life's uncertainties and consolations and indicates the influence of James's English contemporaries, above all Geoffrey Chaucer. Entirely justifiably, this text is now numbered among the greatest achievements of mediaeval Scottish literature.

Events in Scotland itself, however, were less refined. The Duke of Albany, James's uncle who had already had James's brother David killed, ruled as governor (not regent) until his death in 1420. Albany was then succeeded as both duke and governor by his own son Murdoch Stewart.

The elder Albany's tenure was marked by forceful attempts to challenge the growing power of the Lord of the Isles. He also made periodic efforts to defend Scottish interests against the English, including besieging Berwick in 1417 and commanding a force sent to France two years later. Albany even had the distinction of being the earliest of Scotland's rulers to oversee the founding of a university, when the kingdom's first, at St Andrews, was established in 1412.

Whether Albany tried very hard to bring about James's release is, however, less clear. After all, it was scarcely in his interests to do so. Indeed James's release only came about after the elder Albany's death and because he had achieved a good personal relationship with Henry V, accompanying him in his French campaigns and even marrying one of Henry's cousins, Joan Beaufort.

The younger Albany's life, as well as his rule, was then cut short by James's return. On 24 May 1425 he and two of his sons were executed at Stirling by the newly crowned James I, having been convicted of treason. James was undoubtedly helped by the fact that the Albany faction, strong supporters of the French alliance, were weakened both numerically and politically by the defeat of a Scottish army at Verneuil-en-Perche in August 1424. James had also built a power base among Scots who had visited him in England which helped him re-assert his authority on his return.

James's subsequent reign, which really only began when he was already 30 years of age, was broadly successful. Diplomatically he plotted an independent course, allying with France in 1428 (and betrothing his daughter to the French dauphin) but avoiding having to wage war by also signing a truce with England. In addition, enemies and rivals at home felt the full force of James's desire for greater royal authority. He clipped the wings of the Albanys' allies, such as the Douglases, and reined in traditionally disobedient regional leaders, like Alexander, Lord of the Isles, who was defeated and forced to submit at Holyrood Abbey in August 1429. So effective was James in pressing his claims that for some time many of the leading Scottish noblemen were unable to muster meaningful opposition.

Tensions within the Stewart family itself, however, eventually proved James's undoing, just as they had undermined his brother and his father. This time the problem was the direct legacy of Robert II's complicated private life. In 1348 Robert had belatedly married his mistress Elizabeth Mure, James's grandmother, in an attempt, endorsed by Parliament in 1371, to legitimize the nine children, including the future Robert III, he had already had with her. But after Elizabeth's death the king had married Euphemia, daughter of the Earl of Ross. This marriage had produced a further two sons. It was therefore always open to Euphemia's male offspring to claim the crown as Robert's descendants through the only unambiguously legitimate line.

When this dispute caused James's murder at Perth, his own son James, not yet seven, inherited in the most difficult of circumstances. The guardians loyal to the senior Stewart line fortunately stood firm, ensuring the prompt elimination of the chief culprit Walter Stewart, Euphemia's son and Earl of Atholl, together with his fellow conspirators: Atholl endured three days of hideous torture before his execution – far worse even than the standard butchery of hanging, drawing and quartering – in the hope of deterring anyone else from daring to kill a King of Scots.

Unfortunately the power vacuum created by yet another royal minority, necessitating yet another prolonged guardianship, gave Scotland only further instability and factional infighting.

The fiery king

The early years of James II, nicknamed 'fiery face' because of a red birthmark on his cheek, were dominated by the shifting alliances among the leading noblemen who surrounded the young king and sought to govern in his name.

In this situation the Douglas family, whose interests had been closely intertwined with those of the Bruces and the Stewarts ever since Robert I's time, inevitably played a crucial role. It could thus have been no surprise when Archibald Douglas, 5th Earl of Douglas, was initially appointed lieutenant-general and regent. But after Douglas's death (apparently from natural causes) in 1439, things deteriorated rapidly as various rivals scrambled to replace him.

William, Lord Crichton, the Chancellor, was one who exercised considerable influence. So too did Sir Alexander Livingston, warden of Stirling Castle where James resided. Both men wanted to curtail the power of the Black Douglases and to advance their own families' interests. The Earl of Douglas and his brother were duly murdered. A co-conspirator was James Douglas, Earl of Avondale, the great-uncle of the leading victim whose suddenly vacant earldom Avondale conveniently inherited.

> **Insight: Guess who's coming to dinner?**
> Invited to supper with James II in Edinburgh Castle on 24 November 1440, William Douglas, 6th Earl of Douglas, and his younger brother David, suddenly found a black bull's head, the symbol of death, presented at the table. They were swiftly overpowered, subjected to a brief mock-trial and beheaded by Lord Crichton and Sir Alexander Livingston in front of the presumably horrified ten-year-old king. The grisly episode came to be known as the 'Black Dinner'.

This barbaric act was typical of the mixture of extreme violence and naked ambition among near relations that characterized the Scottish elite in the mid-15th century. But what happened next was no less predictable. The Livingstons decided to make common cause with William, 8th Earl of Douglas, Avondale's son, and turned against Crichton, in a brazen attempt to share power between them.

The chronic factionalism was not ended even by James's growing independence as an adult political actor. Not surprisingly, he resented being dominated by the Black Douglases, who by this time had jettisoned the Livingstons and taken almost complete control. James's decision to confront the 8th Earl at Stirling Castle on 22 February 1452, accusing him of leading an aristocratic plot to seize absolute power, ended with a characteristic loss of temper by the king and several of James's servants helping stab Douglas to death. Allegedly the body was afterwards found to have had no fewer than 26 wounds.

Subsequently James gradually reduced the overbearing power of the Douglases. Indeed, so potent had been their influence, especially in the south, that James was forced to proceed with great care, sometimes removing the properties and titles of major offenders but at other times rewarding and trying to win over the Black Douglases' allies. By 1455 the 9th Earl had fled into English exile, leaving James effectively in control of Scotland for the first time.

Unfortunately James II's reign, despite all these intriguing signs of a royal assertiveness not matched for more than a century, soon came to an unexpectedly decisive end. On 3 August 1460, while besieging Roxburgh Castle in an attempt to rid his country of the last vestiges of the English occupation, he was killed when a large cannon that he was standing beside exploded. Killed in a ball of flames that superstitious contemporaries considered had been foretold by his fiery birthmark, James was just 29 when he was laid to rest at Holyrood.

Like father, like son

James II's son and heir, James III, experienced even greater difficulties than his father.

He inherited as a minor: historians disagree over his date of birth but he was certainly not yet nine when he succeeded. Before reaching adulthood his relationships with his close family had deteriorated to such an extent that his reign saw almost continuous instability. His attempts to assert royal authority and to reduce the power and influence of his leading subjects were therefore probably doomed from the start. That James III would die young and violently – this time at the hands of his near relations and rebellious magnates – ought to have surprised no one.

Endemic factionalism at the heart of government, a problem exacerbated by the tendency for different groups to jockey for position in the absence of a strong adult ruler, was vividly displayed during James's early years. Mary of Gueldres, his Dutch mother, initially controlled affairs as regent, and helped Scotland temporarily reclaim Berwick from England by providing limited Scottish support for the Lancastrians during the Wars of the Roses. But following her death in 1463 a number of regents shared responsibility, including James Kennedy, highly respected Bishop of St Andrews, who died in 1465, and his brother Gilbert, Lord Kennedy, both of them grandsons of Robert III.

Soon, however, power fell into the hands of Robert, Lord Boyd. A descendant of one of Robert I's close allies, in 1466 he managed to abduct James into the custody of his brother Sir Alexander Boyd and then to persuade Parliament to make him sole guardian. So confident was Boyd that he even had his own son created Earl of Arran and married him swiftly to James's sister. The teenaged king, meanwhile, was betrothed to Margaret of Denmark. Orkney and Shetland were pledged to Scotland against a dowry that was never subsequently paid: perhaps unintentionally, Boyd had therefore achieved the extension of the kingdom as far as the Northern Isles.

As had happened with his father, however, James III, as he acquired greater age and experience, reacted strongly against these encroachments on royal power. By 1469 Sir Alexander Boyd had been executed for treason and Lord Boyd had fled the country. Yet there was little sign that James had prudent ideas as to how to use his new-found authority. He sought an English alliance, underpinned by marrying his son James to the daughter of Edward IV. But this was a step too far for most of the Scottish nobility, adamantly hostile to England. James's taxes, applied rapaciously to people not accustomed to such exactions, further damaged his relationship with powerful vested interests.

James III's greatest difficulties, though, were with his own immediate family – especially his brothers Alexander, Duke of Albany, and John, Earl of Mar. The latter died suspiciously in 1480 and Albany fled to

France to escape questionable treason charges. There he joined with Edward IV, who had also fallen out with James, and took part in the English invasion of 1482: this damaged James's prestige by re-taking Berwick. It was during this campaign that James, attempting to lead an army to defend his kingdom, instead found himself arrested at Lauder Bridge by disaffected nobles and imprisoned in Edinburgh Castle while Albany established his own government under English protection.

The king, though, was lucky in his allies. The Earl of Huntly, married to James's aunt, played a leading part in successfully challenging Albany's regime which many Stewart loyalists could not stomach. Albany was expelled and James's power restored by 1485. But the underlying unpopularity of James's III's kingship remained unresolved. He continued to make overtures to England, annoying many within Scotland. He rewarded his own favourites (or 'familiars', as they were called), like the notorious Thomas Cochrane, lynched by James's victorious enemies at Lauder Bridge. He ignored the interests of many leading landed magnates, such as Huntly, whose support went largely unrewarded. Worst of all, he seemed uninterested in traversing the kingdom to administer justice – a key obligation for a mediaeval king.

Contemporaries responded to weak government in ways that made perfect sense within a feudal society. The vulnerable signed 'bonds of manrent' with the powerful to provide military service in return for protection. Individual landowners also built the defensible tower houses that increasingly dotted the landscape.

James's inadequacies were clearly at odds with what the population expected – and demanded – of a King of Scots. Many of his most prominent subjects must have heaved a sigh of relief when news came of this divisive figure's death at the Battle of Sauchieburn, fought close by the hallowed field of Bannockburn, on 11 June 1488. James in fact died as he had lived, warring against powerful noblemen aligned with elements of his own family – in this case his eldest son, James, Duke of Rothesay, a 15-year-old whom the king, in a fatal misjudgement, had been marginalizing in favour of a second son.

Pride before a fall

James IV, as the beneficiary of Sauchieburn became known, was the greatest king since Robert I. Arguably he was also one of the most successful rulers of mediaeval Scotland. He took the finest traits of his Stewart predecessors and blended them with his own unique strengths. The result was a ruler with political judgment, personal bravery and genuine royal charisma, as well as considerable intellectual abilities and cultural sophistication.

Like James I, he was a Renaissance prince – though his contributions were of even wider and more lasting benefit. Scottish printing started under James's enlightened stewardship when the bookseller Andrew Millar and the merchant Walter Chapman received letters patent in 1507 to set up shop in Edinburgh's Cowgate: the first books, mainly poems and including Blind Harry's *Wallace*, rolled off the presses the next year. James himself was also impressively multi-lingual, speaking German, French, Latin, Italian and Flemish, as well as Gaelic and Scots.

By an Act of Parliament in 1496 he commanded the nobility to have their sons educated in Latin and law – the first of several legislative attempts by Scottish governments to improve literacy and raise formal educational standards (effectively undermining Gaelic-speaking oral culture among the Highland elite). His great Bishop of Aberdeen, William Elphinstone, founded that town's first university in 1495, appropriately naming it King's College: at a time when England only had two universities, Scotland, with Glasgow having been added to St Andrews during James II's reign, already had three.

Most importantly, a group of talented poets known as the 'Makars' (i.e. makers or creators) were associated with James's court. They included William Dunbar, responsible for the deep reflection on mortality *Timor Mortis Conturbat Me* and the obscene and humorous *The Flyting of Dunbar and Kennedie* (whose reputation spread rapidly after Millar and Chapman published it) and Gavin Douglas, Bishop of Dunkeld, whose magnificent Scots translation of Virgil's *Aeneid* was the first complete vernacular work of its kind in northern Europe.

Another of James's enduring legacies was his enthusiasm for the latest architectural fashions.

Insight: Crowned heads

Visitors to St Giles's Cathedral in Edinburgh and King's College Chapel, Aberdeen, should look up at the unusual stone crowns that take the place of conventional spires or steeples on the main towers. They were constructed in

James IV's time and capture not only the Renaissance architectural exuberance of the reign but also the sense of growing royal authority and Scottish cultural self-confidence. A similar feature at St Michael's in Linlithgow, another church with strong royal associations, was dismantled in 1821 for fear of collapse, but in 1964 a lightweight timber and aluminium crown replaced it.

It is to this that we owe Scotland's great Renaissance royal buildings at Edinburgh, Stirling, Falkland and Linlithgow: Stirling in particular, where James had several structures erected that survive to this day, remains powerful testimony to his commitment to placing his kingdom, previously a cultural backwater, closer to the cutting-edge of contemporary European style. He also built the royal palace of Holyroodhouse, adjacent to the old abbey, which would be the main focus for Scottish politics and government not only in the 16th century but also, once again, in the 21st.

James's political conduct was notably well-considered – dramatically so after his father's ineptitude. He won a far better reputation for active kingship, delivering justice firmly and fairly throughout the country. In 1493 he was even able to revoke the Lordship of the Isles, which thereafter remained in the crown's possession: symbolizing James's control over the far north and west, the last independent holder of the title, John MacDonald of Islay, was exiled to the Lowlands. James also maintained acceptable relations with England for most of his reign, signing the Treaty of Perpetual Peace with Henry VII in 1502 but also creating new dockyards and developing Scotland's navy: in 1511 the famous *Great Michael* was launched, and, at 240 feet long and displacing 1,000 tons, she was at the time Europe's largest ship.

Given James's wisdom and prudence, it is ironic that his reign should have ended prematurely after a single bad decision. With the outbreak of a new Anglo-French war, he agreed to invade England under the terms of Scotland's traditional alliance with France. This was a catastrophic error. Confronted by the Earl of Surrey's army at Flodden Field in Northumberland on 9 September 1513, the Scots, although more numerous, were utterly routed, over-confidently advancing across unhelpfully boggy terrain and being felled en masse by English arrows and cannonballs at a distance and then by English billhooks at close quarters. Between 5,000 and 10,000 Scots perished. Nine earls – Argyll, Bothwell, Caithness, Cassilis, Crawford, Errol, Lennox, Montrose and Rothes – were killed in the bloodbath. So too were the Archbishop of St Andrews, the bishops of Caithness and the Isles, two abbots, the French ambassador, and numerous other noblemen, their heirs, clan chieftains and lairds.

James himself lay dead on the battlefield by nightfall. It was the most one-sided battle ever fought between the two old enemies, conducted on a scale hitherto not seen. Not just a king's reign but also a kingdom's elite had been destroyed in an afternoon.

When the 18th-century poet Jean Elliott composed 'The Flowers of the Forest', a lament for the fallen of Flodden, popular even today as a folk song and pipe tune, she was literally commemorating a national disaster that still scarred the collective memory.

The waning of the middle ages?

Historians disagree over when the mediaeval period really ended. 1492 and Columbus's 'discovery' of the New World is a strong candidate if lasting global impact is the test. 1453, the fall of Constantinople to the Turks, finally terminating the eastern Roman Empire, also has its advocates. 1517, when Luther initiated the Reformation, is obviously another plausible contender. And in a British context there is a case for 1485, the year of the Battle of Bosworth Field, whose victors, the Tudor dynasty, ended feudal challenges to royal power and created the modern English state.

For Scotland, however, no such convenient date exists. 1513 saw the unnecessary deaths of a king and much of the kingdom's leadership. But the turbulence of the previous two centuries meant that the resulting minority, regency and disorder were scarcely novel. Nor did new kinds of politics and government emerge: 16th-century Scotland remained a feudal society prone to periodic and sometimes successful aristocratic assaults on royal authority. Yet this is to miss an important feature of the next 30 years. For key trends that would dominate for another 300 years, and help define modern Scottish history, now began to impose themselves – albeit for reasons largely unconnected with James IV's demise.

James V was just 17 months old when he succeeded his father. His mother Margaret Tudor, sister of Henry VIII, served as regent for a year until she married the Earl of Angus (a Red Douglas). The role was then taken on until 1524 by John Stewart, Duke of Albany, his father's cousin, the French-born son of Alexander, Duke of Albany, and James's own heir at that stage.

The regency proved deeply contentious. Partly the problem was personal, with rival individuals seeking advantage. But another cause of tension was the hostility of Angus towards Albany, who represented France's influence in Scottish affairs. The result, inevitably, was conflict. Margaret's regency was ended by Albany's seizure of all James IV's children in 1514, forcing her to flee to London. Angus and Margaret's relationship, however, deteriorated, and she subsequently made peace with Albany. In 1524, when James V was 12, Margaret had Albany removed, but Angus was able to persuade Parliament to appoint him Guardian. After 1525 Angus was effectively running Scotland, helped by James Beaton, Archbishop of St Andrews, until James escaped, sided with his mother and had Angus exiled to England in 1528.

Throughout the first half of James V's reign Scotland therefore suffered from the same chronic factionalism and instability, often generated from within the royal family, which had scarred James III's time. Yet after freeing himself from Angus's control there was actually a greater resemblance to James IV. He was a Renaissance prince: he built imaginatively at the royal palaces; he patronized playwright Sir David Lyndsay of the Mount and composer Robert Carver; he even played the lute.

James also faced down challenges from the country's outlying regions. In 1532 he inaugurated the College of Justice, a central judicial institution to develop and administer laws. James himself toured Dumfriesshire, Galloway and Ayrshire, overseeing the trial and execution of outlaws such as Johnnie Armstrong of Staplegordon and of notorious 'reivers' – organized Border gang leaders specializing in cattle theft and blackmail – such as William Cockburn of Henderland. In the Highlands congenitally disobedient figures such as the MacDonald and Maclean chieftains also submitted rather than face the military consequences from a determined monarch.

James's drive to strengthen royal authority was also reflected in his religious policies. This was an increasingly critical policy area, given that the Reformation was proving so divisive not only between nations but also, and perhaps especially, within individual European societies. Scotland, with strong cultural, educational and intellectual ties to France, Germany, England and the Low Countries, where

Protestant activities were mainly concentrated, was unsurprisingly exposed to the new ideas at an early stage.

James's response to Protestantism was severe and was reinforced by his personal piety and devotion to the Catholic faith. There were numerous executions. Patrick Hamilton, for example, who had returned from France and Holland with a strong commitment to Lutheranism, was tried by Beaton and burned at St Andrews in 1528. Six years later James personally presided over the incineration of two heretics outside the walls of Edinburgh Castle.

James also dealt confidently and competently with England and France – and this too would have lasting significance. He maintained the Auld Alliance and in 1537 and 1538 married two French wives in quick succession (the first had died tragically on her arrival in Edinburgh). The second was Mary of Guise, a favourite of the King of France, and she bore James two sons, who died in infancy, and one daughter, Mary. Peace with England was encouraged by his English mother and it was only after her death in 1541 that, as Anglo-French relations also cooled and Henry VIII's attacks on Catholicism repelled the devout King of Scots, James renewed hostilities.

As for his father this was to prove fatal. The Scots were soundly beaten at Solway Moss on 24 November 1542. James, who was not present, took to his bed in Falkland Palace. Evidently seriously ill as well as just depressed, he died unexpectedly on 14 December, aged just 30.

James was succeeded by Mary, not yet a week old. As queen in her own right she would soon be overwhelmed by the violent social and political forces unleashed by the Scottish Reformation. And ironically, because of her own intimate connections with the French court, she would unintentionally bring about Scotland's isolation from France and its reconciliation – even its eventual royal union – with England.

This, above all, is why we can say that with the dramatic reign of Mary, Queen of Scots, the modern history of Scotland had begun.

THINGS TO REMEMBER

▶ The emergence of the Stewart kings was the triumph of a family of Norman origin that had successfully linked itself to the cause of Scottish independence.

▶ Scotland's late-mediaeval rulers struggled to contain the traditional threats posed by jealous kinsmen and over-mighty barons as well as by English monarchs.

▶ Several of the early Stewart kings died violently at the hands of ambitious rivals and internal foes, though some were also just plain unlucky.

▶ The invariable consequence of a premature royal death was a premature accession, leading in turn to the greater instability associated with regencies.

▶ The late-mediaeval kings were notable for their learning and patronage of the arts, helping establish the Renaissance in Scotland.

▶ Despite everything, the Stewarts achieved two critical things in testing circumstances – maintaining the autonomy of the kingdom and keeping the crown for themselves.

8

Reformation and rebellion

In this chapter you will learn:
- *about the dramatic and difficult reign of Mary, Queen of Scots, who succeeded to the throne as a small baby*
- *about the Scottish Reformation and John Knox*
- *how Mary was forced to abdicate, and the crown given to her son, one-year-old James VI.*

Two queens and two regencies

Along with Mac Bethad, who won and lost Scotland's crown, and 'Bonnie Prince Charlie', who failed to reclaim it, Mary, Queen of Scots, is one of the three best-known figures in Scottish history. A heroic royal trinity, they were elevated to full-scale tragic victimhood because their own flawed characters, along with cruel misfortune, ultimately swept them to defeat.

Born on 8 December 1542 just six days before her father's unexpected death, Mary's early reign was once more, as so often with the unlucky House of Stewart (or Stuart, as it was re-spelled under the influences of Mary's French associates), dominated by the problems of minority and regency. For 12 years Scotland was ruled in her name by James Hamilton, 2nd Earl of Arran, James II's great-grandson and Mary's own heir. In 1554, her French mother, Mary of Guise, became Queen Regent. But soon there was growing opposition to Guise's rule. A crisis of authority therefore already existed when Mary finally came to govern in her own right.

Religion was the gravest of problems. Arran was a Protestant, and on 1 July 1543 he signed the Treaty of Greenwich which restored peaceable relations between Scotland and England and agreed that Mary would be married in due course to her cousin, Henry VIII's son Edward (the future Edward VI). Henry, of course, had recently imposed the Reformation on England, while Edward was being raised a pious Protestant.

In Scotland, however, closer ties with England, especially ones creating a joint monarchy, were predictably unpopular. Cardinal Beaton, for whom the traditional alliance with Catholic France remained of prime importance, also opposed a scheme that would clearly have placed Scotland decisively in the Protestant camp. Beaton had already tried unsuccessfully (based on a forged will of James V) to claim the regency, and was closely associated with the disastrous Solway Moss campaign. But he was eventually able to have the treaty annulled by the Scots Parliament late in 1543.

This understandably angered Henry VIII. But worse was to follow. Arran now embraced Catholicism, aligning himself with Beaton and Mary of Guise. Henry responded with the so-called 'Rough Wooing', applying military pressure to force the Scots to fulfil the treaty's terms.

There were successive invasions. In 1544, the Earl of Hertford attacked Edinburgh. Three years later, on 10 September 1547, 'Black Saturday', in a battle to the east of the capital, the Scots were defeated at Pinkie, again by an army commanded by Hertford (now the infant Edward VI's protector and Duke of Somerset). In 1548 the English captured Haddington, devastating the surrounding countryside. All the while Mary of Guise kept the young Queen of Scots safe by moving her from fortress to fortress.

England's aggression, rather than weakening the Scots' resolve, actually had the opposite effect. Accordingly on 7 July 1548 they signed a new treaty that promised the marriage of Mary to Prince François, the dauphin. The next month Mary sailed for France. The 13 years that followed, during which Mary was reared as a French princess and as a consort fit for the occupant of the French throne, completed her transformation into an essentially French rather than a strictly Scottish queen in the eyes of many of her own subjects. This mutation had unforeseen but dramatic implications when she finally returned to govern Scotland as a young adult.

Mary's time in France was at least not wasted. She emerged a poised, confident, accomplished and widely admired figure, recognized for her linguistic proficiency and her artistic skills as well as for her grace and beauty. What she did not acquire, though, were any real political skills or insights.

Nor did she learn much about Scottish society and politics. This was a crucial gap in her education, especially as scepticism about the Guise regency, which placed Frenchmen in charge of key government offices and relied on the highly visible presence of French military forces in Edinburgh, intensified quickly after 1554. At the same time, and intertwined with anti-French feeling, pressure from a growing Protestant faction for religious reform in Scotland, a demand backed by powerful noblemen as well as by energetic preachers, was steadily increasing.

In France, this may have appeared not to matter. Mary's position at the heart of the French state, after all, seemed secure. In 1558 she married François. On 10 July 1559, when Henri II died and her husband was crowned, she became Queen Consort of France. Adding to the complexity of her position, however, was her Tudor ancestry. For Mary now also became the focus of long-standing French claims to the crown of England which, with her cousin Elizabeth, a Protestant, on the English throne, was regarded in Paris as being held unlawfully by a heretic. Mary and François were duly presented in French propaganda as England's legitimate monarchs – something that from the outset undermined the relationship between the Catholic Queen of Scots and the Protestant Queen of England, with ultimately lethal effects for one of them.

Events soon took an unexpected turn in both Scotland and France. By 5 December 1560 Mary was already a 17-year-old widow, François having died of a cerebral abscess. His brother Charles succeeded and Mary was suddenly without an obvious French role.

In Scotland, too, developments were running unexpectedly out of control. Mary's mother had died in June with the Guise regime and its French backers facing open rebellion. This was led by disaffected Scottish aristocrats who called themselves the Lords of the Congregation – the religious connotations of the name indicating their Protestant affiliations – who had allied with Queen Elizabeth and wished to end French and Catholic domination of Scottish affairs. Fronted by the earls of Argyll, Glencairn and Morton, this group signed a covenant in December 1557, binding themselves to each other and to God for the defence of the Protestant cause.

The opposition movement also had a dangerously popular, public dimension. By 1558 Protestant preachers, most famously John Knox, a follower of the French reformist theologian John Calvin, had been urging comprehensive change on the Scottish Church. Attacks on religious sculpture and stained glass, symbols of what the more radical Protestants saw as Catholic idolatry, had broken out in towns like Perth, encouraged by the inflammatory sermons delivered by Knox and his colleagues. More importantly but less visible, individual Protestants across the country, some wealthy and influential but many humble and obscure, were rejecting the authority and structure of the unreformed Church, getting for themselves religious ministers who had enthusiastically embraced reformed ways.

The Scottish Reformation, in other words, was already happening by stealth. Among Mary of Guise's last acts as regent had been an attempt to confront this problem by demanding that Protestant preachers meet her at Stirling to receive firm instruction. But this only worsened the situation. The Lords, whom Arran formally joined in September 1559, seized the initiative. By Christmas 1559 they had effectively taken Edinburgh, having first ejected French troops from Perth.

In the last six months of her life Mary of Guise was therefore in desperate political difficulty. The more obviously dependent her regime became on French military resources, the less legitimacy it enjoyed. It also became easier for her opponents to recruit additional support, not least from England. French forces did push the Lords back to Stirling in January 1560. But the timely arrival of an English fleet in the Forth and then of an English army soon led the French to fall back on the port of Leith.

The outcome was the Treaty of Edinburgh, signed by the Lords on behalf of Scotland. This made the Scots and English allies, allowed the calling of a Scots Parliament which Protestants would dominate and also promised peace between England and France. Guise's convenient death clearly helped matters. Mary, Queen of Scots, refused to endorse it but she could do little to prevent its implementation.

Widowed and marginalized at the French court and with her mother dead, Mary came back to Scotland. But when she arrived at Leith on 19 August 1561, the circumstances could hardly have been less encouraging.

A revolution of faith

In most countries where the Reformation occurred, it remains hard for historians to disentangle the material and political self-interest of Protestantism's supporters from their sincerely held spiritual convictions. Scotland is no different. And Mary's opponents were a decidedly mixed bunch.

Some, like Arran and several of the Lords, were clearly interested in restoring their own earthly power at the expense of the Stewarts and their French allies. Others, inspired and energized by Knox's famously volcanic performances from the pulpit, or by contact with the radically new theology of Calvinism, were genuinely concerned to revolutionize not just the Church and its practices but also Scotland's people and Scotland's government. They wanted to create a more 'godly' society, ahead of what they believed were the last days, the final clash at the end of time between God and Satan. Catholicism and adherence to Papal authority, seen in this light, were not only irrational and immoral. To many, they were positively diabolical.

In this context Mary's personal devotion to Catholicism could not be anything but deeply troubling to many Scots. With so many having converted to Protestantism, including not just Arran but also her own illegitimate half-brother James Stewart, created 1st Earl of Moray by Mary in 1562 and a key early ally, her religious stance was difficult in the extreme. Wisely, and taking heed of Moray's guidance and that of William Maitland of Lethington, her secretary who became her closest advisor, she chose initially to compromise with her enemies. She carefully appointed several Protestant nobles to the Privy Council. She also agreed to practise Catholicism in her private chapel while tolerating the *de facto* triumph of Protestantism in the public domain.

There seems little doubt that Mary would actually have preferred to re-impose the old faith. But this was no longer realistic. Her military and political weakness, and the fact that she was an inexperienced female ruler dependent upon older male advisors who differed from the queen in matters of religion, meant that this was simply not possible in the circumstances.

This is why the Scottish Reformation rooted itself strongly during Mary's personal reign, even though she discouraged its most extreme manifestations. Parliament formally declared an end to Papal jurisdiction in Scotland and accepted Calvin's Confession of Faith, though Mary did not ratify these moves. Anti-Catholic measures proposed by Edinburgh's town council were also blocked. And despite Knox's violent rhetoric, to which Mary was personally exposed on occasion, it seemed that her own religious preferences would be tolerated, providing that she did not threaten her subjects' Protestantism.

The number of reformed clergy in Scotland, and the number of Scots attracted to Protestant theology and practices, continued to grow. A particularly important milestone was the move in 1561, led by Knox and endorsed at Privy Council, to require a school to exist in every parish – the intention being, of course, that elementary education should include clear instruction in the new faith.

If she could do little to prevent the rising tide of Protestantism, a more fruitful focus for Mary's efforts at this time seemed to be the English succession. For with her cousin Elizabeth unmarried and childless, it was widely assumed that the next ruler of England would have to be nominated. In Scotland, though significantly not in England, it was also presumed that Mary was the most likely nominee.

This issue understandably dominated Anglo-Scottish relations throughout Mary's reign. She tried to secure Elizabeth's endorsement. Elizabeth, suspicious of Mary's motives and in particular of her Catholicism, was equally determined not to grant it. For her part Mary refused to approve the Treaty of Edinburgh, which would have meant renouncing her own claim to be the legitimate Queen of England already. Neither woman would budge. Both were strong-willed enough to think that they would eventually browbeat the other into submission.

Mary's hopes of the English crown were also dealt a major blow by her own pursuit of a new husband. In order to placate the English elite and reassure them about her accommodation with Protestantism, the last thing she should have done was to consider Don Carlos of Spain, a prominent European Catholic – which is precisely what she did in 1563, although without success.

Only slightly less damaging was her actual marriage in 1565 to her cousin Henry Stewart, Lord Darnley, whose religious affiliations were notoriously ambiguous. Elizabeth was particularly alienated by this union because, since Darnley too had a claim to the English throne, it looked like a clumsy attempt to strengthen Mary's case to be named as Elizabeth's chosen heir.

The queen of hearts

The Darnley marriage marks the end of the first and more successful part of Mary's Scottish reign and the onset of the greater difficulties that would ultimately destroy not only her credibility but also her rule.

One immediate consequence was that Moray and several of the other Lords of the Congregation, fearing that Darnley might increase Catholic influence at court, decided to challenge Mary's power. The so-called Chaseabout Raid in late August 1565 was unable to rally sufficient forces and it fizzled out, forcing Moray into English exile. But it was a worrying sign, as Mary's earlier accommodation with Scotland's leading Protestant noblemen began to unravel.

Another unhelpful development was Darnley's imprudent behaviour. He alarmed many of Mary's previous supporters by demanding a greater political authority when strictly he was only the queen's consort. He was also centrally involved in the killing of David Rizzio, an Italian private secretary and musician at her Holyroodhouse court, in March 1566. Rizzio had become a favourite of Mary and a certain amount of salacious gossip had emerged about the exact nature of their relationship (not least because the queen was pregnant with the future James VI). Darnley's own jealousy merely fuelled the suspicion of many Protestants that immorality was, as they had always feared, rampant in the Catholic culture of the court. Unsurprisingly, his role in blackening Mary's reputation and in the dastardly murder of her close friend also destroyed her relationship with her husband, the father of her baby son.

Darnley's ambitions, meanwhile, proved lethal. His disdain for other people of rank made Darnley dangerously unpopular. Mary's own private affections had also turned to a new man, James Hepburn, 4th Earl of Bothwell. The result was another sensational murder in the queen's circle. On 10 February 1567 Darnley died in highly suspicious circumstances in an explosion at Edinburgh's Kirk o' Field. Bothwell, at whom fingers naturally pointed, was believed to have supplied the gunpowder, while many also saw the queen's own hand in the affair. It would be hard to think of an episode less likely to quell suspicions among her opponents that Mary was a dangerous and deceitful woman who simply could not be trusted.

Insight: The small ball game

No one could have imagined that hitting a ball with a stick towards a hole, a game played on the sandy seaside 'links' at places like St Andrews as long ago as the 12th century and later enjoyed by Mary during her otherwise troubled reign, would have evolved into a lucrative spectator sport as well as attracting mass participation internationally. The 2010 Open Championship at St Andrews was alone worth at least £80 million to the economy. Four other Scottish links currently host the Open – Carnoustie and Muirfield on the east coast, Troon and Turnberry on the west – while spectacular courses such as Gleneagles and Dornoch are among the world's most hallowed.

What little was left of Mary's active rule in Scotland can be swiftly described.

A hasty marriage to Bothwell, further incrimination in many people's eyes, took place on 15 May. And although performed in the Protestant fashion, this ceremony proved the spark that ignited the tinderbox. The Lords, suspicious of the married couple's intentions and sensing an opportunity to strike, raised another rebellion. At Carberry Hill near Musselburgh on 15 June they confronted forces loyal to Mary and Bothwell.

In return for permitting Bothwell to escape, Mary was imprisoned on the island in Loch Leven in Fife. But a more decisive turn of events was the discovery five days later of the so-called Casket Letters, widely thought to confirm Mary's involvement in Darnley's murder. Bothwell was declared guilty and a bounty put on his head. An outlaw, he died ten years later, insane and friendless, in a Danish jail.

Mary, who miscarried twins in the succeeding weeks, was finally forced to abdicate on 24 July 1567. Her only surviving child by Darnley, the one-year-old James, was proclaimed King of Scots, under Moray's regency.

Despite an attempted fightback the following spring, when Mary escaped from Loch Leven and her supporters fought an unsuccessful engagement at Langside near Glasgow against Moray's army, her troubled reign was effectively over. By the summer of 1568 she had fled to England. There, given that she was a focal point for Catholic opposition and that she also had an unrenounced claim to Elizabeth's throne, she ought not to have been surprised to find herself under arrest.

A long imprisonment followed. At an early stage there were English demands that she be investigated for complicity in Darnley's murder.

Insight: Proof positive?

Allegedly found in Edinburgh Castle in 1567 and presented by Moray to Queen Elizabeth, the Casket Letters comprised eight notes in French from Mary to Bothwell, a love poem by the queen and two marriage contracts. Collectively they indicated Mary's adulterous attachment to Darnley's killer as well as her prior approval of the crime. But was the discovery of this incriminating material simply too convenient? There was great controversy among 18th-century historians, who, noticing certain linguistic peculiarities, mostly pronounced them clever forgeries. Today, opinion remains divided, with many claiming that, although certainly tampered with, their guilty substance was real enough. Unfortunately the originals disappeared in the 1580s and only supposed English copies survive, so we will never know.

Later there were accusations that Mary had been active in various plots, with the aid of foreign Catholic powers, to take the English crown. The culmination came with the Babington plot by English Catholic aristocrats in 1586. Implicated by letters unwisely written in her own hand that were intercepted by Elizabeth's spies, Mary was put on trial at Fotheringhay Castle in Northamptonshire. Found guilty of treason against Elizabeth, she was sentenced to death. And although her cousin hesitated before signing the death warrant, Mary was beheaded on 8 February 1587.

Later generations would remain bitterly divided over Mary. For the first 200 years, when conflict between Protestants and Catholics remained crucial, attitudes were determined mainly by religion: to Protestants from Knox onwards she was an immoral and dishonest tyrant justly overthrown by the defenders of Scottish and British liberties; but for Catholics she was more sinned against than sinning, a pious martyr for the faith. From the mid-18th century onwards, however, as religious tensions lessened, an appreciation of Mary's human qualities, together with a greater awareness of the challenges she had faced, became more typical. She has more recently been seen as a tragic victim of her own failings, as an ill-starred romantic heroine – even a feminist icon – who fell foul of a hostile male-dominated world.

There is every reason to believe that future ages will continue to re-interpret Mary's enthralling story according to their own lights.

Two kings in one?

With Mary's son James we enter a decisive new phase in Scotland's history.

In the later middle ages, English kings' claims to rule the Scots had been the main force behind the kingdom's development. The result, of course, was regular cross-border conflict and, though clearly the opposite of what had been intended, reinforcement of the Scots' powerful sense of their own distinctiveness. James VI's reign partially reversed these trends. Inheriting his mother's claim to Elizabeth's throne, the King of Scots himself became King of England in 1603, re-styled thereafter as James VI and I. His so-called Union of the Crowns – by which one individual now ruled the two separate kingdoms – laid the groundwork for his descendants to complete the process of forming a single British state.

Contemporaries were perplexed by James and later ages have also found it difficult to get to the root of the man. For his life is full of contrasts and apparent contradictions. A fiercely proud Scot, he died a much-loved King of England. He was the clearly Protestant son of a pious Catholic mother who allowed the persecution of the old faith while quarrelling regularly with the more aggressive supporters of the new. He was a devoted husband and father who also liked the company of good-looking men, leading to inevitable speculation over his sexual orientation. He faced upheaval and rebellion in Scotland in his youth yet somehow emerged later as 'Good King James', a ruler long remembered for the stable government that he provided. He displayed great learning and culture but was a robust personality whose Scottish origins and coarse manners easily offended delicate English sensibilities. No wonder it has sometimes been tempting to see James as two completely different monarchs, the division lying geographically at the border and chronologically in or around 1603.

In truth many of the paradoxes of James VI and I stem from the challenging circumstances of his childhood. First, his mother had probably connived at his father's murder while he was a baby. She had subsequently been absent and was eventually executed by the cousin to whose throne James himself hoped to succeed. James was also the heir to a ruler who in the white heat of the Reformation crisis had managed to be on the wrong side in the eyes of many of her most influential subjects. Finally he had succeeded not just as an infant but actually as the result of a *coup d'etat*. Its leaders had used him as a figurehead providing cover for their actions. They had also tried to turn him against his mother and to impress upon him his complete reliance on their own goodwill and support. Tensions and contradictions were hardly surprising in a man whose character and approach to kingship were obliged to evolve in such testing conditions.

Particular emphasis needs to be placed on the effects of James's unusual upbringing. Cruel circumstances not only denied him parental contact and affection. They also placed him in the hands of his mother's enemies. As a result James's education was controlled by the famous George Buchanan: Europe's greatest living Latin poet and a scholar of international repute, Buchanan was also a militant propagandist for the coup of 1567 and a zealous convert to Protestantism.

The schooling James received from Buchanan was exceptionally intellectually rigorous. It exposed him to some of the most advanced political and cultural ideas. It also helps explain his sincere lifelong love of literature, learning and the arts – as an adult he would sponsor that timeless monument to the English language, the *King James Bible*. But his teacher was also a harsh taskmaster and an unyielding ideologue. James was beaten into submission: when the Countess of Mar thought Buchanan's violence excessive, his tutor reportedly snapped 'Madam, I have whipped his arse: you may kiss it if you please'.

Such severity allowed James to be force-fed not only Protestant teachings but also Buchanan's revolutionary notions about the duty of patriotic subjects to resist over-mighty (but especially Catholic and therefore godless) tyrants. Indeed, James's childhood seems to have been one long programme of deliberate indoctrination by his mother's opponents. Rather indicating what they had in mind for him from the outset, John Knox, Mary's nemesis and still the country's leading Calvinist preacher, even gave the sermon at James's coronation at Stirling in 1567. The intention was clearly that he would eventually be in no doubt about the strict limitations placed on him by God – and in Scotland by God's chosen lieutenants on earth, the Presbyterian party.

The last king in Scotland

Regency formed a familiar part of the complex set of problems affecting James's early years. Unavoidable in 1567, with the king barely a year old, the struggles for power that had traditionally surrounded regencies in Scotland were nevertheless made even worse by the uniquely revolutionary circumstances of James's accession.

Moray, the designated regent, lasted not three years before being shot dead at Linlithgow in 1570 by James Hamilton, a Catholic supporter of the Queen's Party, as Mary's allies were known. The assassin was the nephew of John Hamilton, Archbishop of St Andrews, who was opposed by Knox and the Protestant movement. The murderer escaped to the Continent but the archbishop, nominally still Scotland's senior cleric, was hanged for his complicity.

A succession of regents followed – their short tenures a reminder of the violence and instability for which Scotland was notorious. Matthew Stewart, 4th Earl of Lennox, Darnley's father and thus the king's grandfather, was next: he survived barely a year before dying from wounds inflicted by Mary's supporters at Stirling. John Erskine, 17th Earl of Mar, followed Lennox but was likewise dead within the year, this time falling victim to a suspicious poisoning in which all fingers pointed at the dead man's host, James Douglas, 4th Earl of Morton.

The latter was a Lord of the Congregation, had participated in Rizzio's murder and had subsequently helped oversee Mary's enforced abdication. It was thus no shock when Morton himself acquired the regency, a role in which he served until his execution in 1581 – ostensibly for involvement in Darnley's assassination but as much because his power had become too great for other leading noblemen to bear.

The Morton regency, by far the longest-lasting of James's minority, proved of wider importance for three reasons.

First, it saw the final defeat of the Queen's Party. This was important, and only occurred when, with English help, the government re-captured Edinburgh Castle from Mary's die-hard partisans in 1573. James, once he took effective charge around 1584, therefore enjoyed real legitimacy, despite his mother still being alive. This in turn allowed him to shore up his authority in the time-honoured fashion, by confronting challengers and suppressing disorder.

Second, Morton's last years witnessed the emergence of James's French cousin Esmé Stewart, soon created Duke of Lennox (and so, to vast native irritation, holder of Scotland's first dukedom). Like some of Mary's liaisons, this relationship isolated the monarch from other allies, particularly as Lennox enjoyed considerable power – it was he who brought about Morton's demise.

It was as a direct result of the apparent threat Lennox posed to royal morality and royal religion that a group of strongly Protestant noblemen, led by William Ruthven, 1st Earl of Gowrie, captured James on 22 August 1582. Keeping the king imprisoned at Ruthven Castle near Perth for ten months, they effectively controlled the kingdom. Under duress, James banished Lennox to France, where he soon died. James himself was free by July 1583 and the next year executed Gowrie for his presumption. But the so-called Ruthven Raid had confirmed James's continuing vulnerability to aristocratic pressure.

The third key development that emerged during Moray's regency, closely connected with first two processes, was the successful entrenching of the Reformed orthodoxy in Scotland – which would have lasting consequences for the country. Protestant ideas, supported personally by the courtiers and other leaders who had overthrown the French-backed Guise regime and who had then brought down Mary's government, were steadily imposed over much of the Scottish Church and most of its people. If the coup of 1567 was indeed a revolution, then its motivating ideology, to which everyone was now required to subscribe, was unquestionably Calvinism.

This entailed the Scots embracing the peculiarly rigid and dogmatic theology that Calvin had developed at Geneva. It teaches that every person, regardless of their actions or intentions on earth, is already preordained to experience a specific spiritual destiny. The fortunate ones who belong to the 'elect' will eventually receive the supreme gift of resurrection and everlasting life, granted by God and clearly demonstrated during their earthly lives by the sincere faith that they display in Christ. The remainder, the 'reprobate', lack that defining belief and unavoidably face only death and eternal damnation.

This famous doctrine of 'predestination', irreconcilably dividing believers from unbelievers and the saved from the condemned, was what ultimately gave such towering confidence, consolation and inner strength to those Scots in the succeeding centuries who genuinely believed themselves blessed to have been chosen to be among Jesus' true followers.

These theological foundations of Scottish Protestantism, strongly advocated by Knox and his allies in the early 1560s but for obvious reasons not formally endorsed by Mary's government, were finally approved on James VI's behalf in 1572. Calvin's Confession of Faith became thereafter the official definition of acceptable religious belief in Scotland.

Yet Calvinism also brought with it some rather more practical implications that were less easily translated from the newly formed city republic of Geneva to the ancient kingdom of Scotland. Above all, it involved implementing a new and controversial form of church organization known as Presbyterianism. In place of the familiar ecclesiastical hierarchy of bishops and archbishops appointed by the crown – Episcopalianism, or Episcopacy, as it is called – the introduction of Presbyterianism required a complex structure of local and regional church courts, staffed by a mixture of clergy and lay members (called 'presbyters') and exercising wide-ranging powers over religious, moral and social life.

The main result of such an arrangement would have been to render the Scottish Church effectively independent of royal control. This, understandably, was not something that James's advisers, let alone the king, would permit, and the Black Acts, passed in 1584, expressly confirmed the king's right to appoint bishops.

This unresolved issue over the control of a broadly Calvinist church was the main problem with which James had to wrestle during his personal rule. Things were certainly not helped by the emergence of an assertive younger generation of radical clergy, led by Andrew Melville, a brilliant scholar, university teacher and inspirational leader at Glasgow and St Andrews.

Melville, like several leading Presbyterian clerics, tended to view James himself as merely an over-ambitious layman who had arrogantly forgotten his own subordinate place as just one of Christ's many sinful followers. In one famously undiplomatic outburst in

1596, Melville is reported to have gripped the royal sleeve and told James to his shocked face to remember that 'ye are God's silly vassal' ('silly' being colloquial Scots for 'weak' or 'feeble'). To be fair, James gave as good as he got from the fundamentalists, responding to one ear-bashing from a Presbyterian minister, whose sermon against royal authority the king had found especially unpalatable: 'I will not give a turd for thy preaching.'

In 1592 Melville and his supporters in Parliament even achieved the Golden Act which partially reversed the Black Acts and formally endorsed Presbyterianism in the Scottish Church – though given James's personal position the appointment of bishops largely continued as before.

We should also be careful not to over-state the differences between James and even the most militant Protestants. It was true that he tolerated prominent Catholic subjects, like his favourite George Gordon, 6th Earl of Huntly, who was forgiven for his violent activities in the north-east and even, astonishingly, for open rebellion against the king himself in 1593–4: such leniency was hardly calculated to impress Presbyterian observers. But James was nonetheless a godly king and a committed Protestant who agreed with the Calvinist radicals on many points of policy – such as on burning witches (there was a spate of executions in the early 1590s) and on the importance of education (Edinburgh University was founded in 1583, with Marischal College, Aberdeen, following ten years later).

By this time, however, James's Scottish reign, despite his on-going tussles with the Presbyterians, was dominated by one factor above all: the long-anticipated death of Queen Elizabeth and the resulting vacancy on the English throne. James had harboured ambitions since his childhood. And with the passing years, as Elizabeth failed to marry or nominate an heir, the prospect of becoming King of England more and more preoccupied him.

The inevitable finally happened on 24 March 1603. With Elizabeth's passing, the English Privy Council offered James the crown. Gratefully accepting, he prepared to ride from Edinburgh to London, to begin a new chapter not only in his own life but in that of the kingdom of Scotland.

THINGS TO REMEMBER

▶ Mary, Queen of Scots, was dealt a bad hand – a woman in a man's world, inheriting as an infant and raised overseas as a foreign princess.

▶ Mary was also responsible for some major errors – involvement in Darnley's murder, her marriage to Bothwell, and her choice of advisors.

▶ Protestantism in England helped bring about Protestantism in Scotland, but in the latter it took a different, more radical form, worsening Mary's problems.

▶ Mary's deposition was a revolutionary moment inspired and justified by revolutionary ideas – Calvinism and the notion of royal accountability.

▶ James VI's early reign seemed like a repeat of his predecessors' experiences – the older Stewarts' problem of regencies and aristocratic resistance allied to his mother's struggle against Presbyterian radicalism.

▶ James nevertheless emerged triumphant, a skilled and pragmatic king of Scots well able to confront the challenges the crown faced.

9

....

Two crowns united

In this chapter you will learn:

- *about the Union of Crowns and the beginnings of absentee monarchy*
- *about James's continuing difficulties with the Scottish Church*
- *how James was succeeded by his son, Charles I, whose own reign ended in civil war.*

The accidental inheritance

The most important point to bear in mind about the Union of the Crowns – important because it created problems that dominated British politics for the next 100 years and more – was what it was not. For when James VI also became James I, in no real sense were Scotland and England themselves being united.

They remained, as they had always been, two separate kingdoms. There were still two peoples and two nations with deep-rooted identities and longstanding antagonisms; two parliaments, with contrasting histories and traditions; two markedly different Protestant churches, though neither now commanded the support of everyone in their respective kingdoms; two largely incompatible legal systems; two parallel sets of governmental machinery; even two armies and two coinages.

So what happened after Elizabeth's death was really only a personal union, the result of the biological accidents which had seen the same individual inherit first the Scottish and then the English crown. In practice its wider constitutional and political implications had to be worked out painfully, step by step, in the years ahead.

Good King James

The most striking feature of James's rule after 1603 was his re-location to London – the largest and wealthiest city in his two kingdoms and home to their most powerful political institution, the English Parliament at Westminster.

At a stroke this rendered Scotland physically a kingless kingdom. On his sole return visit in 1617, James was surprised to hear genuine hurt about his absence. As the poet William Drummond of Hawthornden asked in a verse written for the occasion:

> *Ah why should Isis only see thee shine?*
> *Is not the Forth as well as ISIS thine?*

These sentiments, referring to James's residence beside the Thames (known up-river as the Isis), expressed wounded Scottish pride at the king's preference for the English capital. But there were practical implications too. When it was still impossible to ride between Edinburgh and London in much less than 14 days and it took the best part of a month for any meaningful two-way communication, the very nature of James's rule was seriously affected by his sheer remoteness from Scotland. One result was that James became more detached from Scottish events.

Equally predictable, and another source of friction, were James's attempts to harmonize the two kingdoms. For the self-styled first King of Great Britain (as he declared himself in 1604, to widespread irritation), this made sense not merely in terms of personal vanity but as a solution to the political havoc that continuing differences would cause for someone with obligations to both sides.

Symbolically James experimented with a single flag, merging the Scottish cross of St Andrew with the English cross of St George: this was finally introduced for shipping in 1606, though over continuing opposition from English and Scottish critics. More important was James's successful promotion of a scheme which saw his subjects in each kingdom granted the legal right of naturalization in the other: in effect, a common Anglo-Scottish citizenship emerged.

In 1605 he also established a joint commission to oversee the Borders, or the 'Middle Shires' as they were now called in deference to James's view that he ruled over a single polity. This was an especially wise move given this wild upland region's notoriety for lawless behaviour. Inside the first year the commission had hanged no fewer than 79 offenders, the notorious Armstrong family had been exiled to Ireland and by the 1620s the age-old criminal tradition of reiving had been ruthlessly expunged. More generally, James bore down on the traditional practice of violent feuding between kin groupings.

James also tackled the Highlands, the part of mainland Britain that least conformed to the kinds of behaviour expected by a London-based ruler for whom south-east England increasingly defined the norms. The Statutes of Iona were imposed in 1609. In a striking attack on the distinctive foundations of Celtic culture, the Statutes banned the bards – the singers of traditional oral songs and poems – whose words inspired Highlanders to emulate the heroic deeds of their ancestors and required chieftains to educate their sons in Lowland schools (further undermining the Gaelic language).

James also made sure to have a significant number of Scottish allies with him in London. The arrival of some of Scotland's leading aristocrats displeased their English counterparts: soon there were 158 Scots in paid royal employment, each taking up a position previously occupied by members of England's elite. But this did at least help maintain James's relationship with the ruling families of the native country he had left behind.

Not content with creating a genuinely Anglo-Scottish court, James even wanted to bring about the formal political unification of the two kingdoms, as he told the English Parliament in 1604 and again in 1607. But his hopes were dashed. Accustomed to debating in person in the Scots Parliament, which was really just a gathering of people whom James knew, he could not use the same device to overawe the much larger House of Commons and House of Lords, England's separate, well-established and often independent-minded chambers. When Westminster threw out James's scheme, suspicious that it threatened English identity and interests, he was angry but could do nothing about it.

Clearly union still had severe limits.

The church militant

It would not have surprised James that the Scottish Church remained a major problem even when he was resident in London.

In organizational matters, an uneasy compromise still continued. The Church contrived somehow to be simultaneously Presbyterian, having the necessary hierarchy of courts, and Episcopalian, with the king's bishops, who generally tried to be tactful and inoffensive, working closely with those elected bodies. Indeed, historians have generally been impressed by the surprising harmony of this hybrid arrangement, noting how it only imploded once monarchs lacked James's established personal authority in Scotland as well as his intimate first-hand knowledge of Scottish conditions.

But in other policy areas James remained on a collision course with the Presbyterians, a trajectory that eventually produced the controversy over the Five Articles of Perth. These were regulations on worship and religious observance which, although compatible with moderate Protestantism and with English practice, outraged James's Presbyterian critics when he tried to impose them in Scotland.

The General Assembly duly rejected the Articles in November 1617. Furious, James had them proclaimed publicly by the Privy Council in October 1618. And it took considerable pressure and political manoeuvring from James and his officials to secure the Scots Parliament's approval in 1621. The whole episode, with James clearly underestimating the degree of resistance to his plans, was a classic illustration of the problem of absentee monarchy, with the ruler detached from local events and increasingly unable to read the very obvious signals about serious trouble ahead.

When he died in 1625, James VI and I was in many ways as much of an enigma to those who surrounded him as he had been when he first emerged from his peculiarly intense and restricted childhood – a rough-tongued bully but also an international diplomat and peacemaker; a sincere supporter of the Reformation who bickered constantly with his fellow-Protestants and had numerous good Catholic friends; an experienced and generally flexible politician who could still make appalling mistakes.

His successor Charles I, who inherited the challenging legacy of the Union of the Crowns, was a delicate and prudish man who lacked some of his father's cruder vices. Crucially, however, he also lacked James's winning charisma, his political astuteness, and, not least as things turned out, his good fortune.

The native who was a stranger

One of the many ironies of Charles's rule, given the disasters that subsequently unfolded in his relations with the Scots, is that the future king entered the world in 1600 every inch a Scottish prince, at Dunfermline, with its enduring associations with the Canmore dynasty and where the Bruce himself lay buried. By a further quirk of fate, Charles was even baptized at Holyroodhouse by a Presbyterian minister. Yet no other Scottish monarch would ever betray such suicidal ignorance about the nature and limitations of his power in Scotland, particularly in questions of Church and faith.

A key explanation for Charles's behaviour as king again lies in a peculiar childhood. First, Charles was not born to rule. Only the sudden death of Prince Henry in 1612 turned a sensitive younger son into an ill-at-ease future monarch desperate to live up to the rich promise displayed by his popular but tragically lost sibling. Second, Charles had disabilities, including a limp (possibly from rickets in infancy) and a speech impediment that never left him. His adult obsession with status and his inability to absorb constructive criticism both look like the results of an underlying lack of confidence and of a desire to compensate – perhaps over-compensate – for these handicaps. The same factors also make good sense of Charles's arrogant decision to run England personally from 1629 onwards without calling a Parliament to Westminster where his opponents and critics might congregate.

A further trait that Charles I possessed, in this case much like his father, was a taste for the arts and learning. Mainly this was a good thing. The wonderfully human triple-headed portrait by Van Dyck is probably how we now most often remember Charles's appearance; he knighted Rubens, who decorated the ceiling at the new Banqueting House in Whitehall; and, as a connoisseur with impeccably progressive tastes, he made the royal collection of paintings Europe's greatest concentration of top-class contemporary art. More troublingly, however, Charles also acquired an intense interest in theology and church history. As a result, he learned to view these deeply controversial matters from the doctrinaire perspective of an intellectual purist rather than that of a pragmatic ruler. This was to prove a catastrophic flaw in Charles's approach as monarch, particularly in relation to the Scottish Church.

Arguably Charles's greatest weakness, however, was simply the result of 1603. For he was the London-based monarch not only of England but also of the distinctive, distant and – to Charles at least – largely unknown kingdom of Scotland. He paid his only adult visit, for an inexcusably late Scottish coronation, fully eight years after actually succeeding. And like James in 1617 he heard a welter of complaints, articulated once more by poets such as William Drummond, which reflected the tensions created by absentee monarchy.

All of these problems converged as Charles attempted to deal with the most difficult and contentious policy area of all: the forms of worship and internal organization of the Scottish Church.

It would have seemed far-fetched as Charles paraded proudly through the streets of Scotland's capital in 1633 in a splendid royal pageant. But in the final analysis, these issues would literally be the death of him.

THINGS TO REMEMBER

▶ The Union of the Crowns placed one person on two kingdoms' thrones but did not bring together the peoples, nations or cultures of Scotland and England.

▶ James VI and I had ambitions to integrate his kingdoms after 1603, even to merge them, but, facing strong resistance from both nations, he achieved little.

▶ James's re-location to London caused resentment in Scotland and created a problematic system of long-distance, out-of-touch Scottish government.

▶ James's Scottish reign continued to be dominated by quarrels with the Presbyterians over the Church.

▶ James's son Charles I was born in Scotland but never really knew or understood the country, a fatal handicap as things transpired.

10

The conflict of the covenant

In this chapter you will learn:
- *about civil war and religious strife that spread contagiously throughout Great Britain*
- *how Cromwell's republic occupied and governed Scotland for nine years – until the Restoration of the monarchy.*

Clumsy beginnings

The personal and political calamity which was Charles I's reign as King of Scots gave out a number of early signals that all was not well. These should have indicated that a monarch who was poorly informed about Scotland was stumbling unwittingly into avoidable disagreements with important traditional interest groups. But the signs were ignored.

One error that caused immediate and lasting friction was the Act of Revocation of 1625. In one sense, this was unremarkable. At the end of a minority adult monarchs had traditionally annulled all grants of lands and offices previously made in their name. Either these were then re-assigned or, more likely, a fee would be paid by the holders to maintain the status quo. But Charles was scarcely a minor when James VI and I died, even though he was still strictly just under the customary age limit for revocation of 25. And his legislation was audaciously wide-ranging, stretching back all the way to 1540.

Clearly this was intended to include the huge number of grants of Church property made during the Reformation, Charles's aim being to use the resulting income to create a better funded Scottish Church.

However, to Scottish landowners whose acquisitions were being challenged many decades after the event, the revocation was provocative, instantly alienating Charles from the kingdom's most powerful men.

The coronation itself also fanned the flames of discontent. For the visit could not have been better designed to anger Presbyterians. Henrietta-Maria, Charles's French queen, was herself a Catholic and celebrated mass privately in Edinburgh: the king was inevitably suspected of, at the very least, Popish sympathies. The ceremony too was conducted in the spirit of the Five Articles of Perth: ornately dressed clergy, including English bishops, and lots of kneeling before the altar, were red rags to the Calvinist bull, visible hints that Scotland's new king was not one of them. Finally, one of James's proposals was revived by his idealistic, theologically obsessed son. This was for a new English-style prayer book whose use would bring about uniform practice in religious services.

Let us pray

The mastermind behind Charles I's religious policies in both kingdoms was William Laud, his scholarly and ambitious Archbishop of Canterbury, who, like a number of other leading theologians in Holland and England, favoured a form of Protestantism, often seen as substantially modifying Calvinism, called Arminianism.

At its core lies a theological teaching which suggests that it is because God knows we will have faith in Christ that He predestines us to salvation, rather than, as Calvin had proposed, God giving us that faith only because He has already chosen us to be saved. Most of us today are liable to look at these words and find it hard to appreciate the difference. But to contemporary Presbyterians, versed in the fine theological details and passionately committed to Calvin's insistence that their spiritual destiny rested entirely and exclusively with God's grace rather than with their own decisions, the shift of emphasis promoted by Arminianism was certainly ungodly, seemingly crypto-Catholic, and perhaps even directly diabolical in origin and intent.

Taken together with the Arminians' general bias towards episcopacy and royal authority in the church, this struck at the heart of what large numbers of Scottish Presbyterians believed their own eventual victory in the Reformation – the triumph of God's elect – had achieved.

From this point onwards the ability of Charles's religious reforms in Scotland to generate not merely heated academic debate but profound public hostility and outright physical resistance becomes more intelligible. Despite what was later claimed, the new prayer book, finally distributed in 1637, was actually mainly drafted out by the Scottish bishops. But it was certainly corrected and approved by Laud and Charles. And it was an open secret that Laud's Arminian beliefs were the driving force behind a document, which, his Scottish opponents pointed out, had been approved neither by a Scots Parliament nor by a General Assembly.

The rebellion began at a service in St Giles's Cathedral on 23 July 1637 when, it is said, Jenny Geddes, a local market trader, hurled a stool at the presiding clergyman while accusing him of leading a new Catholic form of worship: 'daur ye say Mass in my lug?' ('dare you say mass in my ear?'), she supposedly asked.

Entertaining though the story is, it is, like so much else in Scottish history, a colourful mixture of hard fact and later embellishment. Geddes herself is not named in any near-contemporary source. There is also real doubt that she spoke those particular words. Yet the commotion does indeed seem to have been begun by a female objector.

Whoever it was who cast the first stone, the vast exposed glasshouse of Charles's prayer book and the Arminian reforms now came under attack – so much so that a degree of co-ordination surely lay behind the campaign. Certainly the hostility was both widespread and ferocious. Edinburgh was in ferment, the Privy Council at one point seeking refuge at Holyroodhouse. The changes nearly saw one Glasgow clergyman torn limb from limb. The Bishop of Brechin took to sporting a pair of loaded pistols when performing communion in the new style.

Large-scale petitioning also occurred. Most importantly, an organization emerged late in 1637 called the Tables, led by the earls of Rothes and Montrose and opposing the innovations. The Lord Advocate, the leading Scottish law officer, advised a climb-down but Charles refused. Indeed, his response, typically convinced that a bold assertion of royal authority would unnerve his opponents, was simply to stand firm and issue proclamations demanding obedience.

Joining with God

The Presbyterians' reaction was in many ways a revolutionary political development. Meeting at Greyfriars' Church in Edinburgh for three days starting on 28 February 1638, the Tables oversaw the mass signing of a document called the National Covenant – drafted by the lawyer Archibald Johnston of Warriston and the Fife clergyman Alexander Henderson. Copies were also made and sent for signing by people across the kingdom. Its text was of immense importance, for it bound the signatories to each other and to God in the cause of true religion: the event, as Warriston proudly boasted, capturing the spiritual fervour of the moment, seemed to be 'The great Marriage Day of this Nation with God'.

Soon a sizeable proportion of the Scottish people had taken this solemn oath to band together to fight their king's religious programme. They were very careful, however, not explicitly to denounce Charles himself: indeed, the Covenant affirmed their loyalty, claiming that they opposed only the king's advisers on church policy.

Charles, privately convinced that he would need to fight what he recognized was effectively a rival Scottish government, allowed a General Assembly to meet in Glasgow in November 1638. This strongly Presbyterian gathering again proved violently hostile. It abolished episcopacy and deposed the remaining bishops. It also repudiated the new prayer book (in a revealing rhetorical flourish they accused it of being 'heathenish, Popish, Jewish and Arminian' – as though any religious text could somehow be such different things at once).

Charles refused to accept these decisions, even though, with the ambitious Presbyterian nobleman Archibald Campbell, 8th Earl of Argyll, emerging as the Tables' leader, it was now a national government in all but name. He prepared a royal army in northern England and moved them towards the border. The Covenanters, as they were increasingly called, gathered arms and prepared their defences.

So began what were to become known as the Bishops' Wars. Led by Alexander Leslie, a battle-hardened Scottish veteran of the recent Continental wars, and by the Earl of Montrose, the Covenanters' superior forces successfully blocked the advance of Charles's army near Berwick in June 1639 in what was later seen as the first phase of the war. Rather than fight at a clear disadvantage, Charles conceded further negotiations, and permitted meetings of the General Assembly and Scots Parliament. The former predictably repeated the decisions made in Glasgow; the latter also declared episcopacy abolished and agreed to end royal control of parliamentary business. Charles again was indignant and unmoved.

The second phase of the Bishops' Wars saw Leslie's army advance on Newcastle and Durham in August and September 1640, which they occupied as Charles's feeble forces melted away. It was this humiliation that finally compelled Charles to call a new English Parliament, the first for 11 years and the body of angry and frustrated MPs at Westminster who would shortly themselves begin a civil war against him.

The Scottish dimension to the final months before open warfare broke out in Britain was in one sense minimal. The Covenanters remained in control of a part of northern England until late in 1641, doing no real physical damage but causing the king huge embarrassment. Charles gambled on yet more concessions – unerringly offered, as was his way, just too late to be either convincing or effective, and probably in any case calculated to shore up his position in England, which remained his absolute priority, by agreeing to give ground in Scotland, which ultimately mattered much less. To this effect he spent the period from August to November 1641 in Edinburgh during which he accepted the recent decisions of the General Assembly and Scots Parliament. Leslie also became Earl of Leven and the Earl of Argyll a marquis.

But Charles's ploy failed because events were now spiralling wildly out of control at Westminster. The king and his English opponents, divided over his religious policies but also over the proper relationship between crown and Parliament, were soon at daggers-drawn. On 22 August 1642 Charles I raised his own standard at Newark in Nottinghamshire: England, at least, faced civil war.

How would the Scots, still antagonistic to the same ruler, respond?

Allies against the king

The Scots' approach to the English conflict was complicated in the first place by pronounced differences of opinion among Charles's Scottish opponents. In particular, not all were willing to join with England's parliamentarians, much less to risk provoking a civil war in Scotland itself, especially given the concessions that the king had offered.

Another issue was Ireland. For several decades Scots had been settling there as part of royal policy. A rising in 1641 by Catholics, with massacres of Protestant immigrants followed by vicious reprisals by both sides, therefore became an acute problem for the Covenanters, who quickly despatched an army to Ulster to help protect Scottish settlers.

In the event the Scots only properly committed themselves after the English Parliament formally asked for assistance. Crucially, however, this request was accompanied by a suggestion: in return for Scottish help, Presbyterianism could become the official church settlement in England.

A formal treaty, the Solemn League and Covenant, was agreed in September 1643, though Presbyterianism was alluded to rather than explicitly mentioned. This was because many English parliamentarians were actually Independents, favouring a radical Protestantism that allowed individual congregations to follow their own consciences: as the Scots would later discover, people like this – the as-yet-unknown Oliver Cromwell was one – thought that accepting the harsh authority of Presbyterian church courts was no better than bending to the will of the king's bishops.

With this somewhat vague but promising-sounding agreement in place, the Committee of Estates, the Scottish parliamentary body that had emerged to run the country's affairs, entered the English war. Importantly, however, there were now Scots willing to fight actively on the king's side. The most prominent was Montrose, who had fallen out with Argyll, the leader of Clan Campbell and the dominant figure in the Covenanting aristocracy. Indeed, Montrose wanted to maintain Charles's authority in Scotland as a bulwark against either Presbyterian dictatorship or outright anarchy. He was assisted by Alasdair MacColla, a Catholic and Gaelic lord from the Hebrides with strong connections among the MacDonalds of both western Scotland and northern Ireland and a deep instinctive loathing of the Campbells.

The period between 1643 and 1645 therefore saw something of a paradox. In England the Scottish Covenanters, with their greater military experience, proved a vital aid to Parliament, playing a key role in winning some of its greatest victories. Most famously, at Marston Moor outside York on 2 July 1644, a force of 14,000 Scots under the Earl of Leven and 11,000 Englishmen commanded by Lord Fairfax crushed the king's roughly equal-sized army:

Charles thereafter abandoned northern England, previously an important area of strength for him.

But in Scotland itself things were far less encouraging for the Presbyterians. Montrose, made a marquis by Charles in 1644, humiliated the Covenanting regime in its own backyard. Less than two months after Marston Moor, the army of Montrose and MacColla, a motley assortment of Highlanders, Irishmen and Lowland Royalists, defeated a superior force of Covenanters at Tippermuir near Perth; 12 days later they repeated the feat near Aberdeen; and the following February they defeated a larger number of Campbells at Inverlochy in the Highlands. As if this were not enough, three more stunning Royalist victories followed: Auldearn, Alford and Kilsyth, all fought and won in the summer of 1645. Confident, determined and flexible, Montrose and MacColla formed a formidable partnership that cut a swathe through the military resources of the Committee of Estates, some of whose members had by August 1645 been forced to seek refuge in Berwick.

Montrose, seemingly dominant in Scotland, was appointed lord lieutenant and captain-general by a grateful king. But Charles's weakness in England soon undercut his unexpected strength north of the Border. Having defeated Charles at Naseby on 12 June 1645, the main Covenanting army was able to spare David Leslie, another of the Scots' veteran commanders, to return home. Leslie surprised Montrose on the misty morning of 13 September at Philiphaugh near Selkirk in the Borders, defeating his Highlanders and, in the aftermath, massacring Irish women among the Royalist camp followers (the killing of Irish people engaged in the fighting in mainland Britain being a particularly repellent feature of the civil war period).

This one setback shattered the newly minted myth of Montrose's invincibility, which in any case had never made him widely popular. In particular, his reliance on imported Irish troops and on Catholic Highlanders, together with his own status as a former Covenanting turncoat, had always limited his appeal throughout Presbyterian and Lowland society.

Leslie then executed a successful mopping-up operation. By September 1646 Montrose had fled to Norway. Charles, defeated in a longer and bloodier civil war than anyone had ever expected, appeared finally to have run out of options.

Covenanted kings

If Montrose's meteoric campaign of 1644–5 had taken everyone by surprise, what happened next in Scotland was even less predictable.

We have already seen how the Solemn League and Covenant had originally promised the spread of Scottish-style Presbyterianism to England. The Westminster Assembly of Divines had even convened in 1643 to devise a uniform system of church government and common services for both kingdoms. By 1646, however, its members had failed to deliver. The main problem was that the Independents, especially strong in Cromwell's New Model Army which had acquired the upper hand in England during the war, rejected the Scots' vision of a Presbyterian structure imposing hierarchical authority over individual groups of believers. An agreed Calvinist statement of belief and form of worship was finally produced – the Westminster Confession of Faith, long afterwards used by the Church of Scotland. But the gulf over church government was clearly unbridgeable.

The resulting acrimony had seismic implications. It split England's Presbyterian parliamentarians from their increasingly dominant Independent comrades. This offered Charles, a prisoner of the New Model Army by 1647 but with no final peace settlement agreed, the chance to re-open the war against a now-divided enemy. More extraordinary still, the rupture between Parliament and the Scots even created the thrilling possibility – inconceivable in 1638 or 1642 or even 1645 – of Charles doing a deal with the Covenanters and using Scottish military power against Cromwell and the radicals who had captured the English parliamentary leadership.

The result was a secret treaty signed in December 1647, known as the Engagement. In this Charles agreed to impose Presbyterianism on England himself in return for Scottish support. Many Covenanters, including Argyll, Leven and Leslie, disliked the deal, either on principle or out of suspicion for Charles's motives, and so did not participate. It fell to the king's kinsman and supporter, the Duke of Hamilton, to lead a Scottish army.

The second civil war in England began early in 1648 in south Wales and in Kent, as Royalists and some English Presbyterians rose against Cromwell. For his part Hamilton marched south in July with

20,000 men under his command. This was met by Cromwell and just 8,000 men near Preston. But in a complicated three-day engagement on 17–19 August the numerically superior Scots were easily beaten.

Hamilton was captured and subsequently executed in London. The strategic and political consequences, however, were far-reaching. Preston effectively strangled the second civil war at birth, simultaneously proving to Cromwell that neither Charles nor the Presbyterians could be trusted. This left the New Model Army, its commanders and the Independents in total command. The Engagers' failure therefore had a quite unintended (and, to most Scots, unwanted) outcome, hastening the culmination of England's crisis that came with Charles's beheading on 30 January 1649.

Charles's death changed everything and it changed nothing. It was and remains a great constitutional turning-point. Even if never repeated, it firmly established a new understanding of the relationship between ruler and ruled – a reigning monarch being tried as a traitor to the English people and put to death for his crimes. In Scotland, however, it did little that the Engagement had not already made likely.

In particular, it commenced the Scottish reign of Charles II, the late king's son and heir. Though in a Dutch exile, he was duly proclaimed king by the Scots Parliament on 5 February 1649. But like his father, the new ruler found that there were strings attached: specifically, a requirement that he embrace Presbyterianism throughout Britain and sign the Covenant himself.

This was not easy to accept, and while negotiations proceeded slowly he encouraged Montrose to land in Orkney to apply a little pressure to the Scots. This ploy went badly. Montrose, lacking major support, was defeated at Carbisdale in Sutherland on 27 April 1650 by an army loyal to Argyll and the radical Covenanters. Hiding with Neil Macleod of Assynt, who betrayed him, Montrose was conveyed to Edinburgh where he was tried and hanged by the Covenanting government.

With no other alternatives available, Charles II duly accepted the Covenanters' terms and returned to Scotland in June 1650. Cromwell and the New Model Army, however, were alert to any sign of Stuart revival. On 3 September 1650 they smashed the much larger Scottish army led by Leslie, now fighting for the king, at Dunbar to the east of Edinburgh. The capital was soon securely in English hands. Prisoners from Dunbar were marched off to Durham, perhaps 3,500 dying en route or in captivity.

Formally signing the Solemn League and Covenant, Charles II was crowned at Scone on 1 January 1651. But it was an empty victory. The king despised and mistrusted his Scottish allies. And they had already effectively lost control of their country to Cromwell.

Charles II was able to persuade them to mount one last desperate attempt to defeat Cromwell. The broader strategic aim was to invade England and to bring together an unlikely grand alliance, rousing English Presbyterians and old Royalists to fight alongside the Scots, all in the cause of a Covenanted king. Charles's Scottish army, closely monitored by Cromwell, got as far as Worcester where on 3 September 1651 it was destroyed. Leslie was fortunate only to have to spend the next few years in the Tower of London; the king, after hiding up an oak tree, escaped to France.

A strangely constructive dictatorship

Substantial Scottish resistance to Cromwell was now largely over.

Edinburgh was already firmly under English control. General John Lambert defeated the last significant Scottish force at Inverkeithing on the Fife coast on 20 July 1651, opening up the way northwards; and then General George Monck, who had fought for Charles I in the Bishops' Wars but was now a respected subordinate and friend of Cromwell, had taken Stirling, Perth and Dundee – in the latter case storming it when it held out for King Charles, killing 800 citizens in the process and burning every vessel in the harbour. A few remote strongholds – the Bass Rock in the Forth, Dunnottar Castle perched on a Kincardineshire cliff top – were reduced in the coming months.

Scotland, arguably for the first time since Edward I, found itself by late 1651 an occupied country, governed by an English administration backed by overwhelming military force. The way was therefore clear for Cromwell to resolve the key problem in Anglo-Scottish relations since 1603. He now did so, and was uniquely free to do so, at the point of a republican sword.

In October 1651 Cromwell issued what came to be called the Tender of Union – 'tender' suggests merely an offer but it was definitely not one that the Scots, who were not consulted, would be able to refuse. Under its terms Scotland would cease to be independent. A single expanded Commonwealth would come into existence, with a Parliament at Westminster in which Scotland would have 30 representatives. All forms of Protestantism (except for Episcopalianism) would also be tolerated.

Small-scale resistance to Cromwell's regime continued. Indeed, at least until 1655, when Monck finally squashed all remaining appetite for military adventurism by Royalists, there were local risings and minor engagements that indicated significant levels of opposition to occupation by the English republic. Charles's principal agent was the Earl of Middleton, an able soldier, assisted by the Earl of Glencairn. But disagreements between Charles's supporters, together with the government's military strength, ultimately made this insurgency more a serious irritant than a grave counter-revolutionary threat.

Meanwhile the Cromwellian regime was busy reforming the reach and efficiency of government – again without consultation. As commander in chief until 1655 and thereafter as the dominant figure in Cromwell's hand-picked Council of Scotland, Monck could actually re-shape the country's politics and administration as he saw fit. And historians have generally agreed that he chose well. Justice and taxation in particular were more fairly run: 'honest general George', as he became known, was more impartial than any native Scot had been, even though his Englishness still attracted some resentment.

As chance would have it, Monck would also do more than anyone else to bring the Cromwellian dictatorship and the English republic to a close.

As the military commander in Scotland, he became the key figure who, after Oliver Cromwell's death and the accession of his insubstantial son Richard Cromwell in 1658, decided to throw his considerable weight behind a return to full parliamentary decision-making and, eventually, a Stuart restoration. Marching a select force from Coldstream on the border on 1 January 1660 – these men, previously Royalism's sworn enemies, would soon become the king's prestigious 2nd Foot Guards, today's Coldstream Guards – he arrived in London, helped reinstate Parliament and began negotiations for Charles II's return.

In that very specific sense the Restoration throughout Britain had direct origins in a small Berwickshire village. This did not, however, guarantee that Charles II would be welcomed with open arms by everyone in Scotland.

THINGS TO REMEMBER

▶ Charles I's relations with Scotland were undermined by his location in London and by his insensitivity and lack of local knowledge.

▶ Charles had particular problems because his Arminian religious preferences placed him at odds with orthodox Calvinist Presbyterians.

▶ The Covenant was the result, literally an alliance binding the Presbyterians to each other and to God in opposing Charles's religious policies.

▶ The Covenanters caused the English civil war, fighting against Charles, invading England and forcing him to convene the Long Parliament that would eventually defeat him.

▶ The Covenanters and English Parliamentarians fell out because of the Scots' Presbyterianism, leading the Scots, remarkably, to ally with Charles.

▶ Charles's final defeat and execution led most Scots to embrace Charles II, but they were easily crushed by Cromwell's formidable military machine.

▶ Cromwell's republic occupied and governed Scotland for nine long years – without consent and usually without consultation.

A restoration and another revolution

In this chapter you will learn:

- *how continuing religious differences in Scotland led to the black period known as the Killing Time*
- *about the exile of James VII, the arrival of William and Mary, and the consequences for Scotland*
- *about the catastrophic financial loss to Scotland resulting from the ill-fated Darien venture.*

A merry monarch has the last laugh

The Restoration was a major turning point in British history. It marked the failure of a radical constitutional experiment and the end of a period of unprecedented political upheaval. The republic was over. But, because of what had happened since 1642, most believed that monarchy too would never be the same again.

There were also differences between what the Restoration meant north and south of the border, with important implications for what would happen next.

First, although Royalists naturally insisted that Charles II's reign had begun at the precise moment of his father's death in 1649, he had never been crowned King of England. In Scotland, however, Charles's coronation had occurred a decade earlier. He had also had the opportunity, during some difficult first-hand experiences in 1650–1, to form a distinctly unfavourable impression of many of Scotland's leaders.

Second, Charles returned to become, as English monarch, the supreme head of the Church of England. This helpfully reflected his own Episcopalian preferences. In Scotland, though, as a consequence of his dealings in 1650, Charles was now that most unlikely (and uncomfortable) of creatures: a Covenanted king. The problems created by this crucial difference were worsened by the fact that Charles never saw Scotland again, reverting to the absentee rule that had generated so much mutual misunderstanding between the Scots and his father and grandfather.

On 1 January 1661 a Scots Parliament convened in Edinburgh. An early decision was the Act Rescissory which voided all legislation since 1633 – making it as if the laws of the Covenanting revolution and Cromwellian occupation had never happened. Middleton and Glencairn, helped by their support for Charles in the 1650s, initially held political sway.

Some of the business of the restored royal government was essentially personal. There were wrongs to right and scores to settle. The Marquis of Montrose's remains were reassembled and paraded solemnly through Edinburgh for re-burial in St Giles's Cathedral on 11 May 1661. Montrose's old nemesis, however, received the opposite treatment just 16 days later. Argyll had been charged with treason for collaborating with Monck's occupying forces and he was now beheaded. Interestingly the two enemies were eventually joined in death as they had been in life, Argyll today lying in St Giles's, his tomb directly facing Montrose's.

Johnston of Warriston, the joint author of the National Covenant and scourge of royal government, was similarly singled out. Hiding in France, he was handed over to Charles's officers and tried for treasonable collusion with the regicide regime. Warriston was hanged in Edinburgh in June 1663 and his severed head placed on a spike on the city's Netherbow.

Aside from chilling retribution against prominent individuals, the Restoration government, coming after the long reign of the Covenanters, had far bigger fish to fry, especially in relation to religious policy. In September 1661 an intention to restore Episcopacy was proclaimed. By 1662 bishops had also been reinstated, the Presbyterian courts abolished and all of the clergy required to repudiate the Covenant.

This was doubly controversial. Episcopalianism was obviously anathema in principle to many Presbyterians, and especially to hardcore Covenanters. But it was the accompanying sense of betrayal that made things even worse. A monarch who had himself endorsed the Covenant had now gone back on an oath taken before God – not only revealing personal untrustworthiness but also committing an act of sacrilege. The new leaders of the Episcopalian church were despised for the same reasons: James Sharp, minister of Crail in Fife who in 1661 became Archbishop of St Andrews, was especially widely loathed by former Covenanter allies as an unprincipled traitor.

Practical opposition was widespread. Many Covenanting parish ministers either had to be ejected for refusing to accept the new requirements or simply walked out themselves. Those who left, however, did not vanish into thin air. Instead they often re-appeared as independent 'field preachers', addressing like-minded Calvinists in 'conventicles' – unlicensed gatherings which, worryingly, sprang up across the country after 1661. It therefore soon became clear that, rather than achieving uniformity in Scotland's religious life and effective royal control of its Church, the government's policies had actually created what was in effect a worryingly militant and entirely unofficial form of Presbyterianism.

Middleton was chiefly responsible for this initial period and to him should be attributed much of the blame for what followed. But by 1664 he had been eclipsed by John Maitland, 2nd Earl of Lauderdale (and 1st Duke from 1672), a former Covenanter who had helped negotiate the Engagement in 1648 and who had been imprisoned by Cromwell since Worcester. As secretary of state, Lauderdale, a skilled political operator, was easily able to dominate matters affecting Scotland, although he was, of course, also left to deal with the bitter legacy of Middleton's policies.

Lauderdale, it appears, had not favoured the ruthless re-imposition of Episcopacy. But this did little to help make the government and its religious policies more palatable to committed Presbyterians and conventiclers. Indeed, in 1666 open warfare erupted in the form of the Pentland Rising by armed Presbyterians. They were defeated by the Royalist cavalry officer Tam Dalyell at Rullion Green near Edinburgh on 28 November. Severe punishments were handed out – hanging for dozens; banishment to the English colonies in the New World for others. Yet this only supplied new martyrs to keep the radical flame of the Covenant burning.

Killing Time

Under Lauderdale genuine attempts were actually made to modify the Restoration religious settlement. In particular he was associated with a more balanced approach. Specific concessions were now made, aimed at wider opinion, whilst seeking to isolate and eliminate the regime's more extreme opponents.

In the late 1660s some moderate Covenanting clergy were re-embraced and, under what were termed 'indulgences', retained in their parishes – to the annoyance of the more doctrinaire bishops. An indemnity was even granted to former rebels. So confident was Lauderdale that this would draw the Presbyterian opposition's teeth that he felt able to have the Parliament of 1669–70 pass the Act of Supremacy. This made Charles II the head of the Scottish Church and made attending illegal conventicles punishable by death.

This two-pronged strategy continued into the next decade. Late in 1672, for example, another 80 Presbyterian clergy received parishes. Yet this approach always had its limits, given that hostility to Episcopacy remained widespread in the south.

Conventicling also continued. It was not only troublingly radical in religion but also politically dangerous – its practitioners often being armed and having an essentially paramilitary character. It was probably this that eventually led Lauderdale to favour a return to repression. Accordingly the Privy Council issued decrees in 1674 against unlicensed gatherings. Even then Lauderdale tried to interest the bishops in balancing this harshness with further targeted concessions. Neither side, however, really wanted compromise. A tougher line thus became even more necessary.

This reached its epitome in 1678 when Lauderdale commissioned a force of 5,000 soldiers, mainly from the reliable Episcopalian and Catholic clans of the north and west. Known as the Highland Host, they were then quartered in the Covenanter-dominated south-west, to deter the conventiclers from armed activities. Unfortunately it soon proved counter-productive.

On 3 May 1679, riding from Edinburgh to his St Andrews home, James Sharp, long a symbolic hate figure, was assassinated by Covenanters on Magus Muir in Fife. The murder of Scotland's leading cleric was a sensational event. The perpetrators were soon tried and executed, but again they became martyrs to the cause. Charles's government now faced not merely civil disobedience but low-intensity civil war involving significant parts of the population.

Another measure of the scale of the problem was offered at Drumclog in Lanarkshire on 1 June, as 200 conventiclers defeated government forces under James Graham of Claverhouse. The victorious radicals were exhilarated at having struck a body blow against an ungodly government – against the Anti-Christ, as some irreconcilables saw Charles II's regime. But their triumph was brief. On 22 June Claverhouse, assisted by Charles's illegitimate son the Duke of Monmouth, smashed them at nearby Bothwell Brig in the Clyde valley. As after Rullion Green, the harsh punishments caused lasting Presbyterian resentment: a thousand Covenanters were imprisoned wretchedly in Edinburgh's Greyfriars' churchyard.

There followed what has become known, thanks to the meticulous documenting of it by Robert Wodrow, an 18th-century clergyman and historian with strong Covenanting sympathies, as the 'Killing Time' – a period of intensified state persecution of committed Presbyterians. Some resisted to the end, arguing not only for non-submission but also for the violent overthrow of a king whom they reckoned was doing the work of Satan. The most significant of the diehards were the armed followers of the field preacher Richard Cameron, from Falkland in Fife, known for his fiery temperament and extreme views. The Sanquhar Declaration, read out at that Dumfriesshire town by Cameron on 22 June 1680, which rejected allegiance to Charles II and his government, was little short of an open declaration of war. As things transpired, Cameron was killed in an encounter at Airds Moss in Ayrshire the next month. But the Cameronians, and his uncompromising ideals, lived on.

Ill-health as well as royal doubts about his effectiveness against the Covenanters had by now cost Lauderdale his position. His place was taken by the king's younger brother James, Duke of York. Residing in Edinburgh from October 1679 and serving as the figurehead for Scottish policy until March 1682, he has subsequently acquired much of the blame for the Killing Time. Also closely associated with the cruel misdeeds carried out in Charles II's name between 1681 and 1685 were Dalyell ('Bluidy Tam' to his many enemies, who whispered that he played cards with the Devil) and the charismatic but ruthless Claverhouse.

That military commanders in particular should have taken a leading role in disciplining civilians in matters of religious conviction might seem strange. But the Scottish Privy Council, horrified at the conventicling movement's revolutionary potential, had authorized the summary execution of anyone possessing unlicensed weaponry or refusing the oath of allegiance to the crown. Officials who despised the Presbyterians therefore had a free hand in rooting out disloyalty by terrifying whole communities into submission.

Some of the individual victims became widely known, not least because Wodrow's writings depicted several unforgettable martyrs. John Brown of Ayrshire died in May 1685 in front of his children and pregnant wife, allegedly shot by Claverhouse himself, for rejecting the oath. Even more heartrendingly, that same month Margaret Wilson, an 18-year-old Covenanter, and Margaret McLauchlan, her elderly companion, were tied to stakes on the beach at Wigton and left to drown in the incoming tide of the Solway Firth: there is even a marvellously affecting 19th-century painting of the scene by John Millais – though some historians insist that the women's awful sentence was never in fact carried out.

There is scope also for arguing over the numbers actually killed and over where responsibility for these excesses ultimately lay. But there is no doubt that the Killing Time traumatized many who lived through it. It poisoned the minds of subsequent generations against the late Stuart kings and helped further radicalize a substantial number of Presbyterians in their rejection of the crown's power in matters of Christian faith and religious observance.

A king much misunderstood?

On 6 February 1685 Charles II died and James, Duke of York, succeeded him as King of England, Scotland and Ireland.

James by this time had already spent the best part of three years in Edinburgh. Essentially he had been in exile from the acute political tensions in London over his likely succession, as an avowed Catholic, to Charles II who, though a prolific father of bastards, lacked a legitimate child. As a result, when he finally became King James VII and II, he actually knew Scotland better, and certainly had more extensive personal connections among its leading figures, than any monarch since James VI.

James VII's residence at Holyroodhouse had several implications for a rounded assessment of the man. One is that his genuine interests in learning and the arts led him to endorse or directly to contribute to a number of far-sighted new developments. It is to this period, for example, that we owe two key modern Edinburgh cultural organizations – the Advocates' Library (now the National Library of Scotland) and the Royal College of Physicians. James also oversaw the creation of the new offices of Historiographer-Royal in 1681 and Geographer-Royal in 1682, both royal appointments intended to reward and dignify Scottish exponents of these important disciplines. For similar reasons the Physic Garden (for the study of medicinal botany) was created in Edinburgh in 1670 by the all-round talent Sir Robert Sibbald. As well as being the first Geographer-Royal, the latter became the first professor of medicine at the university in 1685.

Remembering James's involvement in enlightened cultural developments is all the more crucial because so many people's opinion of him has been coloured by the accusation that he was the evil genius behind the Killing Time. Yet this view of James owes as much to hatred and suspicion of Catholicism as it does to what is known about his personal role in the early 1680s. Indeed, he may well have been a relatively pragmatic and moderating influence and certainly does not deserve his reputation as a sadistic anti-Protestant fanatic.

James had tried, for example, to encourage toleration of those unlicensed conventicles held in private houses: after all, unlike the large-scale armed gatherings out in the fields, they were obviously no threat to peace and order. He had also been willing to pardon any who could be persuaded to say the words 'God bless the king' – though given the intense zeal of the more extreme Covenanters, takers were few and far between.

But we cannot exonerate James from all charges. He was a man and a prince of his time. And his occasional flexibility on questions of loyalty, obedience and religious belief did not extend anything like as far as we might want in the 21st century. He made some serious mistakes, such as the Act pushed through the Scots Parliament at the start of his reign making attendance at conventicles or harbouring their participants a capital offence. Another error was his plan not merely to achieve toleration for Catholicism but actually to re-establish it in Scotland and England on at least an equal footing with Protestantism.

How difficult it would be to fulfil such contentious objectives was shown in the year of James's succession. For in June 1685 occurred the co-ordinated rebellions that in England were raised by the Duke of Monmouth, James's illegitimate Protestant half-brother, and in Scotland by the 9th Earl of Argyll, the latter the son of the executed Marquis and Covenanting leader. The new king's religious preferences provided more than enough opportunity for both men to claim that they were simply the righteous defenders of Protestantism.

The risings, as it happened, went badly. Monmouth and Argyll quickly shared the same experience of defeat, capture and execution. In Scotland in particular the outcome seemed to confirm that James enjoyed sufficient support, especially among the Highland clans, to see off comparatively easily an under-resourced challenge from a Protestant nobleman. Yet the episode should also have been a warning – a reminder that the king's devout Catholicism, his desire to give his faith official status, and his already toxic relationship with radical Presbyterianism, together left his sovereignty open to challenge.

Developments in Edinburgh soon bore this out. For James's commitment to promoting Catholicism even split his leading advisors right down the middle. James Drummond, 4th Earl of Perth, the chancellor, an Episcopalian and then a Catholic convert, was encouraging. But William Douglas, 1st Duke of Queensberry, a Protestant and lord treasurer (who later claimed that James had offered him £20,000 to convert), was horrified. Anti-Catholic rioting in the Scottish capital in 1686 further underlined the scale of the problem for a monarch seeking to reverse the single most important consequence of the Scottish Reformation in what had until recently been an explicitly Covenanted kingdom.

James VII and II also had problems persuading the Scottish and English parliaments to approve toleration both for Catholics and for those Protestants who had rejected the official churches. In the end he simply declared those measures lawful by royal proclamation. Accordingly in February 1686, Scottish Quakers and Catholics were allowed to worship at home. Twelve months later moderate Presbyterians were granted the same right. James also freed Scottish Catholics from the various legal restrictions imposed at the Reformation. But the political damage inflicted by appearing to confirm that this was indeed an aspiring absolute monarch bent on overriding parliamentary processes and imposing his own religious vision by extra-constitutional means outweighed any possible gains for James among the individual beneficiaries of these policies.

The not-so-glorious revolution

The backlash, when it came, actually had its focus in London rather than in Edinburgh. For it was James's English subjects who first concluded that their king had made himself dispensable and that they therefore needed to find an acceptable way of getting rid of him.

This was the genesis of what in England was and is known as the Glorious Revolution of 1688. It was 'glorious' not least because it was quick and cost few casualties – for the English, at least. In Scotland and Ireland, which were dragged along in England's wake, the process of replacing a bad king with a good one was neither smooth nor peaceful.

Not for the first time, the immediate trigger for crisis was the royal succession. Since 1685 it had seemed that James, without a male child, would be succeeded by Mary, one of his Protestant daughters by his first wife. But on 10 June 1688 James and his second wife, a Catholic, finally had a son, James Francis Edward, opening up the likelihood of a permanently Catholic monarchy. This prospect being intolerable to many in England, particularly in view of the royal policy of seeking to re-establish Catholicism as an official religion, a group comprising leading members of the Whig and Tory factions in Parliament decided that it had to be prevented.

An approach was made to William, Mary's husband and leader of the Dutch republic. Like his wife William was a grandchild of Charles I and third in line to the throne before the new royal baby had been born. He was also not merely a Protestant but the emerging leader of the grand European alliance of Protestant states against Louis XIV of France: as a proven ruler with the right religion and the right blood flowing through his veins, William's credentials as a replacement for his father-in-law were obviously strong.

In November 1688 William landed in Devon and over the next few weeks England gradually fell in behind him. Many towns declared their support. Leading allies of James deserted. A couple of very small military engagements were fought, both won by William's forces. And when told that William could not guarantee his safety (clearly the aim being to encourage him to flee rather than have to fight him and then worry about what to do with him), James conveniently left London in early December and headed for France, in effect abdicating and creating a vacancy instead of standing and fighting for his throne. A Convention – a parliamentary gathering not formally authorized by the reigning sovereign – then gathered at Westminster to hammer out a response. In February 1689 this body duly declared William and Mary joint monarchs of England.

In Scotland, where English events had been observed with understandably keen interest, the revolution took a completely different shape. The Scottish Privy Council hurried to declare for William as soon as James had fled. But a Convention also met in Edinburgh to decide what should be done following their king's abrupt departure from Britain. The Scots' options were narrowed by letters received in March 1689 from both James and William: the former threatened reprisals for disloyalty while the latter was tactful and hinted at concessions to the Convention in return for support.

On 4 April the Convention voted to end James VII's reign – in itself a dramatic moment in Scottish history since it involved accepting the principle, already implicit in Queen Mary's deposition in 1567 and long advocated in George Buchanan's radical political theories, that Scotland's parliamentary representatives could indeed terminate the reigns of the country's hereditary monarchs. This decision was justified by reference to the Articles of Grievances in which the Convention listed James's many faults and accused him of defaulting on his obligation to observe the kingdom's laws and constitutional customs. They also issued the Claim of Right, which set out the conditions on which a replacement monarch would be accepted. The crown was offered to William and Mary on those terms. They formally became co-sovereigns of Scotland on 11 May 1689.

Yet this could not be the end of the matter, since the Convention certainly did not speak for all shades of Scottish opinion. It had been dominated by Presbyterians only because Episcopalians refused to participate after mid-March 1689 in what they saw as an illegitimate process that was being manipulated by people determined to remove a lawful king and replace him with a usurper. Given their deep attachment to hereditary monarchy as much as to a church governed by the king's bishops, most Episcopalians put loyalty to the king, and their previous oaths to uphold his divine right to rule, ahead of their own religious reservations as Protestants about James's Catholicism. This decision, principled but naive, allowed the Presbyterians, James's bitterest opponents, to make the running in Edinburgh through the spring of 1689.

Having abandoned the constitutional machinery to the Presbyterians, the Episcopalians became the main contributors to a new opposition movement committed to reversing the revolution by force if necessary. Its Scottish members became known as the Jacobites – from *Jacobus*, the Latin for James. Claverhouse, now Earl of Dundee (and henceforth known in song and story as 'Bonnie Dundee'), took the lead in making Jacobitism a military as well as merely a political phenomenon, raising support among those Highland clans who had previously been bulwarks of James's power in Scotland. What resulted was a specifically Scottish civil war over how to respond to a British revolution that had initially been conceived and pushed through in the south-east of England.

Dundee's forces fought a successful engagement on 27 July at the strategic point of Killiecrankie, in the pass on the River Tay above Perth that carries the main road from the Highlands down into the Central Lowlands. Facing Hugh Mackay, the commander of Presbyterian forces loyal to William, the Jacobites won a stirring victory. But in a disastrous moment, Dundee himself was hit by a single musket shot and died on the battlefield.

Without his skill and talismanic status, James's supporters were fatally weakened. This was proven on 21 August when a second battle took place at nearby Dunkeld: this time the Jacobites failed to dislodge a much smaller occupying force of Williamites and Cameronians led by William Cleland – at 28 already a veteran of Drumclog and Bothwell Brig – who died in the fighting. The Jacobite clansmen thereafter fell back on their Highland heartlands where in a third battle at the Haughs of Cromdale, fought in Speyside the following spring, they were finally defeated and their forces dispersed.

In effect, therefore, the revolution had been resolved in Scotland, albeit by a rather different route, and with broadly the same outcome as in England. William and Mary were monarchs. James and his allies had been removed from power. The dependence of the crown upon parliamentary approval had been made clear. Catholicism had been defeated and Protestantism saved.

As the next 15 years proved, however, the situation was actually far more complicated, and the circumstances far more difficult for Scotland in particular, than this superficial description makes it sound.

When William met Mary

As we have seen, William II (or William III in his English style) was, in a sense, a very modern kind of king. This was especially so in Scotland, where he was crowned only after having been endorsed by Parliament. And even then William only ascended the throne because he accepted – or at least he finally did early in 1690 through gritted teeth after being threatened with non-payment of taxes – a series of explicit conditions intended to make him govern as a constitutional ruler.

Yet a number of difficulties peculiar to Scotland had also been inherited from before the revolution. These continued to cause William serious problems north of the border.

First, like his predecessors since 1603, he ruled from London, and there was no doubt where his priorities lay. Indeed, William became the first (though not the last) King of Scotland never even to see the country at all. This meant that his Scottish policies were often ill-informed. Royal decision-making remained peculiarly prone to misreading clear signals from Scotland, generating mutual suspicion between crown and people.

Second, the revolution had created as many problems as it had solved. Above all, the fact that the Presbyterians were the new regime's principal backers and that the Episcopalians remained attached to the exiled Catholic dynasty meant that William was presented with a contradiction. He already knew Presbyterianism well: most of the Dutch, like most Scots, had adopted it at the Reformation. But he disliked Presbyterian church government, understandably hankering after the firm royal control of religious matters that only Episcopacy could offer. William's reign was therefore marked by tensions between what the king really wanted and what was achievable given the nature of his own Scottish support.

This divergence was clearly seen from April 1689 onwards. For the Presbyterians predictably sought to extend the revolution in constitutional matters into the organization and culture of the Church. This they accomplished with the help of the Convention, and then the succeeding Parliament, which passed a series of laws that it must have seriously pained the new sovereigns to have to ratify.

Most important was the Act of Settlement of 1690. By this the entire paraphernalia of Episcopacy, including bishops, bishoprics and the doctrine of royal supremacy, was abolished. A Presbyterian system of church courts, wholly independent of the crown and the government, replaced it (and indeed survives to this day). The Scots Parliament in addition endorsed the Westminster Confession of Faith in 1690 as the legal basis of a thoroughly Calvinist theology for the post-revolutionary Church.

Parliament also abolished 'patronage'. This was the crucial right, previously enjoyed by landlords, town councils, universities and the crown itself, to appoint suitable candidates – usually safe, politically inoffensive clergy – as parish ministers. A radical Presbyterian alternative was imposed. Individual parishes would now make these vital decisions for themselves, thereby increasing the chances that enthusiastically Calvinist candidates would be successful. In the same spirit of enforcing strict adherence to Presbyterian principles, Parliament even set up 'visitations' to ensure that the university professoriate embraced the new order.

Not surprisingly, these measures triggered a substantial turnover in institutional manpower. Around 200 Episcopalian ministers either left their parishes voluntarily or, in strongly Covenanting districts, were aggressively 'rabbled' – hounded out – by local Presbyterians because they were 'non-jurors' who refused to take the Williamite oaths. Some professors suffered the same fate and were replaced with more compliant alternatives. It is easy to see how this purge drove new members directly into the arms of the Jacobite movement: the experience of persecution has always been a useful recruiter for oppositional movements.

The 1690s, even though the preceding revolution had been founded on the modern principle of government by consent, were therefore distinctly illiberal. Much of the unpleasantness was caused by

Presbyterians seeking revenge for the crimes previously committed against them, especially in the Killing Time. They also wanted to prevent any possibility of a counter-revolution. The problem, however, was that understandable caution easily breeds needless paranoia.

In such a situation even the slightest appearance of dissent can readily generate an extreme response. One notorious instance was the trial and hanging of Thomas Aikenhead in 1697, an Edinburgh student charged with making a joke about the Christian doctrine of the Trinity. The massacre of several dozen of the MacDonalds in Glencoe on 13 February 1692 by government-supporting Campbell soldiers acting under ambiguous orders from John Dalrymple, the lord advocate in Edinburgh, was another shocking example.

Insight: Murder under trust

Supposedly justified because the MacDonalds were slow to take the Williamite oaths, the killings in Glencoe attracted lasting outrage. Partly this was because the victims had unwittingly offered refuge and hospitality to their killers amid a winter blizzard. But it was also because government officials were clearly implicated in a heinous crime for which no one was ever punished. The setting – a gloomily magnificent glen with towering snow-capped mountains and deep defiles – added a backdrop fit for melodrama to a shocking human story.

Also adding to the gloom shrouding William's Scottish reign was what became known as the 'seven ill years'. This was a period of successive weather-induced harvest failures and consequent famines that swept across the country from 1692 onwards. Scotland's primitive agricultural and commercial systems were certainly key factors, though this was also a wider problem: a third of Finland's population died, for example. But faraway events in the Baltic were not what people focused upon. Nearby England and Holland had obviously avoided disaster while perhaps 15 per cent of Scots starved to death.

The famines therefore highlighted a broader problem. This was Scotland's chronic under-development, especially compared with England. The Act of Parliament in 1695 which established the Bank of Scotland (whose branches are still a familiar sight on the Scottish high street) was one part of the response – an attempt to create a financial institution that would kick-start economic growth through lending. The Education Act of 1696 also arose from similar progressive instincts, finally delivering the parish school system that earlier Presbyterians had already sketched out.

The Darien scheme was conceived as yet another contribution to the country's urgent modernization. An Act in 1695 founded the Company of Scotland Trading to Africa and the Indies, the intention being to establish the Scots in lucrative colonial trading of the sort that had manifestly boosted the English, French and Dutch economies. The focus was to be a commercial outpost at Darien in what is now Panama.

The whole venture, however, was badly planned and poorly executed. Darien, never properly surveyed, was in fact a malarial rainforest. The first shipload of settlers in 1698 was dead before the second arrived. The territory itself was also claimed by the Spanish. Madrid understandably complained to William, who required peaceable relations with them in his wars against Louis XIV. The man who was also King of Scotland therefore declined to support the Scots' scheme, while the English, who saw Darien as a cheeky attempt to rival their own commercial activities, refused to help.

The consequences were drastic. So poor was Scotland that around one-quarter of the cash in the kingdom had been pooled together and invested. Darien's failure thus dealt a devastating blow to the nation's limited wealth. It also severely damaged national confidence in the future viability of genuinely independent economic and foreign policies.

This was the situation in which Scotland entered the 18th century. The structural disadvantages of the existing regal union were now increasingly difficult to ignore. And, conscious of their economic backwardness as well as of their political weakness, many influential Scots were starting to conclude that fundamental change was imperative.

The far-reaching consequences of this realization form the subject of the next chapter.

THINGS TO REMEMBER

▶ Rule from London continued under Charles II, bringing the same old difficulties.

▶ Restoration politics were dominated by the crown's attempts to re-impose Episcopacy on a widely Covenanted and Presbyterian country.

▶ Government persecution created Presbyterian martyrs during the Killing Time and provoked further resistance from the Covenanters.

▶ James VII, widely blamed for the oppression, made grave political errors, but, in Edinburgh as Duke of York, had been a great patron of Scottish culture.

▶ James was ejected by the English elite first and only then by the Scots, some of whom were his strongest supporters.

▶ James's removal divided Scotland between his unsuccessful Jacobite defenders and those Presbyterian enemies who embraced revolutionary political ideas in deposing him.

▶ William and Mary, who succeeded James, maintained the absentee monarchy but had to accept Presbyterianism, the creed of their main Scottish supporters.

▶ William's reign saw disaster heaped on disaster as remote rule, economic failure and crushing episodes like the famines and Darien converged to create a growing sense of national crisis.

12

Union and Jacobitism

In this chapter you will learn:

- *about the Union of the Scottish and English parliaments and the creation of Great Britain*
- *about the Jacobite risings*
- *how power and prestige bound the Scottish elite into Britain and its growing empire*
- *how dissatisfaction with the constitution, and particularly the electoral system, flared up in radical demands for reform.*

The national crisis

The intertwined political and economic misfortunes of the late 17th century may have forced many Scots to look to the future with growing anxiety. The immediate cause of the changes that would soon transform Scotland's relations with England, and in their own way be a genuine attempt to resolve the Scots' numerous difficulties, was in fact much more short-term.

With neither William and Mary nor the latter's younger sister Anne able to produce an heir, the question quickly arose as to who should eventually succeed. Two factors lent this special urgency in English eyes. One was the existence of James Francis Edward Stuart, the Jacobite claimant who, on his father James VII's death in 1701, enjoyed significant support, particularly in Ireland and parts of Scotland. The second was the international situation: Louis XIV, at war with England, was providing a base and active encouragement for James – the Old Pretender, as he became known.

All of this made it imperative that the ultimate destination of the crown of England be settled clearly, neatly – and promptly. The Act of Settlement, passed at Westminster in 1701, duly decreed that Anne's successor as Queen of England would be Sophia of Hanover, a German Protestant princess and, crucially, a granddaughter of James VI and I.

Yet the Scots were not consulted. And politicians in Edinburgh were livid at having once more been ignored on a matter with vital consequences for their own country. In the context of the heightened anxiety about their increasingly peripheral status, the insensitive way in which this matter had been handled by the English confirmed all of the Scots' worst fears about Scotland's apparent irrelevance in key decision-making processes in London.

The Scottish response, slow but determined, was two pieces of legislation, the first of which was the Act Anent Peace and War ('anent' being a Scots legal term for 'concerning'). Passed in 1703, this stated that after Anne's death no future Scottish ruler would be able to declare war or otherwise run the Scots' foreign policy without the express approval of the Edinburgh Parliament. This would stop Scotland from automatically being forced to co-operate with future diplomatic and military strategies developed by and for English interests.

The second measure was the Act of Security. In this case Queen Anne actually refused royal assent in 1703 when the Scots Parliament first approved it but it became law the next year when the Scots declined to grant further taxes unless the crown relented. This act stated that Scotland reserved the right to select its own successor to Anne from among the eligible Protestant candidates but that this should not be Sophia unless specific concessions were made by the English – essentially guarantees of free trade and access to the English colonies.

England, not surprisingly, reacted badly to what it interpreted as Scottish blackmail, effectively holding English foreign policy and the British succession to ransom. Worse, the Scottish legislation hinted at the possibility of the northern kingdom hosting a rival dynasty with a claim to England's throne and of the Scots' assertively independent diplomacy undermining London's hard line against Louis XIV.

Westminster retaliated with the Alien Act of 5 February 1705, which was little more than an ultimatum. Cunningly it threatened the Scots with the reverse of what they had been demanding – the ending of free trade with England in key exports like cattle, sheep and coal – unless they either repealed the Act of Security or entered negotiations for a full political union. The latter, as English politicians well knew, by creating a single parliament, would secure both a unified foreign policy and a common royal succession in perpetuity.

Initially the Scots were appalled by this aggressive attitude. But they were also keenly aware that their under-developed economy was utterly dependent on trade with England. Without this, a country already unable to feed its population in the bad years would be even worse off. Accordingly, the Scots Parliament finally agreed to commence discussions with a view to forming a constitutional union between the two kingdoms.

An arranged marriage

The ensuing debate within Scotland, for which the Scots Parliament provided the natural focus, was energetic, acrimonious and deeply fascinating. It had two distinct phases. The first, late in 1705, focused on the selection of Scotland's negotiators – a critical matter affecting the potential for any kind of agreement with England. The second, at its peak between November 1706 and January 1707, revolved around the draft treaty which the Scottish negotiators had brought back. Both debates revealed how complex and contradictory were the arguments both for and against union.

Opponents were numerous and diverse. There were hardened Jacobite enemies of the Hanoverian succession like George Lockhart of Carnwath, the sole anti-unionist negotiator. There were old Williamites like Andrew Fletcher of Saltoun, whose eloquent hostility towards union is remembered and honoured by Scottish nationalists even today. All of the doubters were intensely patriotic Scots. Some were also loudly Anglophobic. Many were concerned that union with a much larger and more powerful country would lead inevitably to Scotland being ignored when key decisions were being made.

Certain vested interests also opposed union for their own reasons. Arguments were heard, backed up by petitions, that Scotland's manufacturers and royal burghs would be ruined by superior English competition. Lawyers complained that Scotland's distinctive legal system would be lost. Others objected that Presbyterianism would be jeopardized by the powerful position of the (essentially Episcopalian) Church of England.

Collectively these criticisms almost certainly enjoyed majority support in the country at large – though this mattered little since Scotland was not a democracy and it would be Parliament alone that would be making the decision.

Pro-unionists such as Sir William Seton of Pitmedden and the 2nd Duke of Queensberry also saw union from a variety of different perspectives. Some were primarily motivated by fear of the alternative: further poverty, further marginalization. Those of a sunnier disposition optimistically looked forward to peace and plenty with the Scots finally being granted a seat at the top table, as part of a Protestant, commercial superpower on the world stage. Again, self-interest was an important factor for some. In particular, disappointed Darien investors were tempted by an English offer of compensation built into the draft treaty.

Significant numbers of pro-unionists were also swayed by bribery: titles and money were undoubtedly offered so as to change minds (the 4th Duke of Hamilton, for instance, acquired an English dukedom, while sceptical noblemen owed cash by the crown suddenly received assurances about repayment). It is common – though not necessarily fair – also to see the English offer of free trade and funds to pump-prime the stagnant Scottish economy as just another form of bribery. After all, certain Scottish parliamentarians with business interests clearly anticipated reaping disproportionate benefit in due course.

Partly because of the gradual movement of key individuals from the anti- to the pro-camp, with bribery often but not always the cause, the parliamentary votes were ultimately won by the unionists. The Treaty of Union, implemented on 1 May 1707, therefore tells us much about what the dominant groups in each country most wanted.

Scotland received numerous concessions, mainly but not exclusively economic, which were necessary to get the treaty through the Edinburgh Parliament: free trade, access to the colonies, promises on taxes, Darien compensation, plus guarantees of continuing independence for the Scottish Church and legal system. For England, however, the union delivered on the Hanoverian succession and on the creation of a single British parliament: these were what really mattered to London, preventing future uncertainty over the crown and foreign policy.

Scotland had at the stroke of a pen finally ceased to be an independent self-governing nation. So too, at least in theory, had England. A new and larger state, Great Britain, had been invented, as well as a new Parliament at Westminster, with 45 Scottish MPs in the House of Commons and 16 Scottish noblemen in the Lords. But there had been surprisingly little prior discussion on many of the other implications not covered in the treaty's mere 25 articles. There is even a plausible argument that Scottish history ever since has been mainly about working out the details required to make the Union function in ways that the two countries might find acceptable.

In the short term, however, the political unity envisaged in 1707 faced one major obstacle that had particularly deep Scottish roots. For Jacobitism, rather than dying back because of the agreement on the Hanoverian succession, flourished with a vengeance in the years immediately afterwards. And it did so in a new and potent guise, as the main vehicle for Scottish anti-Unionism.

We obviously need to ask how this happened and why.

Flogging a dead horse?

Few subjects have attracted more attention or rooted themselves more firmly in Scotland's modern culture than 18th-century Jacobitism. Virtually no one has not heard of 'Bonnie Prince Charlie'. Ironically, however, it remains hard to know just how substantial and potentially viable this movement really was in the years after 1707.

One aspect that tends to obscure Jacobitism's real extent was its secrecy – wise for people facing execution, imprisonment or exile if discovered. Some also prudently held back, reluctant to show their true colours until victory, and hence immunity, seemed certain. Others, by contrast, enthusiastically embraced the cause, but for the wrong reasons: these individuals hankered after personal advancement, thirsted for revenge for a personal slight, or simply craved the excitement and glory that rebellion offered. Mixed motives and inconsistent behaviour were therefore pronounced features of the movement after 1707.

What we can say is that Jacobitism was definitely stronger in certain quarters. Highlanders, with their rigid social hierarchies, attachment to King James and longstanding suspicion of Lowland and English governments, were especially attracted. So were Tories throughout Britain. After all, they harboured ideological reservations about the

1689 revolution and were frequently treated badly by Anne and the first two Georges. Scots, too, were generally more likely to be taken with the Stuarts' loudly trumpeted Scottish associations.

Catholics, who shared the Pretenders' faith, were another useful constituency, though they were in fact disappointingly few in number in 18th-century Scotland: this explains why so many prominent Jacobites were actually from Ireland. Episcopalians, far more numerous in Scotland, likewise became supporters in many cases because they would not break their previous oaths to defend James and his heirs as divinely appointed rulers. Finally, the Old Pretender's promise to abolish the Union if he were restored should have been unconvincing given the Stuart dynasty's obsession before 1689 with unifying their kingdoms. But in Scotland this argument exerted, as it was meant to, a powerful pull on the heartstrings of many who had never been reconciled to what they saw as the great national betrayal of 1705–7.

Rising ... then falling

It was therefore no accident that March 1708, less than a year after the implementation of the Union, saw the first of several major attempts to raise a Scottish rebellion. Unfortunately for them, a parallel uprising in northern England, where much was expected of the significant Catholic minority, failed to get off the ground. And with the Royal Navy in close attendance, the government's intelligence networks having got wind of the plans, a French naval commander sensibly declined to put the Old Pretender ashore at Burntisland in Fife, where strong support had been anticipated among the county's disaffected Episcopalian gentry.

The 1715 rising ('the 'Fifteen' in the customary Jacobite shorthand) was no more successful – and for similar reasons. It was led by the 6th Earl of Mar, an opportunistic and widely distrusted former supporter of the Union who had fallen out with the recently arrived George I (who, with the prior death of his mother Sophia, became Britain's first Hanoverian monarch in 1714).

This whole venture aimed, again with active French assistance, to take advantage of widespread concern, particularly acute in Scotland, at the accession of a German prince. Mar's standard was raised at Braemar on Deeside on 6 September. Several leading north-eastern aristocrats like the 10th Earl Marischal and clans such as the Mackintoshes and the Camerons loyally converged. The plan was to take Edinburgh while other risings flourished simultaneously in the Borders and in England.

Much of Scotland, however, was militantly hostile. Many Lowland burghs and Presbyterian noblemen were appalled at the prospect of a civil war being unleashed by an ambitious Catholic usurper with the connivance of France's absolute monarch. As a result they roundly condemned the Pretender and his supporters. Worse, Mar himself (mocked as 'Bobbing John' for having switched sides) proved neither confident nor competent. He dallied for more than two months with his army of 10,000 before finally being confronted at Sheriffmuir on the road from Perth to Stirling by the 2nd Duke of Argyll's 4,000 soldiers on 13 November. The tactical outcome after a short firefight was unclear. But the strategic outcome was unmistakable. Argyll commanded the road south and Mar retreated to Perth to lick his wounds.

With the northern English rising also easily suppressed and foreign allies discouraged by Mar's uninspiring performance, James's landing at Peterhead as late as 22 December rather missed the point. The momentum necessary to win over further supporters had not been achieved: the rebellion was therefore still-born. In February 1716 a disappointed Pretender, who had clearly been looking forward to being crowned James VIII and III, boarded a ship back to France at Montrose, accompanied by Mar.

Government punishment for the sheer brazenness of the treachery by some Scottish landowners was in fact comparatively gentle. Viscount Kenmore, who had assisted in the botched English rising, was executed. Some rebels were deported to the American colonies. A few Scottish peerages, like the earldoms of Seaforth and (predictably) Mar, were legally annulled. Several landed estates owned by guilty families were forfeited to the crown.

Westminster also passed a Disarming Act imposing fines for the illegal possession of weaponry by Highlanders – except by the Independent Highland Companies now being raised under trusted landowners to police the region. One result with longer-term implications was the formation of what later became the Black Watch, the British army's first Highland regiment.

In the next two decades George Wade, appointed commander-in-chief in North Britain, spread his 240-mile network of roads across the Highlands, the basic features of which are often still visible alongside major routes like the A9 and A82. Military strongholds like Fort Augustus were strengthened and garrisoned to deter rebels and nip trouble in the bud. As things turned out, however, the most significant development had occurred overseas. The Treaty of Utrecht, Louis XIV's death and the long regency of the Duc d'Orleans reduced France's interest in fomenting discord within Britain. As a result the Old Pretender himself moved to Rome, where he became instead a pawn in the hands of the ambitious Spanish monarchy.

In the short term this new Continental connection produced yet another Jacobite plot with a strong Scottish flavour, the comically abortive invasion of 1719. This began, exotically enough, with the arrival of two frigates, filled with 300 Spanish soldiers and Jacobite exiles such as the Earl Marischal, at Loch Duich in the far north-west, originally intended as a useful diversion for a major assault on the southern English coastline. Owing to bad weather, however, the main invasion had itself been abandoned, leaving this intrepid little band in a remote Inverness-shire glen very much alone.

They were not, however, alone for long. A government force under General Joseph Wightman marched out from Inverness to engage them in Glenshiel on 10 June. Within hours the invasion was stopped in its tracks and many of the Spanish imprisoned – further evidence, for those willing to accept it, of Jacobitism's complete dependence upon fragile co-operation between generally half-hearted foreign allies and a tiny core of active native supporters who were prepared to risk their own lives against the odds.

Just as international diplomacy had marginalized Jacobitism, it was only changes in the wider European scene that eventually revived its prospects. The War of the Austrian Succession, which after 1740 set Britain once again against France, led the adult Louis XV to rediscover his country's traditional interest in the disruptive potential of the Pretender's claims. The emergence of the Old Pretender's Italian-born son and heir Charles Edward – the 'Young Pretender', 'Bonnie Prince Charlie' – was an added bonus. For it provided a credible and articulate leader who would play the central part in the most audacious Jacobite plot of them all: 'the 'Forty-five'.

The last best chance

Once again, the best-laid plans were dogged by painfully limited resources, unrealistic expectations and some rank bad luck. In particular a French fleet intended to assault the English coastline was scattered by a storm in the Channel in 1744 (it was a staple of Williamite and then of Hanoverian propaganda that God periodically provided a 'Protestant wind' to thwart Catholic invasions). This effectively nullified a key part of the multi-pronged attack. Yet, typically confident in the face of a setback that would have deterred a wiser strategist, Charlie pressed on with the Scottish part of the plan nonetheless, certain that victory was still achievable.

Charlie first set foot on Scottish soil on the island of Eriskay in the Outer Hebrides on 23 July 1745, accompanied by the famous 'Seven Men of Moidart' who had come with him from exile. But it was at Glenfinnan on the mainland on 19 August that the campaign really began. It was here, in the traditional Scottish summer rain and mist, that Charlie and his companions oversaw an armed gathering of supportive clansmen from the surrounding glens, led by the Clanranald MacDonalds.

Revealingly, however, many Jacobite sympathizers declined to attend. Some even sought explicitly to dissuade Charlie from raising a rebellion. The Catholic community on the island of Barra, for example, sent no one. Some prominent individuals with the power to rally others behind them, like MacLeod of MacLeod, suspecting that this was merely an invitation to commit suicide, simply refused to participate. One pivotal chieftain, Donald Cameron, known as 'Gentle Lochiel' and a respected veteran of previous risings, was only eventually persuaded to involve himself by Charlie's insistent smooth talking.

The assembled force actually made impressive progress. Passing swiftly south through the Highlands, at Perth they recruited Lord George Murray, an experienced soldier, brother of the government-supporting Duke of Atholl and the perfect military commander for Charlie's enthusiastic but diverse army. The threat they posed to the Anglo-Scottish state, then still very much focused on the continuing Continental war, dawned slowly on their complacent opponents. It was only when 2,400 men under Murray routed General Sir John Cope's force of largely inexperienced new recruits in little more than ten minutes on 21 September at Prestonpans near Edinburgh, where they had surprised the soldiers by appearing from the wrong direction, that the government finally sat up and took notice.

After partying long and hard through October in Edinburgh (the Highlanders living up to their reputation for knowing how to have a good time), Charlie and his army eventually took the high road to England, the inevitable next step if they were serious about placing James VIII and III on his rightful thrones. By now two separate government forces had been hastily assembled to stop their advance. But Murray cunningly avoided both, marching successfully through Lancashire and even collecting a few additional recruits from among Manchester's Catholics before arriving at Derby.

At this point London was just 127 miles away. Some wealthy residents began packing their belongings for a tactical retreat to the country, fearing the imminent arrival of lawless Highlanders. There was also a run on the Bank of England, unmistakable evidence of anxiety among the elite. It appears that informed opinion really did think that a stunning Jacobite victory, against all the odds, was a serious possibility.

What no one expected was that at Derby a fateful decision would be taken in the Jacobites' camp. Murray and several of Charlie's other advisors had long been wary of the prince's over-optimistic outlook. The failure to rally the supposed mass of English supporters to the cause only increased their scepticism. So too had the continuing absence of the substantial French assistance Charlie had repeatedly promised. Government intelligence had also convinced the Jacobites' leaders that another sizeable and well-equipped army actually lay between them and London, making a further advance perilous.

Ultimately these considerations prevailed. Charlie found himself outvoted by his entourage. On 5 December ('Black Friday') the Jacobites decided to fall back on Scotland for the rest of the winter, with a view to a renewed offensive in the spring.

The retreat was orderly. Despite skirmishes with government troops in Lancashire and Westmorland, the Jacobites maintained their discipline. At Falkirk on 17 January, they even defeated another government force under General Henry Hawley, using a classic Highland charge backed by lashing wind and rain. Next month they were safely back on the familiar terrain of the Highlands.

Unfortunately for them, the government's main army, under the command of George II's third son, the Duke of Cumberland, had avoided the same arduous winter march northwards. Four of Cumberland's 16 infantry battalions were actually Scottish, including the 1st Foot (Royal Scots) and Royal North British Fusiliers, recently withdrawn from the Continent to deal with this unexpected internal threat. Conveyed by ship to Aberdeen, rested, well-fed and properly equipped, they kept their powder dry and waited for the moment to strike.

Appropriately, it was yet another delusional misjudgment by Charlie, over-ruling Murray and his other advisors, which led the Jacobites to square up to Cumberland's army on the exposed and boggy high ground of Culloden Moor to the east of Inverness. Here, on 16 April 1746, after exchanges lasting barely an hour, perhaps 2,000 of Charlie's bravest and most loyal followers lay dead in the heather. Subjected on disadvantageous terrain to the overwhelming firepower available from disciplined professional musketry backed by emplaced artillery, the military substance of Jacobitism was simply obliterated.

The Butcher and some bills

The aftermath of Culloden was even more devastating. Cumberland, having won what he considered a civil war against rebels and traitors rather than a conventional campaign against honourable foreign enemies, actively discouraged leniency. Fleeing Jacobites soldiers were brutally cut down. Suspects, genuine or imagined, were rounded up. Even blameless non-participants who happened to live in the wrong areas had their houses burned down.

This is why the king's son is now generally reviled in Scotland as 'Butcher Cumberland'. But it is crucial to note that the Presbyterian, Lowland majority overwhelmingly saw things very differently at the time, because the shock of the rebellion was still fresh in their minds. A relieved University of St Andrews awarded Cumberland its chancellorship for having imposed order on impending chaos. The freedom of Glasgow was also bestowed by the grateful civic authorities.

Longer-term responses mainly took the form of bills passed into law at Westminster. Rebel titles and lands, like the earldom of

Cromartie and Cameron of Lochiel's estates, were forfeited. The Act of Proscription of 1746 banned the wearing of tartan, other than by government forces, and also forbade unauthorized weapons to Highlanders. The Heritable Jurisdictions Act, eventually approved in 1747, then swept away the wide-ranging judicial powers of Scottish landowners which had given them an unusually firm grip on their tenants and potentially a useful tool for raising rebel armies. This last measure attracted furious opposition in Scotland – the reform applied to all landlords, not just Jacobites, and arguably breached assurances in the Treaty of Union about preserving the Scots' legal peculiarities. But the large English majority in Parliament, which considered the traditional privileges of Scottish landowners oppressive and dangerous in a modern society, carried it anyway.

Jacobitism's long-term fate was everything that Parliament could have wished. Above all, the errors of the 1745–6 strategy, the bitter fruits of the defeat at Culloden and the final realization that sufficient levels of foreign and domestic support were simply never going to materialize, had at last destroyed its credibility. Nor did Charlie's unattractive response to his disappointment – a painful, self-pitying descent into alcoholism and abusive behaviour before his eventual death in Italy in 1788 – encourage even his most dogged former sympathizers to continue to put their lives, careers and properties on the line for him. The passage of time also undercut the Jacobite case: Scots who could even remember James VII and an Episcopalian Church were few in number by the late 1740s, and wanting to turn the clock back six decades began to seem not just unrealistic but also, frankly, worryingly eccentric.

Not all of the reasons for abandoning Jacobitism, however, were negative. After all, the benefits of Union were becoming ever clearer, especially to Scots who were wealthy and well-connected. By the 1750s commercial developments, many of them linked to involvement in English and colonial markets, were rapidly enriching Scottish property owners in ways of which their grandfathers could never have dreamed: jobs for sons in India or the Royal Navy, profitable exports to Virginia, marriage to an English heiress or a big townhouse in London or Edinburgh could all transform opinions about the merits of Britain and the House of Hanover. Reconciliation with George II and George III even allowed those with classic Jacobite backgrounds to rehabilitate themselves quickly and effectively: some forfeited privileges, like the earldom of Seaforth for the Mackenzie family, had already been recovered by as early as the 1770s.

Several old rebel dynasties went even further, raising government regiments, like the 78th or Fraser Highlanders – actually established in 1757 by Simon Fraser, the son of Lord Lovat, an incorrigible Jacobite who just ten years earlier had become the last man ever to be beheaded on Tower Hill in London for his part in the 'Forty-five. Such units quickly proved their worth, serving with high-profile distinction in British campaigns overseas. When at Quebec in 1759, as he won Canada for Britain, General James Wolfe, an English veteran of Culloden, engaged the French troops outside the city, he had under his command many former Scottish enemies, still dressed in tartan but now fighting courageously and victoriously beneath the Union flag. No more dramatic demonstration of Jacobitism's neutralization – or of the new loyalty of virtually all Scots to Britain, Unionism and the Hanoverians – could be imagined.

Adjusting to new realities

For many English observers in the first half-century after Union, it is understandable that when they looked at Scottish politics – which, to be honest, few could be bothered to do very closely – all that they tended to see was Jacobitism. It goes without saying that this was an inaccurate perception: at no time were most Scots supporters of the Pretender; and the large majority of those with power in Scotland were always solidly Presbyterian, Unionist and Hanoverian in persuasion.

Yet every single Jacobite rebellion had undeniably had its focus in Scotland. The Pretenders, too, positively flaunted their dynasty's Scottish origins. And there was no doubt that much of the military muscle on which they had relied was provided by tartan-clad clansmen and their chieftains. Accordingly the notion that the Scots as a people were resolute enemies of peace and civil order, and that more generally they favoured the kind of absolute and arbitrary government associated with the exiled Catholic line of the Stuart dynasty rather than the limited parliamentary monarchy and the rule of law confirmed by the revolution of 1688–9 and continued through the Hanoverian succession, lingered long in suspicious English minds.

This prejudice evidently still influenced British politics even after Jacobitism had clearly died. Notably it explains the consistent refusal of the government between the 1750s and the 1790s to allow the Scots, on the same basis as their English neighbours, to form an armed militia of concerned citizen volunteers to defend the coastline against French attack. This issue was like a sore tooth for two generations of post-Culloden Scots. It was an ever-present reminder that the English still did not fully trust them. Indeed, it demonstrated a residual fear in London that the collective noun for a group of Scottish civilians bearing guns was a 'rebellion'.

Related concerns about true Scottish motives also lay behind the unpleasant controversy of the early 1760s when John Stuart, 3rd Earl of Bute, was prime minister to the new king, George III. The real problem with Bute was that he was a Scot – the first after the Union to shin to the very top of London's greasy political pole. To English people opposed to what they believed were the king's plans to increase the power of his government over Parliament, his chief advisor's Scottishness was a gift. John Wilkes, the celebrated radical activist, had immense fun at the prime minister's expense, continually suggesting that Bute wished to undermine the traditional freedoms of Englishmen by helping George introduce an absolute monarchy. Wilkes's magazine *The North Briton* – whose very name reminded English readers where the main danger to English liberties lay – proved a potent weapon in the propaganda offensive against what many saw as the threat posed by Scots who could now dominate government affairs.

Bute, however, was only the highest-profile offender. Another important consequence of the Union was that large numbers of Scots soon acquired powerful and well-rewarded positions outside Scotland that would otherwise have been enjoyed by Englishmen. By the second half of the 18th century, the commissioned ranks that ran the British army had a markedly Caledonian complexion: one-quarter of all infantry officers were Scottish in 1794 and perhaps 40 per cent of the full colonels commanding British regiments. Scots also achieved disproportionate success in India – holding at least a half of all East India Company jobs in Bengal, the most lucrative posting, by the 1770s – as well as in the American and Caribbean colonial administrations.

Individual Scots even reached the upper echelons of England's leading domestic institutions – one became Archbishop of York, another lord chief justice, yet another lord chancellor – despite the fact that Scotland retained its own church and legal systems that were still effectively closed to English entrants. Scottish politicians were soon performing a similar trick in Parliament: an astonishing 120 Scots were MPs for non-Scottish seats just between 1790 and 1820. All in all, it was easy for English critics to conclude that the Union, rather than having permitted a powerful nation of around 5 million people to absorb a smaller and weaker country of just 1 million, had in fact allowed the elites of the poorer country to take over the richer one for themselves.

This, then, was the stereotype to which the Scot now seemingly conformed in British public life, at least as far as anxious English commentators were concerned. Ambitious, dictatorial and ruthless, he was also grasping, clannish, conspiratorial – and unnervingly successful. It is worth pointing out, however, that the reality of politics in post-Union Scotland itself was rather more mundane, not to say parochial. Indeed, a form of Scottish politics continued after 1707, and in many respects it did not really fall substantially into line with English patterns for more than 100 years.

Partly this was because distinctive aspects of Scotland's old politics actually survived 1707 intact. In particular, much of the voting system in force until 1832 was the one inherited from the old Scots Parliament. This was far more restrictive than the procedures used to elect MPs in England.

In 1788, for example, it was calculated that there were fewer than 3000 eligible voters across all of the Scottish counties (the equivalent figure in England, still not very generous but nonetheless vastly better, approached a quarter of a million). These county electors, who only qualified to vote because they held the rights in feudal law to a very substantial parcel of land, returned 30 MPs between them. In most Scottish burghs, meanwhile, which sent the remaining 15 Scottish MPs to Westminster, the electorates, exclusively comprising the members of each town's governing council, were normally barely into double figures. Naturally the survival of such distinctive and restrictive electoral practices regularly produced uniquely Scottish electoral controversies – generally settled in the Scottish courts under Scots law.

The oddities of Scotland's electoral law together with the tendency of these tiny electorates to succumb to direct personal manipulation by candidates and their backers allowed those with both the expertise and the motivation to do so to control Scottish politics in their own interests. Usually, because of the system's legal complexity, this meant Scottish lawyers or those who retained the services of Scotland's finest legal minds.

For the period from 1707 until the 1750s the winners in this obscure but rewarding game were the 2nd Duke of Argyll and his brother the Earl of Ilay (who eventually became 3rd Duke). Allies of Sir Robert Walpole and the Whig party in London, the Argylls worked closely with senior judges and with other major landowners across Scotland. This allowed them to control a large number of the country's contested parliamentary seats, as a result to influence a great many Scottish MPs and so to try to shape government policies as they affected Scotland.

Later in the century it was a lawyer working for himself, Henry Dundas, lord advocate and an associate of William Pitt the Younger, who effectively ran the country by pulling the same levers. The result was that he was half-jokingly known as 'King Harry the Ninth' or 'The Uncrowned King of Scotland'. In practice it was once again Dundas's fruitful relationships with local power-brokers that allowed him to control elections and gave him direct influence over two-thirds of Scottish MPs. Such power also made him a man of consequence in London and the holder of several major roles in the British cabinet.

There were also a succession of peculiarly Scottish political controversies – some completely ignored in England but most provoking mystification in London at the alien ways of the Scots. A few were focused on Parliament but others involved public disturbances and public campaigning. On every occasion the English were forcefully reminded that Scottish politics had indeed survived the Union.

In 1713, for example, there was a failed attempt by Scottish peers in the House of Lords to have the Treaty of Union annulled. This was in part because of anger at two recent pieces of Westminster legislation on Scotland that critics claimed breached the assurances given to protect the character of Presbyterianism in 1707: the Patronage Act of 1711 had taken the right to appoint parish ministers away from local congregations and returned it to landowners; and the Toleration Act of 1712 had given Episcopalians the right to worship in Scotland with impunity providing that they adhered to Church of England usages.

Similar grievances over alleged breaches of the treaty were involved in 1725 when there were riots in Glasgow over a malt tax – a levy on the key ingredient for the whisky distilling – for which the local MP had unwisely voted. In 1736 it was Edinburgh's turn, as disorder erupted over the execution of smugglers whose disregard for the hated customs taxes imposed from Westminster had won them widespread sympathy.

Perceived threats to distinctive Scottish institutions and dislike of heavy-handed government interference continued to provoke strong reactions more than a century after the Union. This always seemed to take London by surprise. In the early 19th century, for example, the reform of the Scottish civil courts, involving the adoption of English-style jury trials, proved unexpectedly contentious before finally being embraced. In 1826, meanwhile, Sir Walter Scott fronted a successful campaign against plans to stop Scottish banks issuing uniquely Scottish bank notes (a practice that, despite regular criticism in England, no British government has yet dared end).

Not surprisingly, however, the most problematic political issue – reform of the restrictive and unresponsive political system itself – also played an important part in Scottish politics in the 18th and early 19th centuries.

Radicalism and protest

The principal cause of rising discontent was a sense that an irresistible force was increasingly coming into contact with an apparently immovable object. The latter was Scotland's electoral system – as we have seen, far narrower and more comprehensively corrupt even than England's and denying all but a few thousand Scots the right to participate directly in the political process. What made this intolerable were the growing political aspirations of key excluded groups, especially among the middle-class professionals and business owners who were increasing in number as well as ambition at the time. The problem became impossible to ignore by the 1780s, when in Scotland as in England there emerged serious efforts, led by responsible and influential people, to modify aspects of the voting system.

In 1782, for instance, smaller landowners in Caithness, Moray and Inverness-shire, who were themselves eligible to vote, organized unsuccessful campaigns aimed at ending some of the most blatant electoral manipulation by Scotland's great aristocrats. A committee also emerged the next year, mainly run by opponents of the government, to demand the extension of votes in the Scottish burghs – the preserve of town councillors – to all who were registered to trade freely in the town: this time Dundas and his friends at Westminster defeated the scheme.

It was the advent of the French Revolution in 1789, however, which gave a new language as well as renewed inspiration to these sorts of reforms. This was particularly so in Scotland, not least because progressive ideas had been a notable feature of university teaching under liberal professors like John Millar at Glasgow and Dugald Stewart at Edinburgh: indeed, it was one free-thinking Scottish academic, William Ogilvie of King's College, Aberdeen, who was an early advocate of that classic revolutionary principle, the common ownership of property (though his views only became widely known much later). Scotland therefore proved especially receptive to the sparks given off by dramatic French events, the flames further fanned by the English radical Tom Paine's *The Rights of Man* (1791) which circulated widely among all social classes.

Organizationally the main vehicle for pursuing domestic constitutional reform was the Scottish Association of the Friends of the People, founded in July 1792 at the Fortune Tavern in Edinburgh. Shopkeepers, craft workers and other skilled workers, all excluded from the political process, were able to join, alongside the middle-class leaders. They found it the ideal focus for their demands for an end to corrupt electoral practices and a widening of the voting qualification. Demonstrations also occurred in towns such as Perth and Dundee, and on the king's birthday in June 1792 there was a riot in Edinburgh, though the Friends' leadership carefully distanced themselves from actual disturbances. Nonetheless, these developments, with the French Revolution descending from pious liberal idealism into a murderous Reign of Terror, steadily detached respectable and wealthier opinion from a movement whose purpose was to destabilize the British constitution in dangerous times. What was left was an increasingly isolated group of radical activists such as the celebrated Thomas Muir.

Muir, a lawyer and Glasgow graduate who had been influenced by Millar's lectures, became a hero for the cause. Tried for seditious libel in 1793 – the offence of fomenting political subversion – he was convicted in an elaborate show trial in front of an openly biased judge and sentenced to transportation to Australia. Less high-profile campaigners, such as the radical English preacher and Dundee activist Thomas Fyshe Palmer, shared the same fate.

So worried was the government that French violence might migrate to Britain because of the often-secretive activities of the radicals that the ban on detention without trial was suspended and unlawful gatherings were prohibited. These measures formed part of what became known to liberals as the 'Dundas Despotism'.

Insight: Treachery in the capital

The discovery of the so-called 'Pike Plot' in 1794, a wildly implausible scheme to capture Edinburgh Castle and trigger a revolution in Scotland, seemed to justify the government's anxieties following the French Revolution. Robert Watt, a former government spy turned radical agitator who was the heart of the scheme, was eventually convicted of treason and executed. But he was the only Scottish fatality of the crackdown overseen by Henry Dundas, the lord advocate, and the threat of revolution seems to have been greatly over-stated.

Small numbers of committed radicals remained active, but they tended to be weak and largely unconnected with the middle-class reformists who had made the cause respectable back in the 1780s. The best known in the 1790s, the United Scotsmen, argued for votes for all men – then an extreme and uncommon demand – as well as annual parliaments. They too were strong in the towns and among the workers. But their lack of clout and evident interest in bringing about what they thought would be a sympathetic invasion by revolutionary France, with which Britain was at war, as well as a failed insurrection that some of them attempted near Perth in 1797, kept them marginalized and without significant influence: George Mealmaker, a Dundee weaver and their leader, was convicted of sedition and despatched to Australia that same year.

One final, vital point is worth making about this era. Because Scotland over the next two centuries, as we shall see, built for itself a powerfully radical, even revolutionary self-image, figures like Muir and Mealmaker and organizations like the United Scotsmen, who made demands that today seem unexceptional, have retrospectively attracted a great deal of historical attention. Indeed, they have frequently been depicted as typifying political opinion at the time.

But this is almost certainly wrong. The evidence suggests instead that very many of their contemporaries were politically conservative, loyal and patriotic. Statistically the Scots were twice as likely as the English to flock to join the Volunteer regiments that defended the coastline in the 1790s. And there is no reason to assume that Scottish conservatism, just because it did not express itself in rioting and plots, was any less sincere than Scottish radicalism, or that it should be taken any less seriously by historians.

For the next 20 years Britain's wars with revolutionary and Napoleonic France dominated the political scene. Any demand for significant change therefore risked seeming unpatriotic, even traitorous. But in the years of peace after 1815, in which unemployment and economic contraction added to the discontent, momentum built once more for constitutional reform.

This was the immediate context to what became known as the Radical War of 1820, in which a group of working-class Glasgow strikers marched on the Carron ironworks to seize weapons. They were stopped and dispersed by cavalry at Bonnymuir near Falkirk: again, 'war' is a retrospective over-dramatization (as is describing Bonnymuir as a 'battle', when no-one was actually killed at the site). Eighteen ringleaders were soon unwillingly in Australia, however, and three men, Andrew Hardie, James Wilson and John Baird, were subsequently tried and executed for treason. These men understandably became genuine martyrs in the eyes of later generations of Scottish radicals.

It is now clear that government agents actively encouraged the insurrection of 1820 to flush out suspected radicals. The outcome certainly helped deter campaigners for a few years. But it could not and did not end the broader desire for some kind of political reform, which, as we shall shortly see, eventually arrived throughout Britain in the early 1830s.

THINGS TO REMEMBER

▶ Scotland by the 1690s had entered a complex, multi-layered crisis – with harvest failures, famines, colonial misadventures and growing political marginalization.

▶ Once England, worried about how Scotland might use control over its own royal succession and its own foreign policy, decided to pursue political union, many leading Scots found the offer of greater wealth and power hard to resist.

▶ Jacobitism remained a credible threat until after 1746, but it was weakened by poor leadership, half-hearted support, dependence on unreliable foreign allies and, eventually, its own repeated failures against a powerful government.

▶ Scottish politics continued along a distinctive path after the Union, and Scottish interests were often successfully defended by Scotland's leaders.

▶ Wealth, employment, power and prestige all bound the Scottish elite effectively into Britain and its growing empire.

▶ Dissatisfaction with the constitution, and particularly the electoral system, flared up in radical demands for reform in the 1790s and after 1820 but, tainted by association with France's bloody Revolution, progress was slow.

13

....

Industry and Enlightenment

In this chapter you will learn:
- *about Scotland's economic development in the first age of industrialization*
- *about the 18th-century Enlightenment in Scotland and some of its greatest figures.*

The shock of the new

If Scottish politics remained surprisingly little altered between the Union and the late 1820s, there were two critical ways in which Scotland became unquestionably different. One was its rapidly transformed social and economic condition: as Sir Walter Scott claimed in 1814, 'the present people of Scotland [are] a class of beings as different from their grandfathers, as the existing English are from those of Queen Elizabeth's time'. Alongside this, a country previously notorious for bigotry and backwardness was now known for its learning and sophistication. Even the philosopher David Hume, with his insider's knowledge, was taken aback, as he confided in 1771:

> *Really it is admirable how many Men of Genius this Country produces at present. Is it not strange that, at a time when we have lost our Princes, our Parliaments, our independent government, even the Presence of our chief Nobility, are unhappy, in our Accent & Pronunciation, speak a very corrupt Dialect of the Tongue which we make use of; is it not strange, I say, that in these Circumstances we shou'd really be the People most distinguish'd for Literature in Europe?*

Such dramatic changes in Scotland's society, economy and culture pose a very simple question: how on earth had this happened?

The fruitful soil

Any attempt to explain Scotland's transformation after the Union must begin with agriculture – the unglamorous but essential activity that fed, clothed and occupied the vast majority of contemporary Scots. Yet in no area of economic activity did the dead hand of the past lie more heavily on the shoulders of the present.

To start with, difficult geological and climatic histories needed to be overcome. Scotland possesses much uncultivable upland, as well as many lower-lying landscapes where high acidity, often running to bog, makes cultivation particularly challenging. Allied to the harsher weather of the 'Little Ice Age', at its worst as the 18th century opened, Scots who dreamed of extracting regular and bountiful returns from their native soil clearly faced considerable physical obstacles.

Human legacies further hampered progress. A low population density, limited urbanization and agricultural backwardness created a vicious circle. Unreliable harvests and meagre food surpluses kept population growth minimal and made non-agricultural activity precarious.

Feudal social structures and relationships similarly restricted progress. The famous 'runrig' system, where tenants cultivated fields in common, and widespread use of co-operative farming practices, guaranteed that change proceeded only through communal agreement and even then only at the pace of the slowest.

It is now clear that this regime was breaking down from 1650 onwards as landowners became interested in improving productivity. But progress was insufficient to forestall the famines of the 1690s. Only the stimulation provided by increased exposure to English know-how and to the far greater demand from English consumers eventually produced the complete transformation noticed by many observers, Scottish and foreign, in the decades after 1750. Undeniably this was comprehensive, permanent – and, for those with no choice, often as distressing as it was disorienting.

Every aspect of Scottish farming had changed by 1800. The very nature of the land itself was physically altered by manure, liming and large-scale drainage and reclamation. Enclosure – adding fences or tree screens for protection from the ever-present winds and to create clear units of land for production – even made the landscape appear different: the modern 'patchwork quilt' effect familiar to modern observers in the Lowlands became the norm. New crops were also introduced. Peas, beans, turnips and potatoes, for example, varied the previously proverbial reliance of poorer Scots on oats.

In upland areas, where arable farming was less viable, forestry caught the new commercial mood: the 4th Duke of Atholl, who died in 1830, planted 27 million new trees on his Perthshire estates. Elsewhere, complex rotation systems were applied to replenish the soil and maximize yields. Better ploughs, improved steadings (farm outbuildings) and enhanced domestic accommodation for farmers and resident workers also added to the sense of a tangible transformation underway.

Arguably most crucial of all, tenancies and relations between landlords and workers were placed on a new footing. Farmers increasingly tended to be single tenants, recruited for their skills. Encouraged to innovate, they paid commercially determined rents. Waged workers supplied any additional hands, carrying out prescribed tasks as and when required.

Traditional labour-intensive communal farming therefore swiftly disappeared. And by delivering generous surpluses like clockwork, there is no doubt that this new regime finally freed the population as a whole from the age-old threat of starvation. But it also made it easier for people no longer to be directly involved in food production. This in turn made more likely a population shift from countryside to town, and so from agricultural work to the non-agricultural sector. Indeed, mass migration was positively encouraged by many landowners, as customary tenants lost their rights, their homes and their roles.

Towns and cities boomed. Glasgow grew from just 32,000 people in 1755 to be the country's largest city with 147,000 people by 1821. Conversely, in some rural areas, like Peeblesshire, the population actually fell. Some historians plausibly argue that we might think of this great migration as the 'Lowland Clearances', as irresistible market forces pushed people from rural central and southern Scotland into the crowded towns of the Central Belt as well as to England and the North American colonies.

History has certainly not been slow to recognize the 'Highland Clearances'. Yet this was really only the same experience of large-scale migration propelled by agricultural reforms – a process given a special emotional resonance only because the collateral damage here included the distinctive culture and society of Gaelic Scotland.

Undoubtedly the degree of change required to create a fully-functioning commercial system in these areas was greater. Here customary rights and a non-cash economy had been normal. The chieftain had been less a proprietor exploiting his assets than the wise and benevolent protector of his humble kinsmen. As a consequence, the introduction of written leases and money rents radically disrupted social relations. Chiefs unsurprisingly were the big winners. The 'tacksmen', community leaders who in the old regime were middle-men between the lord and his people, lost out and quickly disappeared.

The restructuring of the Highland economy unquestionably delivered impressive revenue growth: the average owner saw a 300 per cent increase in estate income between 1750 and 1800. Sheep farming, introduced in the inland glens so as to supply the expanding Scottish woollen textile industry, proved particularly lucrative. But it also entailed whole communities being moved – 'cleared' – either to the coasts or onto emigrant ships bound for North America.

This was usually non-violent. It was also frequently sweetened by the realistic promise of a better life, away from the hand-to-mouth existence and periodic famines that had always characterized the Highlands' traditional economy. For many, however, it was an upsetting, and sometimes a brutalizing, experience. After all, people were required to leave their family homes and often their homeland for good. In certain cases, moreover, such as on the Countess of Sutherland's estates after 1806, tenants were definitely evicted forcibly in a notorious sequence of events that remain bitterly contested in Scotland more than two centuries later.

Tenants re-settled on the coast took to a new lifestyle called 'crofting', designed by proprietors to make Highland society both more sustainable and more profitable.

Insight: A cottage and a 'tattie patch'

Crofting, a product of agricultural change in the Highlands, revolved around several unrelated activities. These included working on the landlords' sheep farms and hunting estates, collecting seaweed ('kelp') from the shoreline which, when burnt, turned into a crucial industrial raw material, and engaging in small-scale coastal fishing. Crofters also grew some staple crops for themselves – particularly the apparent wonder-food of the age, the potato.

This way of life, however, as a supposed solution to the Highlands' age-old problems, turned out to have two major flaws, as we shall later see. It unwittingly exposed communities to some entirely new threats to their very existence. And it helped make relations between many tenants and their landlords even more toxic as the 19th century unfolded.

Filthy lucre

The first priority of those wanting to improve commerce and trade in post-Union Scotland was simply to overcome two critical deficiencies inhibiting business and investment: lack of cash, making buying and selling harder; and lack of credit, hampering the borrowing required for innovation or expansion. This is why the development of Scottish banking was so utterly essential to everything else that happened to the country's economy.

Building on the Bank of Scotland's foundation in William's reign, the Royal Bank of Scotland was chartered in 1727 under Lord Ilay's oversight. A series of major local institutions also soon appeared, including the Ayr Bank (which imploded spectacularly in the financial crisis of 1772) and the Dundee Banking Company. As well as growing rapidly, the banking sector experimented with new products, now familiar to us, such as arranged overdrafts (the first was granted by the Royal Bank in 1728) and their own paper banknotes (the Bank was the first private bank in Europe to issue them). Later, the world's first savings bank was opened at Dumfries in 1810 by the local Presbyterian minister, paying interest on ordinary people's deposits. And insurance – of both lives and property – also emerged as a key Scottish specialization. A country whose economy had been drained of liquidity because of Darien was, strangely enough, an international leader in financial services less than 100 years later.

Deliberate improvements to the country's physical infrastructure proved to be another key driver for trade.

Authorized local markets in particular increased dramatically, further encouraging the production of surpluses for sale: astonishingly for a country unable to feed itself in the 1690s, Scotland by 1760 was even exporting excess grain to Norway. The transport system was also augmented to ease the movement of goods. New roads were built and others improved beyond recognition. John Smeaton's elegant bridge across the Tay at Perth, opened in 1771 and jointly funded by private donations and by government, became a symbol of the contemporary commitment to facilitating commerce, as did the Forth and Clyde Canal which opened in 1790 and which Smeaton designed to carry waterborne freight right across the Central Lowlands.

The Scots' intensifying interest in transportation also helps explain why some of them were also responsible for landmark contributions to England's industrialization: Thomas Telford from Dumfriesshire became the greatest canal and bridge designer of the late 18th century, while John Loudon Macadam from Ayr will always be associated with his method for creating durable road surfaces from graded small stones – a technology that, when a modified pitch was later added, became known, in honour of its Scottish originator, as 'tarmac'.

The greater availability of manufactured goods because of industrialization proved another crucial stimulus to trade, especially in the retail sector. Imported goods either for domestic consumption or for further export, such as spices, silks, tea, coffee, sugar and tobacco, were equally helpful. The trade in these products, and above all in tobacco, which alone accounted for more than half of the country's total exports by 1760, were classic examples of the kind of activity that the Darien scheme had originally envisaged – controlling the movement of highly desirable commodities between the continents at a handsome premium.

These lucrative import-export businesses especially enriched Glasgow's merchants. With their fine houses and newly bought country estates outside the city, some became known colloquially as 'tobacco lords'. The same profitability, however, also reinforced a mutually-dependent relationship between the west coast and the slave plantations of America's eastern seaboard. This fact in turn raised profound moral criticisms in some parts of Scottish society as the 18th century progressed.

Dark satanic mills

The most significant long-term result of the commercial ties between Glasgow and America was to be the growth of cotton manufacturing, the activity on which early Scottish industrialization mainly rested. Indeed, the production of cotton goods in Scotland was only possible because the vital raw material, from a sub-tropical plant farmed in the American South, arrived by ship in the expanding ports of the Firth of Clyde – and Glasgow and Greenock especially.

Cotton industrialization had significant precursors. By 1750 Scotland was already familiar with what some historians call 'proto-industrialization' – especially textile production using spinning wheels and looms in workers' own homes, making linen wares out of locally-grown flax. In fact, linen was an important source of part-time employment across the Lowlands by this time. It was also crucial to expanding Scottish trade and increasing exports in the first generation after the Union.

Cotton, however, was different. It was properly industrialized from the time the first mill opened at Penicuik outside Edinburgh in 1778. By the late 1780s large-scale manufacturing was converging on single-site factories where the workforce operated new thread-producing machinery such as the famous 'Spinning Jenny' and 'Crompton's Mule', recent English inventions. Initially these facilities were water-powered, hence their early location on rivers – such as at New Lanark on the Clyde and at Stanley on the Tay – which also provided convenient sites for related processes like dyeing and bleaching.

Once the first steam-powered mill was up and running in 1798, however, sites away from riversides quickly became viable. And by the 1830s mechanization of cotton production was even spreading at great speed to the more complicated weaving process – further lowering costs and increasing output, of course, as it finally threw the skilled handloom weavers out of work.

Insight: What's Watt?

Scottish industrialization produced several engineering heroes, none greater than James Watt from Greenock who started out as Glasgow University's instrument-maker. The man whose name is used today for the standard unit of power, Watt is often wrongly credited with inventing the steam engine. His actual achievement, begun in Glasgow in 1765 and completed ten years later when working with the entrepreneur Matthew Boulton in Birmingham, was to add a separate steam condenser to existing versions, greatly increasing their efficiency and making their widespread industrial application economically irresistible.

Distinctive forms of cotton manufacturing also arose in some areas, as production, in another feature typical of full-scale industrialization, rapidly specialized and diversified: Paisley, near Glasgow, for example, lent its name to a complex new textile pattern that would unexpectedly return to fashion as late as the 1960s.

Taken together, these developments in power engineering and production were what increased output and profitability exponentially in such a short space of time: from 1780 to 1800, for example, the amount of raw cotton processed by Scotland's mills grew 14-fold. But these same factors, with 250,000 people employed in the textile industries by 1800, were also fundamentally altering workers' daily experiences and their relationships with their employers and each other. Labouring for long hours at repetitive tasks, they operated under close supervision in a dedicated workplace for cash wages – and under threat of redundancy in business downturns or as further technological or organizational changes arose.

Comparable transformations were also underway in other industries. Woollens, for example, were important in certain districts, especially in Borders towns like Hawick and Galashiels. Here manufacturers turned abundant Scottish fleeces into attractive mass-produced goods: 'tweed', a twilled woollen cloth named in the 1830s after the area's main river, soon became a characteristically Scottish garment material that was highly regarded internationally. This was only possible because of the scale of production that industrialization had made possible.

Coal mining, as it happens, was less quickly revolutionized. It even took parliamentary legislation in 1775 and 1799 to end a system of indentured labour (found also in the salt-panning industry) which had made Scottish colliers an unusually powerful group but had also severely reduced freedom of movement for what was in effect a hereditary workforce.

A society in motion

The story of Scotland's population in this age of unprecedented socio-economic change is easily told – not least because this is the first period for which accurate contemporary statistics were collected. These tell us that the population grew from around 1 million in 1707 and 1.2 million in 1755 to 1.6 million in 1801 and 2.4 million in 1831.

This would be noteworthy enough in a country which had never before had so many inhabitants and which had recently seen vicious famines kill tens of thousands. But some of the details buried within these data are also striking enough to bear closer examination.

For example, the main underlying trend was clearly not rising birth rates – these remained relatively static – but falling death rates: 30 people per 1,000 were dying each year in the 1750s but only 24 by the 1790s and 21 by the mid-19th century. Similarly, we can see that life expectancy at birth in Scotland was little more than 30 years in 1755 – which it may well have been for all of previous history – but it then suddenly started on an upwards trajectory, passing 40 years by the 1840s.

Such figures cast serious doubt on the belief, common among hostile observers at the time and lazily repeated ever since, that industrialization and urbanization brought only hardship and misery to ordinary Scottish men and women. They also provoke a series of further questions, not the least of which is why death rates actually began to reduce. Again, the contemporary statistics are suggestive, revealing that the decline was overwhelmingly in infant rather than in adult mortality: put simply, children were becoming less likely to die at birth or shortly thereafter. This is a vital clue because it points to some of the more specific factors that surely lay behind the population's sudden growth.

One was the gradual spread from the 1730s onwards of inoculation against smallpox, previously the greatest child-killer of them all. Not everyone liked it or used it. Some Presbyterians even considered it sinful to thwart God's mysterious intentions. But where it was adopted it undoubtedly reduced infant mortality in particular.

Another advantage was the more varied and nutritious diet facilitated by agricultural improvement. Most Scots were now eating more and better food, again particularly benefitting the youngest and most vulnerable. Also important in all likelihood were improved living conditions in rural (though not, crucially, in urban) communities: cleaner and better-built homes again harboured fewer threats to the very young. We might further add that incomes generally rose faster than prices across this period, despite some short-term reversals. This too must have made life easier for the majority of adults and so for their children.

There were nonetheless considerable drawbacks to socio-economic change that we should not overlook. For urbanization also generated conditions where diseases like typhus and cholera could flourish. Increased localized mortality was the depressingly inevitable result: between just February and May 1832 cholera killed 660 people in Glasgow alone, caused primarily by unclean water in slum housing areas.

Moreover, society, as wealth grew, increasingly felt more divided. Animosity between 'clearers' and 'cleared' in the Highlands was scarcely surprising. But tensions also worsened elsewhere as the gap between the richest and the poorest widened and some groups suffered irreversible losses.

A final dimension to changing social experiences in this period must be mentioned. This was the combined effects of immigration and emigration on Scots at home and overseas.

In the first place, large numbers of Irish immigrants now started to arrive. A figure of 300,000 people between 1790 and 1850 is widely accepted, nearly all settling in the Lowland towns and cities. They were to prove a useful source of cheap unskilled labour for 19th-century industries. But they also established a large Catholic community in a strongly Presbyterian country for the first time since the Reformation. As we shall see, this created significant social and religious tensions in succeeding generations.

At the same time, vast numbers of Scots were also leaving (which means, of course, that the contemporary growth in Scotland's population would have been even more dramatic but for these substantial losses). Perhaps 75,000 people crossed the Atlantic for good between 1707 and 1780 – 80 per cent of them probably from the Lowlands. Between 1821 and 1915, as the pace of emigration quickened still further, as many as 2 million more departed for North America, Australia and New Zealand.

Highland emigrants generally remained more recognizable once overseas, often leaving as entire communities. This was the case at Cape Breton in Nova Scotia, where Gaelic-speakers from Barra and South Uist put down lasting roots in 1775. It also happened at Cape Fear in North Carolina, where Argyllshire folk settled in the 1730s but then in the late 1770s found themselves fighting as Loyalists against the revolutionaries. This, together with the emotive connection with the Clearances in some cases, probably explains why Highlanders have tended to dominate most modern perceptions of historical Scottish emigration.

Yet the majority of Scots emigrants actually left as individuals or in single families from the Lowlands. The poor often worked as indentured labourers to pay off the cost of their passage. The better-off, meanwhile, were able to hit the ground running. Most merged deftly into the melting-pot of colonial society, their Scottish origins soon signified only by their descendants' distinctive surnames. But some nevertheless acquired undue prominence in their new homelands.

Nine of the first 13 state governors in the United States, for example, and every single member of the first federal cabinet, had at least some ancestral ties to Scotland. And some first-generation Scottish emigrants even played leading parts in the American revolution: John Witherspoon, a Paisley clergyman who became president of the College of New Jersey, and James Wilson, a Fife lawyer who settled in Philadelphia, both signed the Declaration of Independence in 1776 placing themselves among the founding fathers of a new nation.

Politeness and the life of the mind

Significant cultural change was probably an inevitable side-effect of the extraordinary upheavals that were transforming the Scottish economy and Scottish society in the decades after 1707.

The landed elite were particularly affected. Assisted by their enhanced wealth and growing self-confidence, they increasingly knew England intimately, mingled with their English counterparts, and generally absorbed all kinds of subtle and not-so-subtle southern influences: the 2nd Duke of Argyll, for example, the dominant chieftain in the West Highlands in the 1740s, was born and died in Surrey, had a mother from Suffolk gentry stock and both times married an English wife.

Convergence, though less dramatically, was also happening more widely. Travel, trade and employment, after all, brought many ordinary Scots into regular contact with English people on both sides of the Border. London-centred publishing in a standardized modern English further cultivated a common identity and a British-wide culture, especially among the literate majority.

The potent contemporary propaganda of Protestantism and patriotism doubtless worked a similar unifying effect.

At the five universities, specialist professorial teaching began, new subjects like history and modern literature were introduced and the latest English and European developments, including Newton's science and cutting-edge political and legal theories, were added to revised curricula. By 1750 Scotland's universities had for the first time become an attractive destination for students from other countries.

The Scottish yearning for intellectual novelty also showed itself in the enthusiastic embracing of London literary fashion. The zeal with which Scots took to the popular magazines written by Joseph Addison and Sir Richard Steele, especially *The Spectator* (1711–12), was especially revealing. Their love of Addison's work was an early indication that literate Scots were becoming wedded to the brilliantly seductive vision of modern society that he projected. Like him, they wanted to create a new kind of community, prosperous and at peace with itself. Here people would use intelligent conversation and interaction to promote 'politeness' – meaning greater insight and understanding and mutual tolerance – for themselves and for others.

Some Scots by the 1720s, including some of the Presbyterian clergy, were certainly seeking to extend religious and intellectual freedom. Their aspirations were helped by the passage of time. The dogmatic and suspicious Covenanting ministers who had endured the Killing Time and then hanged Thomas Aikenhead for making a theological joke were fading away. A new generation of confidently liberal and Anglophile clerics was slowly emerging. Tellingly, for men influenced by Addison's notion of politeness, they called themselves the 'Moderate party'.

The Moderates above all accepted the Patronage Act of 1711, which had returned power over parish appointments to secular landowners. Some in the Scottish Church, known as the 'Popular party' or the 'High flyers', long continued to reject this legislation. Many of its staunchest opponents even left the Church altogether, forming their own permanent breakaway Presbyterian organizations – notably the Secession Church from the 1730s and the Relief Church from the 1760s. But the Moderates held firm, insisting that the national Church had an obligation to obey the law of the land.

By the 1750s the Moderates, by dominating the General Assembly, had emerged as the Church's acknowledged leaders. Self-consciously polite and strongly opposed to old-fashioned and dangerous religious prejudices, they also helped make the Church substantially more open-minded. Official harassment of Episcopalians and Catholics ended. Those with unusual opinions were also now protected from the traditional sanction of a heresy prosecution.

Some of the Moderates, indeed, became increasingly active in intellectual circles themselves – and duly faced sniping from the Popular party. William Robertson, for example, their acknowledged leader, was principal of Edinburgh University from 1762 and one of Europe's best-known and best-paid historians. His friend Hugh Blair, minister of St Giles, was another Edinburgh professor and an influential literary critic, whose greatest achievement was to provide encouragement and vital publicity for the emerging young Ayrshire poet Robert Burns.

Insight: 'The Bard'

Scotland's national poet was a farmer who almost emigrated to America. His work, however, soon won him not just recognition but immortality, celebrated by Scots on his birthday, 25 January, at Burns Suppers. His poetry comprises Scots and English verse on a vast range of themes, including romance, the countryside and religious faith. Each generation has claimed him as its own, the current fashion emphasizing his radical politics, proud Scottishness and unconventional love life. Burns remains the acknowledged property of almost all Scots, as a prominent English journalist found in 2008, provoking outrage by dismissing him as the 'king of sentimental doggerel'.

Robertson and Blair were central participants in what we now know as the 'Scottish Enlightenment' – the Scottish version of sophisticated 18th-century culture, characterized in most countries by scientific advances, philosophical free-thinking and progressive ideals.

This development, as Hume was surprised to find, with his Moderate friends to the fore, was what had suddenly catapulted Scotland itself from cultural backwater to intellectual centre-stage.

Some of the Scottish Enlightenment, it might be added, was distinctively and vitally *Scottish*. In particular, because the king's government was accountable to Parliament and to the courts, and because progressive values therefore seemed already to be embodied in the post-1689 British constitution, the Continental Enlightenment's fervour for radical political change and hostility towards the oppressive role of churches and churchmen was not fully reflected in Scotland (or in England). The stark contrasts between Highland and Lowland society and the rapid contemporary commercialization of their country's economy also made Scottish intellectuals more fascinated than their European counterparts by the origins of cultural difference and by the causes and consequences of prosperity.

This richly stimulating context was actually a key reason why the Scottish Enlightenment registered such a wide impact outside Scotland. But another was that some of its greatest achievements provided answers to scientific and philosophical questions that were already being asked elsewhere.

Joseph Black, for example, a chemist at Edinburgh University with strong interests in industrial applications, successfully explained latent heat and was the first to isolate carbon dioxide (or 'fixed air' as it was then called). His friend James Hutton, meanwhile, progressed from expert in agricultural improvement to pioneering geologist: his *Theory of the Earth* (1785) began the dominance of 'uniformitarianism' – the assumption that the planet is subject to basic natural processes that have existed since its formation and which are still in operation.

Some of the Scots' most influential contributions came in the study of man and society. Philosophy, the core of the traditional Scottish university curriculum, was an inevitable preoccupation. David Hume, the century's greatest philosopher, was rejected for professorships at Edinburgh and Glasgow because of his religious doubts. But his sceptical arguments about what we can know about the world around us and what we ought to believe, especially in the *Treatise of Human Nature* (1739–40), would prove the 18th century's most influential statements in the field.

Hume's friend Adam Smith, from Kirkcaldy, also offered new insights in moral philosophy while a Glasgow professor. But it was his subsequent study of economic change in *The Wealth of Nations* (1776), forcing people to re-think their comfortable assumptions about the moral character of economic activities, which brought him fame and influence. Smith's main argument, running against the grain of much traditional Christian teaching, was that it is the self-interest of individuals that leads them to sell goods and offer services. The pursuit of private profit and not a benevolent concern for others is therefore what ultimately creates wealth and maximizes society's material well-being.

Overall, the Scottish Enlightenment lacked a single theoretical standpoint. But its leading contributors typically assumed that extremely long histories interacting with highly specific cultural and environmental situations could explain most of the peculiar features of human societies. This insight was what made them important precursors to the 19th-century founders of the modern social sciences.

In literary and artistic terms the Scottish Enlightenment also brought Scotland and its culture to far wider attention than hitherto. Tobias Smollett and Henry Mackenzie produced some of the age's most entertaining novels, but it was Sir Walter Scott who from 1814 onwards offered some of the most popular and influential stories about Scotland ever written.

Insight: Scott-land

This one-word 19th-century joke makes a serious point. After early fame as a poet, Sir Walter Scott's extraordinary best-seller *Waverley* (1814), the first historical novel ever written, brought the Scotland of the 1745/6 rebellion dramatically back to life. *Heart of Midlothian*, *Rob Roy* and *Redgauntlet* are among his other novels to depict a seductive but old-fashioned Scotland dominated by the Highland mountains, imposing castles, scheming Jacobites, fervent Covenanters, amusing eccentrics, dogged heroes and lost causes. More than anyone else before or since, it was Scott who made the country seem irresistibly romantic.

The poet James Macpherson also achieved worldwide celebrity with his purported translations from the ancient Gaelic poet Ossian. These were a crucial inspiration for European Romanticism and Napoleon kept a copy with him on campaign. Even so, well-founded doubts persisted about whether they were genuine translations or had been substantially invented by Macpherson himself.

The Scottish Enlightenment also reinvigorated the graphic arts. Painters like Allan Ramsay and Henry Raeburn and architects like the Adam family contributed greatly to the cultural improvements that Scotland was now experiencing. Indeed, nothing better symbolised the country's dramatic transformation than the elegant buildings that Robert Adam himself added to Edinburgh's emerging New Town at the end of the 18th centuty.

THINGS TO REMEMBER

▶ The pace and extent of social, economic and cultural change between the Union and the 1830s struck those who lived through it as simply extraordinary.

▶ Agricultural improvements were crucial, with a shift imposed by landowners from traditional communal farming to commercial, entrepreneurial systems.

▶ The rural economy became gradually less labour-intensive, bringing mass departures and even forced clearance of people from Lowland as well as Highland estates.

▶ Scotland's economic infrastructure – banking, insurance, bridges, roads – was developed in order to assist commercial activities in the expanding towns as well as in rural areas.

▶ Industrialization greatly accelerated economic growth as natural resources, new technology and capital investment converged to transform the nature and scale of production.

▶ The Scottish population, encouraged by rising living standards and falling child mortality, more than doubled between 1700 and 1830, with particular growth in urban areas.

▶ The period also saw large-scale emigration, partly caused by changes in the rural economy, while Irish immigrants started arriving in the industrial towns.

▶ A conscious desire to modernize society lay behind the growth of polite culture, the rise of the Moderates in the Church and the philosophical, scientific, literary and artistic achievements of the Scottish Enlightenment.

14

The long Victorian age

In this chapter you will learn:
- *about Scotland's unique experiences of industry, empire, cultural change and electoral reform in the 19th century*
- *about their unanticipated social and political consequences.*

Change and stability

It is conventional to regard the Victorian age as one of success and tranquillity.

The British constitution was widely venerated, the monarchy popular and beyond reproach. The economy, directed by mutton-chopped entrepreneurs and overseen by prudent governments, boomed like never before. The *pax Britannica* prevented major European wars. And a worldwide empire existed whose bounds simply got wider and wider. On this view the period saw a happy balance struck which, at least until things went disastrously wrong on 4 August 1914, made the British wealthy and contented as well as all-powerful.

Yet this is an unrealistic characterization of the Scottish experience in particular. The period between the 1830s and Victoria's death was in fact marked by unprecedented political changes, by further economic transformations, by social upheaval and by profound cultural developments.

Scotland, as we shall see, was fast becoming a quite different country from what it had been at the end of the Georgian era.

The birth of democracy

One reason why a misleading impression can sometimes be given of Victoria's reign is that the most fundamental of the political changes that re-shaped 19th-century Britain actually took place shortly before she came to the throne.

The Reform Acts of 1832, implemented by Lord Grey's Whig government after more than a decade of public pressure and political campaigning, had dramatic effects in Scotland. Previously there had been just 4,500 Scottish voters; but by finally bringing the much narrower Scottish qualification into line with further-extended English practice, the changes enfranchised most well-to-do householders in the burghs and most small landowners in the counties.

At a stroke this created a Scottish electorate of 65,000. Of course, this was still only a small part of the population. But that the vast majority of the new voters were middle-class nevertheless represented a shift in the balance of power. Government policies would in future no longer be dictated by the great landowners. They would increasingly have to reflect the views of urban Britain and the business classes.

Another seminal consequence, crystallized in the reinvention by the 1860s of the Tory Party as the Conservatives and the Whig Party as the Liberals, was the evolution of something like modern party politics. Beforehand, with many Scottish constituencies having just a few dozen electors, private relationships between candidates and individual voters were often decisive. Afterwards the sort of campaigning machinery that only mass-membership political parties could provide became necessary. Politicians were also forced to court the newspapers to reach a wider public. In effect, prospective MPs and potential governments finally had to compete for the support of broad swathes of the electorate.

Insight: Man of the people

The emergence of modern politics in Victorian Scotland was exemplified by the famous campaign of 1879–80 in which William Ewart Gladstone, from a Scottish business family that had made its money in Liverpool and already twice Liberal prime minister, toured the Midlothian constituency in which his father had been born. A series of packed public meetings heard his passionately argued speeches on the moral deficiencies of Disraeli's foreign policy. Gladstone in due course defeated the sitting Tory MP at the polls.

Sceptics at the time and since were, however, correct that the reforms of 1832 were limited in their extent. The signatories of the People's Charter in 1838 and of its subsequent revisions – demanding, among other things, votes for all men over 21, annual elections and equalization of constituency sizes – were only the most organized and articulate of the many critics.

Chartism, as it became known, was a popular radical phenomenon throughout Britain, though it differed in character from place to place. It was especially potent in Ireland and in Wales, where open violence flared in 1839. But in Scotland it was associated with working-class Presbyterian dissenters in the Relief Church and the Secession Church. And they were noted for using peaceful meetings and the arts of persuasion – so-called 'moral force' Chartism – rather than employing sedition and conspiracy to advance their cause.

The Chartists ultimately failed, their campaigns fizzling out everywhere by the early 1850s as the lack of progress eventually undermined their credibility. It took until the Second and Third Reform Acts, passed in 1867–8 by Disraeli's Conservatives and 1884 by Gladstone's Liberal government, for some of the Chartists' main aspirations finally to be fulfilled.

The Second Reform Act enfranchised all urban householders, effectively benefiting the working class: by the 1868 election, Scotland's electorate had reached 150,000. The Third did the same for rural Britain, giving the vote to all householders in the counties. Added to the 1872 Ballot Act which introduced secret voting (thereby preventing the political preferences of employees and tenants being monitored by their superiors), these changes further advanced the politics of mass democracy in Victorian Britain.

The Liberals were the chief beneficiaries in Scotland. The 1886 general election, for example, which saw a Conservative government sweep to power at Westminster, nevertheless yielded 39 Scottish MPs for the Liberals and 16 more for the new Liberal Unionists (dissidents who opposed Gladstone on Irish Home Rule). Just 12 Scottish Tories were returned even in a year of victory UK-wide.

The same skew was seen in the Liberals' famous 1906 landslide victory. This made the Glaswegian businessman Henry Campbell-Bannerman, representing the Stirling Burghs, the new Prime Minister, succeeding his fellow Scot Arthur Balfour, a Manchester Conservative MP from an old Fife landed dynasty. On this occasion the official Liberals secured 58 Scottish seats, the Tories limping home with a mere eight.

In truth, the Conservatives remained hampered in Scotland by being the party of the established churches and the landed class. Accordingly they struggled to attract the working-class vote that they acquired more easily in parts of England. The Liberal Party, by contrast, was high-minded and moderately progressive not just on constitutional matters but on education and welfare issues too – passing, for example, the Factory Acts that stopped children being sent up chimneys and women down mine shafts.

Liberalism thus appealed intuitively to the morally-upright evangelicals and Presbyterian dissenters who were so numerous in Victorian Scotland. More widely, it attracted a powerful (though inherently unstable) coalition of urban voters: both businessmen and unionized workers, who were becoming more important as the economy industrialized, were bastions of Scottish Liberal support.

Scotland, in short, remained a discernibly different society with a different political culture from England. To understand why, we need to consider the further progress of Scottish industrialization since the 1820s.

The workshop of the world

By the 1820s a new phase in Scotland's economic history was dawning. At its heart lay the rapid growth of the coal, iron and steel industries, and soon also of their related manufactures, such as railway engines, girders, boilers, large-scale machinery and, above all, ships. As a result, the shape and overall performance of the Scottish economy by the turn of the 20th century would be dominated by what we would now describe collectively as 'heavy industry'.

The triggers for this new transformation lay in the decades before 1830, when two innovations greatly increased the productive capacity of the iron industry. It was the Glasgow engineer James Neilson who invented a new furnace that injected heated air into the smelting process (at a time when received wisdom insisted that the best results occurred at the lowest possible temperature).

Patented in 1828, the 'hot blast' technique consumed far less coal. But it also delivered more and better-quality pig-iron. This in turn allowed the full exploitation of a superior new ore, the much richer 'blackband' or carboniferous ironstone (50–70 per cent of which could be turned into metal), which had been found in Lanarkshire and Ayrshire by the metallurgist David Mushet in 1801.

The combined effects of these two discoveries were spectacular. In the year of Neilson's patent Scotland produced just 36,000 tons of pig-iron. By 1840 output had already passed 300,000 tons and by the 1880s it exceeded 1.2 million. Since most Scottish iron masters considered the subsequent stages of metal production unprofitable, pig-iron itself soon became an important export as well as supplying the many other local businesses for which it became the key raw material.

Coal output, partly to feed the rising demand from Scotland's metal industries but also to power steam engines, to warm homes, and for sale to England and overseas, charted a broadly similar course. From just 1 million tons dug in 1775 and 3 million in 1830, Scottish miners, of whom there were by then well over 100,000, were excavating 42 million tons annually by 1914.

Other local factors also helped propel these industries forward. In particular, 19th-century Scottish workers, many newly arrived from Ireland, earned significantly less than their English counterparts (perhaps only 75 per cent as much in the 1860s). Labour-intensive processes such as coal extraction and iron-smelting thus enjoyed peculiar advantages in Scotland, since the main production cost was minimized.

The large and well-established metal industry that resulted, densely concentrated to the south and east of Glasgow, where adjacent coal and ironstone reserves existed and 18th-century infrastructure like the Monklands Canal linked related sites together, allowed other specialist businesses to take on the design and manufacture of derivative products like locomotives, rail tracks and their associated machinery and structures.

Trains quickly became a key Scottish export industry. Firms such as Neilson and Company of Springburn and Dübs of Polmadie sent tens of thousands of engines to India, South Africa, Australasia and South America over several decades. By 1870 as much as one-quarter of all of the world's trains were being fashioned in and around Glasgow.

The Scots' contribution to the railway age was, however, most famously embodied in the majestic Forth Bridge: 55,000 tons of carefully assembled steel built by Sir William Arrol & Company of Glasgow; when it finally opened in 1890 it was, as it remains today, an exuberant monument to Victorian heavy engineering at its most confident and bombastic.

Early competitive advantages in producing lower-cost iron and steel in quantity also explain the rise, from virtually nowhere, of what was Scotland's most important industry by the late 19th century. Shipbuilding was transformed in character as Scottish companies swiftly adapted new technologies from elsewhere. Beginning with paddle steamers, they readily embraced the mass production first of iron plating and reciprocating steam engines and then from the 1880s of steel hulls and from the early 1900s of steam turbines too.

Ships of all descriptions thus became the specialist Scottish industrial product par excellence. Leading firms like J. & G. Thomson (from 1899, John Brown & Company) at Clydebank, Denny of Dumbarton, Beardmore of Dalmuir and Fairfields of Govan soon acquired worldwide reputations.

The results were utterly extraordinary. Glasgow and its satellite riverside towns were alone building more iron ships by the 1870s than the rest of the world put together. A generation later, in 1913–14, no less than 20 per cent of the world's newly launched tonnage – more than either Germany or the United States were then producing – bore the prestigious branding 'Clydebuilt'.

Cheap, reliable and prolific, by the turn of the 20th century Scotland's shipbuilders supplied warships for the world's most powerful navy as well as a vast range of vessels for Britain's merchant fleet. They were also securely established as the country's most successful exporters.

The triumph of Scottish heavy industry brought wider gains too. Everything from banking, accountancy and insurance to technical education, joinery and all the electrical and mechanical trades benefited. As importantly, in making possible regular train services and steamship routes, these products also created a truly British economy that was better integrated than ever before.

Local specialist production flourished when linked to much bigger and further-flung markets: granite-quarrying and beef cattle in Aberdeenshire, coal-mining in Fife, trawling for herring (the 'silver darlin's') along the entire east coast and for haddock off Arbroath, milk and cheese in Ayrshire, fruit in Angus, jute production in Dundee (where the necessary raw material actually came all the way from Bengal) and woollen manufacturing in the various Border towns (which exported tweed garments worldwide) all expanded profitably as trains and ships, designed and built in Scotland, made the world a smaller place.

Yet not all the consequences of heavy engineering's central position in Scottish life, nor all the linkages that now tied the country into an international economy, were quite so benevolent. For it had spawned a network of separate, mutually dependent, family-owned companies, in most cases highly specialized and also unusually reliant on exports to foreign and colonial markets.

This made it acutely vulnerable to new overseas competition exploiting higher levels of integration, more extensive natural resources or far greater economies of scale. The lower wages paid to Scottish workers also suppressed domestic economic consumption. This in turn discouraged diversification into consumer items and so further reinforced the focus on an industrial monoculture manufacturing a limited range of high-value capital goods: by 1914, for example, over half a million Scottish workers depended directly on making iron and steel products.

Scotland's conspicuous success in labour-intensive forms of work also had a looming dark side. Especially once again in native-owned heavy industry, it encouraged and rewarded a business strategy that prioritized containing wages and hiring and firing to cope with fluctuating demand. Simultaneously it undervalued risk-taking and investment, which in the long term would threaten the country's early technological leadership in capital goods.

Worst of all, this entire model of industrialization hid a dirty secret. For it had helped generate a series of intractable social problems and worsening class tensions that bubbled away just beneath the apparently serene surface of Victorian Scottish society.

Labouring and living

Large scale and rapid urbanization was certainly the most important factor in transforming Victorian social experiences. Indeed, Scotland was quickly becoming second only to England in the extent to which its people had abandoned their traditional rural way of life. At the 1801 census barely one in five Scots resided in a town or city with at least 5,000 inhabitants. By 1901, however, after a century of industrialization and further agricultural modernization, the proportion already stood at 58 per cent. Urban life, in short, had suddenly become the norm.

Glasgow, the focus of commerce, textile manufacturing and heavy engineering, as well as of immigration (44,000 Irish-born residents were recorded in the 1841 census), had overtaken Edinburgh and was now Scotland's largest city. From just 77,000 inhabitants in 1801, by the First World War its expanded boundaries encompassed over a million souls – more than one-fifth of the country's total, giving Glasgow a proportionately more dominant position than other great cities like London, Paris, Rome or New York. Indeed, if we include the city's many satellite towns, west-central Scotland, later dubbed 'greater Glasgow', was actually home to the clear majority of the national population by the early 20th century.

The pace and scale of Scottish urbanization created a whole new set of social problems. Spatial segregation, a classic feature of modern cities, was one of them.

The well-to-do naturally lived in increasing comfort and style. Housing for the masses, however, was both cramped and insanitary. Mainly comprising unregulated rented accommodation in tall, densely-packed tenements, large numbers of new blocks were built cheaply – though this was convenient for workers whose own wages remained low – and with few if any domestic amenities.

The result on the ground was some chilling contrasts. Dundee's Broughty Ferry and Glasgow's West End, for example, became much sought-after for their fashionable townhouses and gracious living. Yet neighbourhoods only a couple of miles away, like Lochee, the haunt of Irish immigrants in Dundee, and the Gorbals (often described as Europe's worst slum) and the East End in Glasgow, were now notorious for their appalling housing and blighted lives.

The data on working-class accommodation in particular never fail to shock. In 1861 a third of all Scots lived in one-roomed homes ('single ends', in Glaswegian slang). Another third had just two. In such conditions, especially before mains sewerage, clean drinking water and inoculation were made generally available, disease was a regular visitor. Cholera epidemics cut a swathe through Glasgow in the 1830s, 1840s and 1850s. Typhus and typhoid were ever-present for most of the century.

As in England's cities, mortality was consistently higher than in the countryside. On average 28 people per 1,000 were dying each year in urban Scotland in the early 1860s against just 18 in rural areas. In the Gorbals in the 1890s the annual child mortality rate was still running at an astonishing 200 per 1,000.

Most Victorian Scots were, of course, substantially better off than their predecessors. And there can be no doubt that things broadly continued to improve between the 1830s and 1914. Death rates, notwithstanding some appalling black-spots and significant setbacks, declined: 21 Scots in every 1,000 died each year between 1855 and 1860 but only 17 each year by 1900. Life expectancy also increased, from around 40 years for Scottish men in 1850 to 50 by the First World War. These benign averages reflect steady improvements in living standards and living conditions for the majority that cannot be denied.

Yet people did not seem any happier or more contented. Partly this was because Scottish society was increasingly unequal and divided. Some were very wealthy indeed. Just 7 per cent of Scots collected 46 per cent of the national income in the 1860s, with a quarter claimed by just 5,000 individuals. On the other hand, the bottom 70 per cent of earners took home just one-third of the total. At the very top, the richest 1 per cent – including industrialists like David Colville and William Beardmore – enjoyed incomes at least 200 times greater than anyone in the poorest 30 per cent.

The sense of grievance that these contrasts generated was compounded by the fluctuating wage levels and periodic unemployment to which Scotland's export-led industrial economy was particularly exposed. The official system for coping with destitution, the New Poor Law introduced in 1845 (finally replacing the charitable parish handouts of the old Reformation-era regime), was wholly inadequate. Workhouses, meagre payments and a deep reluctance to give anything at all to the able-bodied – based on moral assumptions about the 'undeserving poor' – maintained rather than alleviated poverty.

Mutual support was the natural response of many of the vulnerable. For welfare purposes this meant forming 'friendly societies', as in

England, whose members subscribed to a fund that would support the needy. But to manage relations with employers a rather different kind of collective organization was required.

Following the Trade Union Act of 1871 which legalized them for the first time, Scotland's workplaces began to see concerted union activity. This was partly inspired by socialist ideas. But more commonly it was motivated by employees' desire to strengthen their own hand in bargaining over wages, redundancies and conditions. Organizations like the Ayrshire Miners Union, established in 1886, and the National Union of Dock Labourers, founded in Glasgow in 1889, eventually became a significant presence in many working communities.

Yet another logical response was long familiar in Scotland: emigration. Huge numbers, perhaps approaching 2 million between the 1820s and 1914 – disproportionately the young, the skilled and the ambitious – left for the United States, Canada and Australasia.

Some of those who departed applied their talents overseas with startling results.

Insight: Success stories

Andrew Carnegie, Dunfermline weaver's son turned Pittsburgh steel magnate and philanthropist, was dubbed 'the richest man in the world' by the 1890s and was one of the most famous Scots alive. Allan Pinkerton, too, became a legendary American detective and spy, having started out a mere Gorbals cooper and Chartist activist. The dramatic upwards mobility of some emigrants became a source of much national pride and reinforced the myth of the humble Scot prospering by dint of natural talent and sheer determination.

The vast majority of those who emigrated, however, merely lived decent, blameless lives in their new countries. In practice, railways, engineering, government, the military, education and banking – the stereotypical national strengths – invariably gained disproportionately wherever the Scots ended up.

Even those Victorian Scots least affected by industrialization and urbanization, because they still lived in the most remote rural districts, suffered growing distress and experienced deepening social divisions throughout this period. In particular, relations between Highland crofters and their landlords, already poisoned by the recent Clearances, were worsened still further by two unforeseen developments.

First, the danger of over-dependence on the potato to feed the newly established crofting communities was brutally demonstrated by *Phytophthora infestans* – the blight fungus which also lay behind the great Irish potato famine of the same period. Thriving in the relentlessly damp environment of the north and west of Scotland in 1846–7 and successfully destroying the harvest ahead of what turned out to be an unusually harsh winter, it caused severe deprivation.

Suffering crofters, unable to pay rent, were treated in different ways. Certain landlords helped tenants leave for Canada or Australia. Others organized paid work such as building the 'destitution roads' in remote parts of the Highlands. Some, however, like John Gordon of Cluny, were lambasted in the newspapers for evicting their stricken tenants, while the government made ineffectual attempts to distribute sufficient additional food by ship. In the event large numbers, above all the young, left permanently in the aftermath, reckoning Highland life perhaps unsustainable and certainly unpalatable. The region's total population peaked in mid-century and has been in decline ever since.

The second problem peculiar to the Highlands was that the unusual land economy underpinning crofting also proved untenable. The inadequacy of the agricultural resources available to communities, when so much land was given over to sheep farms and sporting estates, had again been highlighted by the famine. The ease with which crofters could be evicted also rankled, as did rising rents. These grievances caused the Highland Land War of the early 1880s. There were rent strikes, occupations and attacks on owners' properties as the Highland Land League, the crofters' collective campaigning vehicle, attempted to secure additional land and enhanced rights for tenants.

Eye-catching incidents, like the Battle of the Braes in 1882, in which 50 Glasgow policemen were drafted in to confront crofters resisting an eviction on Skye, secured them sympathetic media attention. No one, fortunately, was killed or badly injured – unlike in Ireland, whose own struggles over land provided general inspiration but no precise model for Scottish activists.

The government, however, was forced to sit up and take notice. The Napier Commission duly investigated and made its recommendations.

And Gladstone's Liberal government passed the Crofters' Holdings Act in 1886, giving existing tenants security of tenure and establishing the Crofters' Commission with powers to manage rents.

The political consequences of these specifically Highland troubles were distinctive and yet illustrative of broader Scottish patterns. A Crofters' Party actually returned four MPs in the 1885 election. But as in Ireland, it was the Liberals who derived most electoral benefit, and the Conservatives who suffered most, from widespread anti-landlord sentiment.

The same was true of growing tensions in Lowland society. Collective workplace organization, facilitated by Liberal legislation, broadly aligned industrial workforces, once they secured the vote, with the party of Gladstone.

Yet this was by no means a straightforward political alliance. After all, the Liberals also represented many middle-class Scottish employers. Suspicious of intrusive state intervention in the free market, such people were also hostile to trade unionism, sometimes actually banning them for their workplaces. Many workers, by contrast, were increasingly class-conscious. Growing numbers were also attracted to socialism, with its robustly collectivist prescriptions for the economy.

Increasingly, this basic ideological contradiction led some Scottish workers off in a new direction. A Scottish Labour Party, whose secretary was James Keir Hardie, a Lanarkshire miners' union organizer, was formed in 1888 to field socialist candidates in parliamentary elections. In 1893 its first British-wide successor was established, the Independent Labour Party (ILP), again led by Keir Hardie, by now an MP for a poor London constituency.

With its idealistic worker-friendly manifesto committed to the common ownership of industry and the pursuit of social and economic equality, by the turn of the new century the ILP was becoming the more obvious party for a significant number of unionized working-class Scots to support. No-one could yet have known it – especially with Arthur Primrose, 5th Earl of Rosebery, a Scottish aristocrat, as Liberal prime minister in the mid-1890s – but this shift would soon help bring about the strange death of Liberal Scotland.

Revivalism

Industrialization was so profoundly transformational that its effects reached far beyond the workplace, into the nooks and crannies of everyday life. It altered not just economic structures and political affiliations but also the ways in which people looked at the world around them. It even had the capacity to change how they thought about their own place within it.

This was emphatically so in the religious sphere. Indeed, no mental revolution in Victorian Scotland was more dramatic than the one that began on 18 May 1843. On that day more than a third of the Church of Scotland's clergy, attending that year's General Assembly in St Andrew's Church in Edinburgh, walked out to form a separate Presbyterian church, the Free Church of Scotland.

The immediate cause was, as ever, patronage. Ostensibly this 'Disruption' was the culmination of what was referred to as the Ten Years' War, between a Moderate leadership who still endorsed the Patronage Act of 1711 and an increasingly vociferous Popular party. The latter, evangelical in inspiration and temperament, flatly rejected the state's interference in clerical appointments, arguing instead for a re-born national church whose only legitimate authority would be Jesus Christ.

At a deeper level, however, the Disruption reflected contrasting responses to the new Scotland. The Moderates represented the secularizing tendencies of the Scottish Enlightenment nurtured in a genteel 18th-century world of landowners and polite clergymen in rural parishes. But the evangelicals, led by charismatic figures like Thomas Chalmers and David Welsh, were closely engaged with the challenges of urban, industrial and Highland society – poverty, unemployment, illegitimacy, immorality and a lack of access to churches. Intriguingly, they were also convinced that the solution lay in reviving the spiritual certainties and moral fervour of the Reformation era.

Chalmers and his Free Church colleagues aimed to create nothing less than an alternative national church uncorrupted by political interference. This is why they took 474 of the Church of Scotland's 1203 ministers with them, and constructed 500 new churches in the first two years, often adjacent to the existing parish buildings.

They also founded schools, training institutions, charities, publications and overseas missions. All were financed by their own congregations and other well-wishers. The Free Church quickly attracted most leading Presbyterian theologians, preachers and social activists. And it won particularly strong support in the Highlands, from the urban working classes and among Liberal voters. All in all, the Disruption was a quiet but stunningly effective domestic rebellion – the only really successful one of its kind in the Victorian period – against the British state and the failings of its established institutions.

Even so, the unyielding spirit that had made it possible in the first place, and the habitual preference of strict Presbyterians for a 'stooshie' (Scots for a row or a fight) instead of a compromise, came back to haunt the Free Church in due course. It did itself few favours, for instance, by upholding a heresy charge in the late 1870s against one of its own ministers, William Robertson Smith. A brilliant professor at the Aberdeen Free Church College, his articles for the *Encyclopaedia Britannica* had failed to uphold the literal truth of scripture: the convicted author consoled himself with a position at Cambridge.

Further splits were also always likely given the doctrinal strictness that had originally facilitated the Disruption. After the government abolished patronage in 1874, the Free Church did move closer to the United Presbyterian Church, formed earlier by combining the 18th-century Secession and Relief churches. The negotiated outcome, in 1900, was the United Free Church of Scotland. But one group, later mocked as the 'Wee Frees' (properly it still called itself the Free Church), rejected the deal and continued as before. There had already been another embarrassing rupture in 1893 over the Free Church's gradual dilution of Covenant theology. The opponents of this particular error had also departed to become the Free Presbyterian Church (colloquially the 'Wee Wee Frees').

These two breakaway institutions, again drawing particular support from the Highlands and even becoming the dominant force on isolated islands like Raasay, would long maintain their stricter Calvinist views. Coming on top of the old divisions between Episcopalians and Presbyterians and then between the established Church of Scotland and the Free Church, they also ensured that 20th-century visitors to Scotland would find along its high streets a confusing succession of rival Protestant places of worship, each claiming uniquely to be continuing the godly mission of the Scottish Reformation.

Religious revival in response to disorienting and destabilizing social change was actually a process that stretched far beyond the confines of the Presbyterian churches. The Episcopalian church itself, for example, blossomed once the restrictions on this formerly Jacobite institution were relaxed in 1792. At Perth in 1851 it opened the first post-Reformation cathedral in Britain. Gradually it restored some of its long-lost respectability and influence. With more than 300 parishes and clergy by 1900, Episcopalianism was especially popular among the landed classes and urban professionals.

The re-birth of Scottish Catholicism, once even more under suspicion, was more spectacular still. It was helped, of course, by the mass influx of Irish adherents and by the government's removal of the remaining legal prohibitions in 1829. Parishes were re-founded, particularly in the industrial towns of the Lowlands on which working-class Irish families converged. Proper dioceses were restored by Rome in 1878. And a full-scale seminary was even re-instituted at Blairs in Aberdeenshire.

From just 30,000 mainly native believers in 1800, Catholicism grew to become once more a major national force by 1901, with 244,100 adherents, overwhelmingly of Irish descent. Community tensions, however, were the worrying legacy, especially in Scotland's towns and cities. Traditional anti-Catholic sectarianism was given greater force by new concerns over the effects of cheap immigrant labour on prevailing wage rates and by the divisive culmination of the Irish struggle for independence.

The experiences of all of Scotland's main Christian groups in this period had certain features in common, generally traceable to the industrial and urban setting in which they increasingly operated. Determined to recover ground among the 'godless poor' who had moved to new locations to lead new kinds of lives exposed to new threats, every church understandably became noticeably more energetic and more creative.

The urgency of the challenge meant that spiritual zeal and theological precision seemed to matter more than in the 18th century. Committed pastoral outreach also became a top priority. So did charitable efforts to help the needy poor as well as vociferous moral campaigns to hector them into improved behaviour.

Widely perceived too was the churches' obligation to conduct
missions overseas. The latter extended the views and values of 19th-
century Scotland across a much broader canvas. They were, of course,
exemplified by the much-idolised Dr David Livingstone, the explorer
and evangelical preacher who traversed southern and central Africa
in mid-century. Each of the competing Scottish churches naturally
maintained an institutional campaign of its own. In some parts of
Britain's African empire, like Nyasaland (now Malawi) and British
East Africa (Kenya), Presbyterianism soon became the dominant form
of Christianity, whose imprint is still felt there even today.

Recreation, culture, nationhood

By the late 19th century the different churches' many-faceted
campaign to win converts and retain believers had spread across
much of Scottish life.

The 1872 Education Act formally handed control of school education
to the civil authorities and made attendance compulsory up to the age
of 13. But the Presbyterian churches retained a dominant influence
over the ethos and the strong religious content, while Catholic schools
remained unchanged and outside the system.

The Sunday Schools movement, which had rather earlier beginnings,
was another staple feature of many people's lives by this time,
inculcating Christian teachings among the masses. So too were more
recent innovations, like the Boys' Brigade, founded by the Free Church
in Glasgow in 1883, and the Salvation Army, which arrived from
England in 1879. The latter in particular quickly won over many
additional Scottish recruits to the trademark cause of temperance.

Yet the churches, desperate to attract support and deflect their members from potentially sinful alternatives, also increasingly exploited essentially secular pastimes. Football had the greatest pulling power. Many parish churches formed amateur teams, taking advantage of what was fast emerging as a ragingly popular working-class pursuit, for spectators as well as for participants.

Insight: Only a game?

Football was a popular pastime in Scotland by 1500 and well-attended matches between professional teams had emerged by 1880. A reputation soon grew for exporting great players: Hughie Gallacher in the 1920s, Denis Law in the 1960s, Kenny Dalglish in the 1970s; and formidable managers: Bill Shankly to Liverpool and Sir Matt Busby and Sir Alex Ferguson to Manchester United. But football has deeper significance. The 'Old Firm' clubs Celtic and Rangers, dominant on the field, have sectarian associations off it (Irish tricolours and republican songs like 'We are the IRA' versus Union flags and anti-Catholic lyrics like 'The Sash'). The humiliation of Ally MacLeod's much-hyped Scotland team at the 1978 World Cup traumatized people already fretting over the country's constitutional arrangements. And that many Scots clearly enjoy England's losses more than Scotland's victories speaks volumes about the game's palpable political undertones.

By 1900 bicycling clubs (the contraption itself was actually pioneered by Scottish engineers), choirs and artistic groups were proliferating too. Healthy communal activities always promised much to the churches and their leaders in search of new ways to capture the loyalties of the population.

Yet not all diversions that interested the Victorian public were as easily co-opted in the cause of religion. The theatre, for example, was a common diversion with which religion struggled to compete, a fashion made possible by the modest surplus incomes of workers and by the gradually reducing hours that they worked. Venues such as the Britannia Music Hall and the Whitebait Music Hall, both opened in Glasgow in 1857, played an increasingly important part in the lives of many industrial workers. Such places also provided a venue in which Scottish performers like Arthur Lloyd and Harry Lauder could popularize distinctively Scottish songs and cultural symbolism – tartan, bonnets and endless references to the Highlands – that reflected and accentuated the emphatically Scottish identities of their audiences.

Lauder and his maudlin signature love song 'Roamin' in the Gloamin'', hugely popular in England and North America before and after the First World War (Winston Churchill even hailed Lauder somewhat implausibly as 'Scotland's greatest ever ambassador'), were among the most accessible manifestations of a broader trend in which Scottishness of a particularly sentimental and stereotypical kind became a lucrative and influential cultural product. In a slightly more challenging form this same development was represented by what have become known, not without a touch of sarcasm, as 'Balmorality' and the 'Kailyard'.

These two cultural phenomena, the first alluding to the royal family's infatuation with their Highland holiday home and the second to a form of literature that portrayed Scotland as rural, traditional and deferential, can be seen as yet another response to industrialization and urbanization. For they clearly represented a retreat from the mid-Victorian period onwards into a psychological comfort zone, safely away from the increasingly troubling social and political realities of the age. They indicate a deep cultural yearning in many quarters for a Scotland that was stable, contented and unthreatening – for a country that, in truth, had never existed historically, but which was nonetheless far removed from the bleak industrial towns of Lanarkshire and Clydeside, the poverty of the Gorbals and the conflicts over the ownership and use of land in the Highlands.

In another way, too, the attention garnered at the time and ever since by the increasing sentimentalization of Scottish culture does a real disservice to Victorian Scotland. For the period actually saw a fruitful and engaged intellectual life evolve that was no less distinguished and no less widely influential than that produced by the Scottish Enlightenment. The universities, particularly Edinburgh and Glasgow, remained internationally important: Sir James Simpson's discovery of chloroform anaesthetics in 1847, which transformed the nature of surgery, took place at the first institution, while Lord Kelvin's work on electricity and on the two laws of thermodynamics, one of the foundations of modern physics, occurred at the second.

Insight: The physics of everything

James Clerk Maxwell was one of two great scientific geniuses to pass through Edinburgh University in the early 19th century (Darwin being the other). Born in Edinburgh and a professor at Aberdeen and Cambridge, Maxwell developed the mathematical equations that explain the behaviour of electricity, magnetism, light and gases. His work laid the theoretical foundations for modern physics, made possible colour photography and encouraged many new electrical and electronic technologies: Einstein, who revered him, kept a photograph of Maxwell on his office wall.

In Robert Louis Stevenson and J. M. Barrie, meanwhile, the country produced two of the century's best-loved literary figures – though again, their most enduring works, *Treasure Island* (1883) and *Peter Pan* (1902), timeless escapist fantasies for children, studiously avoided direct engagement with contemporary Scottish society.

More intriguingly, the period from 1850 onwards saw the first dim stirrings of reviving collective concern for national interests and national identity. It was almost as if accelerating industrialization and urbanization, together with the British state's wide-ranging attempts at progressive reform in response, were now being interpreted by some Scots as threatening not just their pre-existing institutions but also traditional Scottish ways of life.

A National Association for the Vindication of Scottish Rights, for example, existed briefly between 1853 and 1856, inspired by a sense among conservative-minded Scots that the Liberal Party had become obsessed with Irish issues. Interest in securing the same form of self-government that Ireland was likely to be offered continued to increase and in time even bore some modest fruit. In 1885 a separate Scottish Office and a Secretary of State for Scotland emerged. And a Scottish Home Rule Association started up the next year, seeking devolution within the Union.

Increasingly, the symbolism of Scottish identity also seemed to require vigorous defending. The totemic monument to Sir William Wallace, funded by public subscription, was completed near Stirling in 1869. This was no anti-Unionist statement but rather about reversing a general neglect of Scotland's own national heroes. Reflecting a somewhat different standpoint about how to preserve the country's threatened identity, An Comunn Gàidhealach, the organization committed to protecting and promoting Gaelic language and Gaelic culture in Scotland, also came into being at Oban in 1891.

These were small but vital signs, probably more significant in retrospect than they seemed at the time. For they indicated that at least some people recognized that Scotland remained a strongly distinctive country and that this might justify positive action in order to preserve it.

THINGS TO REMEMBER

▶ The convention of seeing Victoria's long reign as one of stability and calm misrepresents a period of dynamic change and new conflicts in Scottish society.

▶ The political reforms of 1832 and other legislation that followed created modern party politics, helping Scotland become a Liberal bastion until the eventual rise of Labour.

▶ Industrialization saw Scotland emerge as a world leader after 1850, especially in heavy engineering – notably trains and ships.

▶ With industrialization closely connected with the growth of towns and cities and of large groups of dependent workers, it brought grave social problems – periodic unemployment, low wages, increasing inequality, urban squalor and disease – as well as rising class tensions in its wake.

▶ Economic change also generated worsening problems in Highland society in particular and broadly encouraged the rise of trade unionism and the Labour Party.

▶ Another result of hardship and growing social conflict was the emergence and success of breakaway Presbyterian churches, as well as revived Catholicism among Irish immigrants.

▶ Scottish culture adapted to urban and industrial conditions, with the emergence of mass entertainment, new participatory activities for the public and some striking new literary developments reflecting changing times.

▶ By the end of the Victorian age there were also the first signs of increasing public awareness of the threat to distinctive Scottish ways of life and Scottish identities.

15

Retreat and resurgence

In this chapter you will learn:

- *how global warfare and loss of empire brought deep and prolonged crisis as heavy industry struggled, unemployment rose and growing anxiety promoted both radical left-wing and organized nationalist politics*
- *about the political changes of the later 20th century in Scotland, resulting in devolution, a return to a Scottish Parliament and a distinctively Scottish government.*

Just 44 years passed between Queen Victoria's death and the end of the Second World War. In rather less than a couple of generations, involvement in two titanic global conflicts subjected British politics and society to considerable new stresses and strains. Difficult questions were also posed about the place of Scotland and Britain in the wider world – questions that would still define the Scottish political scene into the 21st century.

Armageddon

The epochal events of the summer of 1914 took place far away from Scotland. But on 4 August war was declared between Britain and Germany. What would soon become the First World War – the Great War – had begun. And Scotland was fully involved from the outset.

As conflict loomed the Royal Navy's key strategic assets were moved to Scottish waters, to keep the German fleet penned in the North Sea and Germany itself blockaded.

Yet it was in the army, where the Scottish regiments each raised dozens of extra wartime battalions, that Scotland's contribution was most obviously seen.

In the final reckoning, 150,000 of Britain's 880,000 war dead were Scots – nearly one-fifth of the total from a country with less than one-tenth of the population: 26 per cent of Scottish combatants, and more than one in ten of all young males in Scotland, had died, as against 12 per cent of British servicemen as a whole. This tragic imbalance arose because the 'poor bloody infantry', where the Scots were traditionally over-represented, bore the brunt of the slaughter in a conflict that, to everyone's surprise, including that of the generals, turned out largely to revolve around interminable trench warfare. It was ironic that Scots were also chief among the senior commanders – Sir Donglas Haig on the Somme and Sir Ian Hamilton at Gallipoli – who took the blame.

There were other important consequences of the war that meant life would never be the same again. Above all, the government, to win the war, had taken unprecedented control of Scotland's heavy-industrial economy. After victory it was therefore harder to defend a return to *laisser faire* and correspondingly easier to demand detailed state direction of manufacturing.

The diversion of manpower into the armed services had also required the mass recruitment of new employees into industries previously dominated by unionized workers. Many of the newcomers were female, and often married – an unheard-of development that greatly aided the war effort. After 1918 this quickly helped women win the long-running argument over the right to vote. Female activists like Helen Crawfurd of the ILP also took the lead in a series of strikes against wartime rent rises, which made urban housing a key post-war electoral issue, especially in Scotland.

In many workplaces, wartime conditions also bred a new militancy. Attempts to depress wages, tie employees to their existing employer and impose 'dilution' of skilled workforces with new wartime labour had led to the emergence of the Clyde Workers Committee to confront the policies of both management and government. Many of the union officials involved in this organization were also anti-war ILP activists. The result was a series of strikes in the Clydeside factories, notably in 1915 (when Lloyd George, minister for munitions, was shouted down at a Glasgow public meeting) and again in the winter of 1917–18. Hinting at a broader political agenda informed by socialist ideas, an anti-war demonstration even saw 100,000 Glaswegians stop work in protest on May Day 1918.

A flawed peace

To say that the early post-war years were a disappointment, particularly in Scotland, would be an understatement.

The shipyards did experience a brief revival as lost merchant vessels were replaced: 650,000 tons of new Scottish-built shipping was launched in 1919. But the collapse of naval ordering, the return of the old problem of increasing technological obsolescence and the existence of steadily-improving larger-scale foreign competition all boded ill. And when allied to the new disadvantages of over-capacity and rigid integration, and placed in the context of a global downturn that became a slump after 1929, the sector was teetering on the brink: in 1933 the total Scottish tonnage launched collapsed to just 74,000. But shipbuilding was no isolated victim. Similar problems of shrinking markets and stiffer competition also beset the locomotive manufacturers and the rest of Scotland's heavy industrial economy. Coal exports, for example, were 20 per cent lower by the mid-1930s than they had been in 1914.

The raw data on output, however, tell only half the story. The human costs were immense. More than 40,000 Scottish shipyard workers lost their jobs in just 18 months in 1919 and 1920. At no time in the 1920s did unemployment in Scotland as a whole drop below 14 per cent. By 1932, as the Great Depression bottomed out, it approached 30 per cent – and a scarcely believable 50 per cent in many mining and shipbuilding communities.

As before, people's responses varied, with emigration remaining a favourite strategy for many: 400,000 people left Scotland in the 1920s alone – roughly eight per cent of the population (when in England the proportion departing was just 0.5 per cent).

A less common but far more visible reaction, which attracted much press comment at the time and has continued to exercise historians, was the series of more or less political activities that earned the label 'Red Clydeside'.

On 31 January 1919 a red flag flew over George Square in central Glasgow at a rally called to demand rent control and a 40-hour working week. This was a worrying portent in the aftermath of the Bolshevik Revolution and it encouraged a nervous government to deploy tanks and soldiers onto the city's streets as a precaution. Yet a sober view suggests that this greatly over-stated the danger. The evidence implies that the movement's wider public appeal rested not on the revolutionary socialism of some of its leaders but on the specific workplace and welfare concerns of many working people.

Red Clydeside had more practical political consequences. In the 1922 general election the Conservatives won power under another Scottish prime minister, Andrew Bonar Law, MP for Glasgow Central, who had been born in Canada into an emigrant Free Church preacher's family. Critically, however, the Liberals were replaced as the main opposition party at Westminster by Labour. The latter's numbers were swelled by several Scottish ILP MPs like James Maxton and David Kirkwood, propelled to fame by events on Clydeside. Overall 29 Labour candidates won in Scotland in 1922, against 27 Liberals and just 13 Conservatives – strong evidence once more that Scottish voting patterns were highly distinctive. That a new Scottish and British politics had been born was confirmed in 1924's election when the first Labour government – the largest party in the Commons but without an outright majority – won power under yet another Scottish premier, Ramsay MacDonald, the illegitimate son of a Moray farm labourer.

Other responses to the post-war challenges facing Scotland had equally significant long-term implications. Poor housing led to large-scale slum clearance. Health too was improving. By the 1930s maternity and child health provision was available across Scotland, while better housing, advances in public medical programmes and higher standards of living all worked their magic effects. As a result, infant mortality still fell despite the economic crisis. Adult life expectancy in Scotland also continued to increase: from the low 50s at the end of World War One to around 60 by the start of the Second World War.

Yet not all inter-war social trends were benign or could rise above the difficult economic challenges of the period. Life in working-class homes and on the streets of Scotland could often be extremely tough.

One dimension to the social tensions of the inter-war years proved especially problematic. For animosity seemed to grow between Protestant and Catholic Scots.

Sectarianism often derived its force from the concern that 'immigrants' threatened 'native' jobs and wage rates at a time of cripplingly high unemployment. But the decision in 1918 to grant state funding to Catholic schools ('Rome on the rates' to critics) hardly helped allay suspicions among poor Protestants.

Even literary figures were not immune to this nagging sense that the Irish threatened Scotland's identity and integrity. The critic George Malcolm Thomson claimed in 1927 that the Scots were a 'dying people being replaced in their own country by a people alien in race, temperament and religion, at a speed which is without parallel outside the era of the barbarian invasions.'

The thistle blooms

The feeling that it was actually Scotland itself that was in terminal decline, and not merely capitalism and the industrial economy, was increasingly widely shared by Scottish intellectuals as the inter-war crisis deepened. The Orkney poet Edwin Muir eloquently expressed this concern in his *Scottish Journey* of 1935: 'Scotland', he wrote, 'is gradually being emptied of its population, its spirit, its wealth, industry, art, intellect and innate character'.

What has come to be known as the 'Scottish Renaissance' was a response to the period's social and economic problems that also tried to address some of Muir's cultural anxieties. Hugh MacDiarmid (the pen name of Christopher Murray Grieve, which helped him sound more Scottish) was the movement's visionary prophet and leader. He emphasized above all that recovering Scotland's distinctive national culture was an essential precondition of the country's much-needed political re-birth.

A slightly more practical response to the feeling that the country itself was in danger, though closely linked to this cultural phenomenon, was the emergence of organized Scottish political nationalism – the first in 200 years, although initially it was very much a minority taste. A National Party of Scotland was duly established in 1928, and its successor the Scottish National Party (SNP) six years later. It made no immediate electoral impact, however, before the Second World War, and in any case was not initially committed to outright independence.

Douglas Young, a poet and academic whose sense of his own Scottish nationality was so intense that he was imprisoned for refusing wartime conscription by the British government, then led the SNP, now finally advocating dissolution of the Union, from 1942 to 1945. In April 1945 the SNP won its first Westminster seat, in a by-election at Motherwell. What this said about the future direction of Scottish politics was far from certain at the time. After all, it was not immediately obvious that a war which had united the British people under Churchill in a desperate but ultimately victorious fight for survival would necessarily assist a party now advocating the voluntary dismemberment of Britain itself.

Finest hour

Scotland's direct military contribution to the Second World War was broadly similar to that made in the First. Scottish regiments again served in all theatres and experienced both defeat and victory along with the rest of Britain's forces.

Scotland was also crucial once more to the war at sea. Scapa renewed its acquaintance with the Home Fleet, the Royal Navy's two finest wartime admirals, Sir Bruce Fraser and Sir Andrew Cunningham, were from emigrant Scottish backgrounds, and the many ports and protected coastal waters of the Clyde were the last parts of Britain seen by many servicemen headed for Africa or the Far East.

Approximately 50,000 Scottish combatants were killed in the war. Civilian casualties were not insignificant but, resulting from targeted air raids, they were unevenly distributed. Clydebank, the jewel in the crown of strategic shipbuilding, was blitzed in March 1941, killing 528 people in just two nights and rendering 35,000 homeless. The city of Dundee, by contrast, suffered just a single death by bombing.

The war's wider effects were similar to those seen between 1914 and 1918. Women once again proved crucial in the heavy engineering sector, and direct state invention in the labour market, in industrial decision-making and in the allocation of resources (everything from food to fuel was rationed) increased dramatically. Victory even appeared to vindicate such approaches, suggesting that governments could and should play the dominant role in directing productive activity. In particular, it was believed that this would avoid a repetition of the 1920s and 1930s and prevent the return of depression and mass unemployment.

As a result, when Clement Attlee's Labour government was elected on a landslide in May 1945 – scooping 37 Scottish seats against the Conservatives' 24 – there was much optimism that a new age was dawning in which economic efficiency, equality and social justice would go hand in hand. It remained to be seen whether the aftermath of another global war in which Britain had emerged on the winning side would be a happier affair second time around.

Building Jerusalem

The most influential and enduring achievement of the Attlee government was the foundation of the National Health Service in 1948 as part of a wider programme aimed at building a comprehensive welfare state. This created a government-run health care system funded out of general taxation and free at the point of use. The 64,000 hospital beds and 900 senior clinical staff in Scotland were brought under a single authority for the first time. Yet despite these UK-wide improvements, Scottish health remained stubbornly worse than England's over the succeeding decades.

A commitment to providing other forms of assistance for the population 'from the cradle to the grave' ensured that a wide range of financial benefits also became available. Payments were offered in all cases of unemployment and were also available for sickness, maternity, retirement, widowhood, disability and other circumstances of vulnerability.

Non-cash benefits also proliferated under Attlee, as they did once more under Wilson, who led the next Labour government from 1964 to 1970. Social services departments emerged, run by local councils, providing social work, childrens' homes and other functions.

Simultaneously the school system, previously the principal responsibility of local government, was further expanded and refined. Legislation in 1945 extended free compulsory education up to the age of 15 and compelled councils to create the first nursery schools. By the early 1960s local authorities were also being required to provide maintenance grants and fees to those qualified to enter higher education. Student numbers in

Scotland were enhanced in part by the foundation of new universities. In 1951 there had been just 15,000 students in Scotland but by 1981 there were 100,000 and by 2010 more than 300,000.

If a panoply of welfare provision and new social institutions were Labour's noblest legacy from the post-war years, one other set of policies, equally determined by the party's ideological convictions, had a less happy effect. Sworn to socialism interpreted in a peculiarly British fashion, Attlee's government began a programme of nationalization, taking ownership of many industries and services. This, however, was an unforced error with damaging long-term consequences, especially in Scotland.

One problem was that nationalization strengthened Scottish industries' habitual disinclination to change. Powerful trade unions, controlling Labour ministers and cowing Tory ones, found it easier to obstruct change once politicians were calling the shots. No less damaging was the fact that the old Scottish predilection for labour-intensiveness was set in stone by the government's explicit pursuit of full employment. Sadly this philosophically based aversion to commercial realities, just at the moment when international economic competition was intensifying after 1945 and the pace of technological and organizational change worldwide was accelerating, would eventually prove not the salvation but the undoing of many of Scotland's major industries.

Another peculiar consequence of the process of building Jerusalem was the further erosion of Scottish distinctiveness. Contrasts between Scottish and English life narrowed markedly. For example, as grants were introduced to help young people leave home to attend university, leading institutions like Edinburgh and St Andrews, with growing English intakes, became much less obviously Scottish in composition. The welfare benefits paid were all the same from Brighton to Berbecula.

Winds of change?

Scotland in the 1950s and early 1960s appears in retrospect a country poised on the brink of radical change.

One area in which substantial transformation was certainly underway was the liquidation of the British empire. Between Indian independence in 1947 and the decision of the Wilson government to pull British forces out from east of Suez, just 20 years elapsed. 'The winds of change' famously detected in 1960 by Harold Macmillan, the Conservative Prime Minister, had therefore frequently attained gale force.

The velocity and direction of these winds caused unexpected structural damage in Scotland. Obviously the jobs in colonial administration from which generations of middle-class Scots had benefitted slowed to a trickle and then stopped completely. The armed forces, especially the army with its strong Scottish affiliations, also shrank, with far fewer outposts to garrison.

At a deeper level, however, and in ways that no one could have foreseen, the loss of empire had uprooted one of the key foundations on which many Scots' relationship with Britain itself had rested. It was, after all, the common experience of imperialism and the shared spoils of empire (of which the Scots had always taken more than their due) that had made the Union so strong. Britain's stature on the world stage – its wealth, power and prestige – was what more than anything else had justified its continuation. But by 1970 it suddenly seemed legitimate to ask whether Scottish interests were still best served by political arrangements with England that had been entered into in circumstances that clearly no longer applied.

Another important change was the political eclipse of Scottish Conservatism. Under Churchill's successor Sir Anthony Eden in 1955, they had secured 50.1 per cent of the Scottish vote, but by October 1974 under Edward Heath they were winning only 24.7 per cent.

Some of the Tories' slow subsidence was probably an unavoidable side-effect of Britain's shrunken post-imperial role; the most strongly British of parties simply appeared less relevant in very different circumstances. Also loosening a traditional identification with the Conservatives was the gradual erosion of Protestantism as an electoral factor in Scotland after the 1960s. Slowly this issue was losing its power to galvanize Scottish voters. So too was Ulster, which had once been critical for many urban Scots, especially those of Loyalist heritage whose families had arrived from Northern Ireland. All of these factors steadily ate away at the Conservatives' voter base long before the Thatcher governments of the 1980s put the final nails in the coffin.

Devaluation and devolution

Some aspects of life in mid-20th-century Scotland clearly still exuded a reassuring calm and stability. Yet the tectonic plates of the country's economy, which underlay everything else, were also generating unnerving levels of seismic activity, with consequent threats to the comfort and well-being of the human population.

Between nationalization and 1979 the number of working mines shrank drastically from 187 to just 18. Coal's fate was symptomatic of a wider malaise in industries which had been world-beating in the late 19th century. Just between 1962 and 1977, for example, Glasgow alone shed 85,000 manufacturing jobs. Scotland as a whole lost 40,000 textile jobs in the same period. That the economy was in very serious difficulty was increasingly hard to deny.

One feature of the growing economic troubles of the period, which may have been encouraged by the evidence that the government could be persuaded to intervene directly in troubled businesses, was a rise in worker militancy. Articulate but abrasive Scottish trade union leaders in fact played a disproportionate part in the strikes and other disruptive activities which from the mid-1960s onwards became what Europeans mocked as 'the British disease'.

Throughout the same period, a quite different response to the parlous economic situation in Scotland was the steady rise of the SNP. Indeed, so much of a broad church did the party eventually become that by the end of the century it had even attracted supporters of an independent socialist republic such as the notable union leaders Jimmy Airlie and Jimmy Reid.

From 0.8 per cent of the Scottish vote and no MPs in 1959, the party, formally committed to independence since the Second World War, began a steady improvement in its electoral performance. Seven MPs were returned in February 1974 and an unprecedented 11 in October of the same year (on 30.4 per cent of the Scottish vote).

Much of the dramatic increase in the SNP's popularity through the 1960s and 1970s reflected public anger at the inability of either of the two mainstream British parties to reverse the fortunes of Scotland's ailing industrial economy. The discovery of North Sea oil also influenced the calculations of some, adding ballast to the claim that an independent Scotland would be not merely economically viable but actually richer once separated from England.

Insight: 'It's Scotland's oil!'

This slogan gave the SNP a powerful electoral boost in the early 1970s. It suggested that an independent Scotland would be enriched by bountiful natural resources while also implying (without tactlessly stating) that the country's wealth was currently being plundered by the English. The government's use of the tax revenues in the 1980s and 1990s to fund Britain's economic restructuring and welfare payments remained contentious in Scotland.

But longer-term factors were also at work. In particular, the places where the SNP was now winning seats, such as the north and east, indicated that many of its new adherents were people who either had or would have voted Conservative 20 years earlier. And the SNP's fortunes were also affected by the emergence of the 'devolution' issue.

Devolution was the term adopted in the late 1970s to describe a highly peculiar form of self-government offered to certain parts of the UK. In essence the Callaghan administration proposed creating elected parliaments or assemblies in Labour-inclining Scotland and Wales (but not, of course, in more Tory-leaning England) which would exercise significant governmental power inside those two countries. This would simultaneously blunt the demands of the Scottish and Welsh Nationalists for full independence, entrench reliable Labour-run administrations in Edinburgh and Cardiff in perpetuity and yet still allow Labour MPs from Scottish and Welsh constituencies to sit at Westminster where they could help the party shape English affairs.

The scheme, however, was not even universally popular. On the Left, some were anxious lest the experience of limited self-government fan rather than douse the unpredictable flames of nationalism. In England, a concern was that restricting devolution to Scotland and Wales was both unfair and ultimately dangerous because it left England wholly governed by the British Parliament. This in turn posed what became known as the West Lothian Question: 'How can it be', Tam Dalyell MP asked, 'that I can vote on matters in relation to health in Blackburn, Lancashire, but not in Blackburn, West Lothian?'

Fully aware that many in Scotland were no more enthusiastic, Labour opponents in the Commons therefore amended the rules of the public referendum on the Scottish scheme. This ensured that not just a clear majority of the votes cast but also 40 per cent of the total

Scottish electorate needed to endorse the proposals. The SNP officially supported the scheme, too, though many Nationalists loathed this watered-down version of self-government and worried that it might actually reduce public support for outright independence. In the event the 'Yes' campaign achieved a slim majority with 51.6 per cent. On a turnout of just 63.8 per cent, however, this represented only 33 per cent of the electorate (in Wales there was a comprehensive 4:1 defeat). Labour's plans for devolution lay in tatters – and what the episode said about the SNP's demands for independence was also unclear (as the party's electoral disappointments during the 1980s showed).

There was, however, a more immediate result of the devolution debacle. An SNP motion of no confidence in the government actually triggered the general election of 1979. Though jeering Labour MPs would never let them forget it, the Nationalists had unwittingly played the initial walk-on part in what would prove to be a drama based on a new and deeply unsettling script.

The empire strikes back

On 4 May 1979, Margaret Thatcher, Britain's first female prime minister, took office, with a strong (though largely non-specific) commitment to confront the grave economic crisis facing the UK. James Callaghan's tired and demoralized Labour government had been convincingly defeated.

Thatcher, the self-conscious embodiment of small-town provincial England, never connected with Scotland: the misunderstanding was mutual, even if the loathing from the Scottish side only produced wounded puzzlement in the prime minister.

The Scottish dominance of Labour and the unions not only institutionally but culturally and ideologically meant that her views never struck a chord with most Scots. Increasingly suspicious of commercial values and inclined to welcome collectivist approaches to life's challenges, they instinctively recoiled from Thatcher's aspirational individualism and no-nonsense homilies on thrift, enterprise and self-reliance. Many thought her moralizing at best archaic, at worst heartless and divisive.

It has to be said, too, that hard statistics counted against her being welcomed with open arms. For Scotland had more people in public housing and in public employment and overall had a greater reliance on publicly owned industries and public subsidies than was the case in England. As a result, the Scots as a nation, and much of the Scottish establishment in particular, ranged themselves against Thatcher once the 'Iron Lady' began her revolutionary campaign to reverse the state's post-war domination of Britain's social and economic life.

'Selling off the family silver'

The nationalized industries – which since 1945 had absorbed £40 bn in taxpayer write-offs and returned an abysmal –1 per cent on the public's £100 bn of so-called 'investment' – bore the brunt of Thatcher's frontal assault on the comfortable previous consensus. The programme was deeply controversial. Above all this was because, especially in Scotland and in the Labour movement, it was never accepted that purely financial judgments based on losses, debts, shrinking markets and the ballooning cost of bailouts were appropriate. For these organizations, for all their many faults, were also major providers of decent jobs and their public ownership was considered to be by definition in the public interest.

Still-rising unemployment, soon at levels not seen since the war, was already a curse even before privatization started. By a bitter irony, this was in some respects the downside of Scotland's oil bonanza. For it was this that stimulated a steep increase in the value of sterling and hence a drop in the international competitiveness of UK exports. High interest rates, imposed to suppress runaway inflation which early in 1980 peaked at 22 per cent, did the rest, further powering the pound's appreciation and punishing both exporters and those seeking business finance.

What resulted was the worst recession since 1945. Around 20 per cent of all remaining Scottish manufacturing jobs were lost in just two years. High-profile casualties included Singer (sewing machines) at Clydebank in 1980 and the taxpayer-subsidized factories at Linwood (cars), Corpach and Invergordon (aluminium smelting), all of which shut down in the *annus horribilis* of 1981 when government subventions were withdrawn.

It is in this context that the social impact of the de-nationalization programme has to be understood. Coming on top of the partly unavoidable industrial disaster of 1979–81, the massive restructuring that privatization deliberately introduced ensured that unemployment in Scotland soon reached crippling levels. Five years later the City of London may have been partying into the night, with a new economic boom, fuelled by financial services and consumer spending, letting rip in much of middle England. But in Scotland's 'rustbelt' industrial communities, formerly reliant on traditional manual jobs in heavy engineering and manufacturing that had become increasingly dependent upon government protection and taxpayer support, the recession just seemed to run and run.

By the mid-1980s 15 per cent of the Scottish workforce was registered unemployed. But more than a decade later, in 1997, with far more Scots now working in tourism and in call centres than in shipbuilding or mining, and with whisky a far more valuable Scottish export than textiles or trains put together, the figure was still a worrying 9 per cent.

Insight: Marvellous malts

The focal point of an industry now worth £4 billion annually, whisky gets its familiar name from the Gaelic *uisge beatha* ('water of life'). Distilled from a mixture of fermented malt and local fresh water aged and coloured in oak casks, the earliest documentary reference to production comes from the reign of James IV in 1495, who reputedly enjoyed a 'wee dram' (small measure) himself. Many regional types exist – the smoky Islays and the diverse Speysides are the best-known – and the 'single malt' versions, associated with specific producers, now have a large and devoted overseas following.

In certain areas, the combined effects of recession and privatization generated levels of permanent unemployment that turned joblessness into a way of life for many working-class Scots.

Unemployment combined with other factors to make Scotland from the early 1980s onwards a by-word for the ills of post-industrial society. Registered disability reached sky-high levels and stayed there. Drug addiction, particularly on the council schemes, was another new problem that intermingled with the familiar old ones of ill-health, criminality and gang warfare.

Trainspotting was a blockbuster 1995 film in which a young Ewan McGregor helped reveal the mixture of nihilism and black humour that had become common on Scotland's urban housing schemes. But even more destructive of the Tory government's reputation was the attempt to introduce a new system of local government finance: known as the 'Poll Tax' because all adults paid the same sum, it provoked rioting in London in 1990 and spawned a mass non-payment campaign across Scotland.

Few would have been surprised, then, when Tony Blair, educated at Fettes College, one of Edinburgh's top private schools, but obviously an English politician effortlessly attuned to the outlook and values of middle England, swept Labour, or 'New Labour' as he had re-branded it, back into power at Westminster in May 1997 in a landslide of historic proportions, leaving the Tories without a single seat in Scotland.

Not-so-New Labour

Blair in truth won few new converts for Labour in Scotland, despite his crushing electoral victories south of the Border. Indeed, 'Old Labour', as it was dubbed, had never suffered the electoral drubbing from the Scots that the party had experienced in England in the 1980s.

As a result, many of Labour's senior MPs by 1997 were Scots. Above all there was Gordon Brown, once Blair's friend but now his rival who became a uniquely dominant chancellor of the exchequer as well as brooding heir-apparent and constant thorn in the prime minister's side. Robin Cook ran foreign affairs and then led the Commons. Donald Dewar, the Scottish secretary, delivered the devolution policy in which Blair (who had unhelpfully likened the proposed Scottish Parliament to a mere 'parish council') was so obviously uninterested. George Robertson, noted for a daring prediction that devolution would 'kill nationalism stone dead', became Britain's defence secretary and later headed NATO. John Reid, a pugnacious political heavyweight, successively ran the English NHS, English home affairs and defence. Scotland also provided Labour with some of its most high-profile back-benchers, troublesome and quotable in equal measure, like Dalyell (in his mid-seventies but still gamely asking the West Lothian Question), Dennis Canavan and George Galloway.

Paradise postponed

Devolution, the cherished ambition of Blair's more left-wing predecessor John Smith, a Lanarkshire MP who had died in 1994, was implemented quickly and smoothly by Smith's old friend Dewar.

Insight: 'The people say yes'

The devolution referendum was held in the first flush of New Labour's triumph late in 1997. With everyone but the still-traumatized Tories in favour, a positive outcome was inevitable. A 60 per cent turnout, intriguingly down on 1979, delivered a thumping 74.3 per cent endorsement. The Scotland Act 1998 duly progressed into law at Westminster: Wales had approved an assembly for Cardiff, though with just 50.3 per cent support, so both devolution packages sailed through Parliament in tandem.

Instead, the greatest complication when a Scottish Parliament met in Edinburgh for the first time in 292 years turned out to be caused by the chosen electoral system. Dewar and his allies had devised a complex mixture of 73 Westminster-style constituency representatives and 56 additional members. This was specifically intended to make the final allocation of seats to each party proportional to its share of the vote. It was also meant to encourage a 'new politics' in which alliances and agreements had a role to play. The result was that no single party obtained a majority of Members of the Scottish Parliament (MSPs) in the first election on 6 May 1999.

With 56 MSPs, Labour therefore formed a coalition Scottish Executive with the Liberal Democrats who had won 17. The SNP, with 35 MSPs, became the main opposition under their long-serving leader, the wily and acerbic Alex Salmond.

The 'new politics' proved in one sense a gloriously diverse kaleidoscope – a claim repeatedly heard amid the orgy of understandable self-congratulation when the Parliament was officially opened by Queen Elizabeth II in July 1999. Yet it was in another sense strikingly monochrome. Despite early talk about a more inclusive and diverse politics, almost all the new crop of parliamentarians were existing career politicians aligned with long-established parties. Furthermore, not only the two parties in the Scottish Executive but also their main opponents inclined leftwards.

To some extent this reflected Scotland's known political preferences. But it was accentuated by the Scottish Executive being funded by a direct grant from Westminster. Hence the Edinburgh parliamentarians' duty was merely to decide how to distribute large sums of public money among their own voters. This further exaggerated the in-built advantages enjoyed by politicians promising even higher levels of spending.

Some of the headline decisions of the Parliament's early years also revealed a determination to extend the reach of government into new areas. Legal prohibitions on a range of hitherto private activities that offended left-wing politicians' sensibilities (though by no means always those of their voters) were quickly imposed: woe betide the Scot in the early 21st century who wanted to smoke in his own office while looking forward to spending the next day fox-hunting. Because the 'new politics' proved gratifyingly receptive to single-issue campaigns demanding blanket bans, everything from pub strippers and horse-branding to air guns, cheap alcohol promotions, caffeinated tonic wines and the parental smacking of children were soon on an impressively miscellaneous list awaiting similar punitive treatment.

Far more constructively but also very expensively, the Scottish Executive promised free care for Scotland's elderly and spared Scottish students up-front university fees – though English observers, footing most of the bill but getting none of the benefits, were often less thrilled. There were also notable achievements in extending the rights afforded to homosexuals.

Labour nevertheless had growing problems, not least caused, strangely, by being unable to shake off the association with Blair, whose credibility was fatally damaged by the Iraq war, which was even less popular in Scotland than elsewhere. Jack McConnell's Labour coalition had continued after the 2003 election, but in 2007 the election resulted in a photo-finish: 46 MSPs for Labour but 47 for the SNP. The implications were initially uncertain, since Labour and the Liberal Democrats could no longer command a majority even between them. But as the smoke cleared, and after a fruitless exploratory discussion with the Liberal Democrats, Salmond announced that, as leader of the largest party, he would form a minority executive (or 'government', as he insisted on calling it).

This brought a whole new dimension to devolution into play – essentially the one that Dewar and Robertson had discounted and Dalyell had long feared. With a Nationalist administration manipulating the levers of power and defining the terms of the relationship with London, would it be possible to use Scottish self-government to begin to unravel the very fibres of the Union? Actually, the reality proved less traumatic than the expectations. Salmond's MSPs were heavily outnumbered by the three large Unionist parties. Accordingly he was unable to do much more than generate opportunistic friction with Westminster.

In particular, the SNP had no hope of legislating for its long-standing main policy: a national referendum preparatory to secession from the UK. And although McConnell's short-term Labour successor Wendy Alexander briefly toyed with the intriguing possibility of calling Salmond's bluff and voting to hold the referendum that every opinion poll suggested the Nationalists would then lose, Salmond himself, ever the pragmatist, openly conceded by 2010 that no such first step on the road to independence would be attempted before the next Scottish election.

The son of the manse

After many years of trying unsuccessfully to force the issue, Gordon Brown had finally managed to become Britain's prime minister following Blair's resignation in June 2007. Gordon Brown's administration enjoyed a couple of brief moments of optimism and managed some genuine achievements. He even persuaded other governments to reduce indebtedness in the developing world. As a party loyalist steeped in Scottish Labour, he also attracted far more genuine affection across his own party than Blair – who regularly challenged and offended its Socialist traditions – had ever managed. Yet Brown always faced an uphill struggle in winning over the wider electorate. And frequently there was little that he himself could have done about it.

His Scottishness, for example, which could hardly be concealed, played well enough in Labour-supporting heartlands, but predictably proved less appealing to many English voters. Brown's transition from number-crunching back-room wizard to media-savvy leader of the nation was also hindered by appearing ill-at-ease in public, and attempts to coach a winning smile only seemed to make things worse.

Yet it was the onset of a deep recession in 2008, with accompanying stock market crash and plunging house prices, that did more than anything else to undermine the reputation of a politician whose catch-phrase during his decade as chancellor had been that he had personally guaranteed the country 'no more boom and bust'.

Brown's defeat in May 2010, by 7 per cent overall, was less punishing than some had feared, given the dire unpopularity which at times in 2009 had created new post-war opinion poll records. But with Labour on just 29 per cent (its second-worst result ever) and largely wiped out across much of England, the outcome was hardly something to celebrate.

Unfinished business

As the Cameron-led coalition got underway and Labour pondered how best to combat it under a new leader, Scotland's own future was shrouded in uncertainty. It was unclear where devolution itself now stood. The Cameron coalition prudently inserted a Liberal Democrat as its Scottish Secretary and signalled a willingness to work constructively with Scotland's SNP administration. It also indicated that 'Calman' would be implemented.

Insight: Calman

The 'Calman Commission', properly known as the Commission on Scottish Devolution, was set up in December 2007 with the support of all three Unionist parties. When it reported back in June 2009 it pronounced devolution a success, but in addition it proposed changes. Along with a welter of minor adjustments to ensure greater co-ordination between Edinburgh and Westminster, Calman also recommended that the Scottish Parliament should take on substantial tax-raising powers. In particular, it was suggested that the UK government ought to reduce the income tax rate in Scotland and allow Holyrood to determine whether and how far to make up the difference with Scottish taxes. This had all the hallmarks of being a messy compromise between several different options. It certainly stopped short of the much-discussed concept of 'fiscal autonomy', whereby Scotland would collect its own tax revenues and pay an appropriate contribution to common UK expenditure. But Calman's idea did hold out the promise of greater power, and, perhaps even more importantly, a chance to develop a greater sense of responsibility.

In some ways this was unsurprising, despite the Tories' earlier hostility to devolution. For Calman's potential to help re-build centre-right politics in Scotland should have been obvious even to the dullest fiscal conservative. Anything that encouraged voters to re-connect their concerns as Scottish taxpayers with their assessment of Scottish politicians' spending promises had to be a good thing. But how the Calman package would work and what its implications would be were left disappointingly up in the air.

There were other possible ways of extending devolution, however, including some dear to certain English Tories that were utter anathema to Scottish Labour MPs. After all, devolution for England itself had always been the most obvious answer to the West Lothian Question. Most importantly, it would eradicate the indefensible asymmetry that left the English alone governed by a Westminster Parliament in which Scottish and Welsh MPs often enjoyed the casting vote. Could England, like Scotland, restore the independent Parliament that it too lost in 1707, leaving the existing UK Parliament for British-wide matters? Or might it be easier just to exclude non-English MPs from such Westminster business as affected only England? Either way – and Cameron showed no early sign of having decided how to play this – it would have potentially dramatic consequences for the status and influence of Scottish politicians in particular.

And what of wider Scottish society, where some developments over recent decades had been so deeply problematic? Joblessness, drug addiction, educational failure and welfare-dependency remained chronic features of too many Scottish lives. Endowing poverty and entrenching inequality, they bequeathed a desperate lack of opportunity to successive generations. Associated with this, a striking number of Scots, as a casual glance at any newspaper letters page showed, also displayed an implacable hostility towards entrepreneurialism and the profit motive, convinced that they were the cause of their country's social and economic problems rather than part of the solution.

These broader questions were overshadowed by the explosive consequences of the Scottish election of May 2011. This produced a result that, according to the Labour architects of devolution, should have been virtually impossible. Losing what had been some of its safest seats in and around Glasgow as well as a slew of its leading figures, Labour was humiliated as the SNP returned 69 MSPs. Having seen his party also conquer long-established Liberal Democrat strongholds in rural areas, Alex Salmond emerged with a stand-alone majority government and the power to pursue his own agenda.

This presented the newly reinstalled First Minister with both an opportunity and a problem. On the one hand the SNP dominated the political landscape and was finally able, if it wished, to conduct a national referendum on independence. On the other hand, opinion polls continued to show that only between one-quarter and one-third of Scots endorsed independence. Voting for the SNP, particularly if it punished Labour and inserted an Edinburgh administration well able to fight the country's corner against Westminster, was one thing. Voting for outright independence remained quite another.

A tactical delay in calling any referendum seemed likely in the short term. How Cameron's UK government would react to the new situation and whether some version of Calman could still satisfy either the coalition at Westminster or the nationalists in Edinburgh remained uncertain. Only one thing was clear. Ahead lay another fascinating but thoroughly unpredictable phase in the long history of the Scottish people.

THINGS TO REMEMBER

▶ Early 20th-century Scotland was at its imperial zenith – its people central to the British Empire's global strength.

▶ The First World War inflicted disproportionate Scottish casualties but also masked the extent of underlying economic, social and political problems.

▶ The inter-war years saw deep and prolonged crisis as heavy industry struggled, unemployment rose and growing anxiety promoted both radical left-wing and organized nationalist politics.

▶ Post-war Scotland was transformed by Labour and its commitment to building a welfare state, nationalizing key parts of the economy and de-colonization.

▶ The electoral decline of Scottish Conservatism after the 1960s and the emergence of the Scottish National Party steadily altered political life.

▶ Margaret Thatcher's governments after 1979 presided over traumatic de-industrialization and privatization and the growth of welfare dependency in Scotland.

▶ Tony Blair and New Labour had limited impact in Scotland which remained staunchly behind more traditional Labour politics and politicians.

▶ Devolution, delivered after 1997, saw a new Scottish Parliament and a new politics emerge – multi-party in composition but ideologically homogenous.

▶ The emergence of an SNP government in Scotland in 2007 produced less change than might have been expected but raised questions about the long-term effects of devolution.

▶ With a Conservative and Liberal Democrat coalition administration in London in 2010 and the SNP in power in Edinburgh, key issues about Scotland's relations with England remained unresolved.

Taking it further

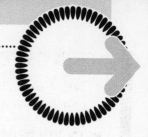

Books

The history of Scotland has spawned a vast body of literature stretching back over many centuries. Much of it focuses on highly particular aspects and some of it is extremely technical, but the following broader studies are useful for developing a better understanding of longer periods and key themes:

Michael Lynch, *Scotland: a New History* (1991).

R.A. Houston and W.W.J. Knox (eds), *The New Penguin History of Scotland* (2001).

Michael Lynch (ed.), *The Oxford Companion to Scottish History* (2001).

Gordon Donaldson and Robert Morpeth (eds), *A Dictionary of Scottish History* (1977).

A.A.M. Duncan, *Scotland: the Making of the Kingdom* (1975).

Alex Woolf, *From Pictland to Alba: Scotland, 789 to 1070* (2007).

G.W.S. Barrow, *Kingship and Unity: Scotland, 1000–1306* (1981).

Michael Brown, *The Wars of Scotland, 1214–1371* (2004).

Alexander Grant, *Independence and Nationhood: Scotland, 1306–1469* (1984).

Jenny Wormald, *Court, Kirk and Community: Scotland, 1470–1625* (1981).

T.C. Smout, *A History of the Scottish People, 1560–1830* (1969).

T.M. Devine, *The Scottish Nation: a History, 1700–2000* (2001).

Christopher Whatley, *Scottish Society, 1707–1830: Beyond Jacobitism, Towards Industrialisation* (2000).

David Allan, *Scotland in the Eighteenth Century* (2002).

T.C. Smout, *A Century of the Scottish People, 1830–1950* (1986).

T.M. Devine and R.J. Finlay (eds), *Scotland in the Twentieth Century* (1996).

Christopher Harvie, *No Gods and Precious Few Heroes: Twentieth-Century Scotland* (1981).

Films

Scotland has attracted much interest from film makers, often inspired by the country's distinctive landscape, rich literary traditions and colourful history. A good selection of leading films about the country – some Hollywood blockbusters, others by significant native directors, and a few strongly whimsical or openly satirical about the peculiarities of Scottish society – include:

The Thirty-Nine Steps (1935)

Whisky Galore (1949)

The Prime of Miss Jean Brodie (1969)

The Wicker Man (1973)

Gregory's Girl (1980)

Local Hero (1983)

Trainspotting (1995)

Braveheart (1995)

Mrs Brown (1997)

Websites

Scotland's history is reflected in a profusion of web-based materials, some of them vital resources with official status. An authoritative starting point for exploration would be:

The National Archives of Scotland: www.nas.gov.uk

The National Library of Scotland: www.nls.uk

Historic Scotland (government heritage agency): www.historic-scotland.gov.uk

National Trust for Scotland (a conservation charity): www.nts.org.uk

The Scotsman (leading national newspaper): www.scotsman.com

History Scotland (magazine and website): www.historyscotland.com

BBC Scotland history: www.bbc.co.uk/scotland/history

Maps

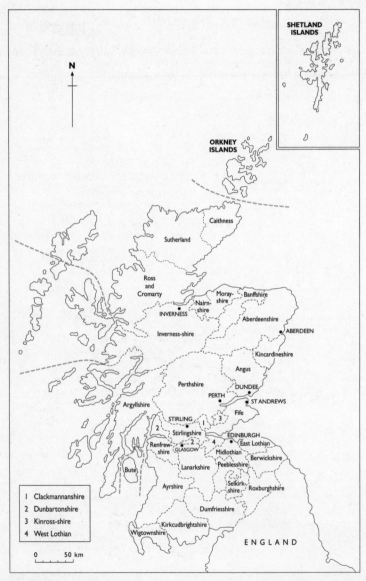

SHETLAND ISLANDS

ORKNEY ISLANDS

Caithness

Sutherland

Ross and Cromarty

Moray-shire Banffshire

Nairn-shire

INVERNESS

Aberdeenshire

ABERDEEN

Inverness-shire

Kincardineshire

Angus

Perthshire

DUNDEE

PERTH

ST ANDREWS

Argyllshire

STIRLING

Fife

3

2

Stirlingshire

1

EDINBURGH

Renfrew-shire

2

4

East Lothian

GLASGOW

Midlothian

Berwickshire

Bute

Lanarkshire

Peeblesshire

Ayrshire

Selkirk-shire

Roxburghshire

Dumfriesshire

Kirkcudbrightshire

Wigtownshire

ENGLAND

1 Clackmannanshire
2 Dunbartonshire
3 Kinross-shire
4 West Lothian

0   50 km

Scotland: major towns and pre-1975 counties.

232

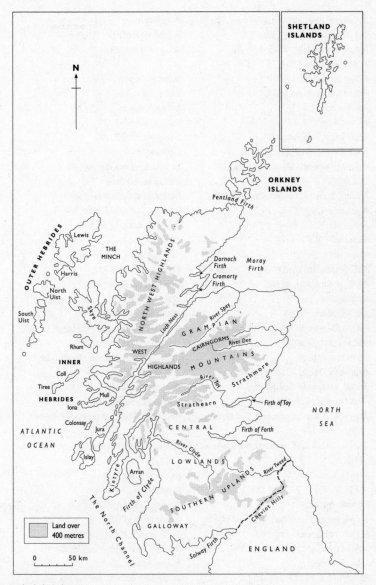

Scotland: physical map.

Index

trade, *148, 175–6*
trade unions, *197, 199, 209, 215, 217*
transport, *175–6, 192–3*
Trapain Law, *3*
Treatise of Human Nature, *184*
Treaty of Greenwich, *98–9*
Treaty of York, *46*

unemployment, *210, 220–1*
Ungus, King of Fortriu, *13*
union, constitutional, *152–9*
Union, Treaty of 1707, *153*
Union of the Crowns, *107, 114–16*
Union of the Parliaments, *213*
United Scotsmen, the, *168*
universities, *182, 205, 214–15, 224*
urbanization, *173, 180, 194–6*

Vikings, *14–19, 23*
Votadini tribe, *3, 4*

Wallace, William, *57–62, 206*
Warriston, Lord Archibald Johnston, *135*
Wars of Independence, *56, 57–62, 64–80*
water power, *177*
welfare state, *214, 224*
Wessex dynasty, *23, 24*
West Lothian question, *218, 227*
Wilkes, John, *163*
William I, King of the Scots, *42, 44–6*
William III of England, *142–3, 145–8*
William the Conqueror, *31*
Wilson, James, *169*
Wolfe, General James, *162*
workhouses, *196*
World War One, *208–11*
World War Two, *213–14*

Young Pretender, *see* Charles Edward Stuart

Image credits

Front cover: © Le Do – Fotolia.com

Back cover: © Jakub Semeniuk/iStockphoto.com, © Royalty-Free/Corbis, © agencyby/iStockphoto.com, © Andy Cook/iStockphoto.com, © Christopher Ewing/iStockphoto.com, © zebicho – Fotolia.com, © Geoffrey Holman/iStockphoto.com, © Photodisc/Getty Images, © James C. Pruitt/iStockphoto.com, © Mohamed Saber – Fotolia.com